THE
ORGANIZATION
OF HOPE

SUNY Series in Urban Public Policy
James Bohland and Patricia Edwards, Editors

THE ORGANIZATION OF HOPE

Communities Planning Themselves

HOWELL S. BAUM

State University
of New York
Press

Parts of chapters 8, 9, and 10 were published earlier in "Community and Consensus: Reality and Fantasy in Planning," *Journal of Planning Education and Research* 13 (4) (Summer 1994): 251–62, reprinted by permission of the Association of Collegiate Schools of Planning.

Published by
State University of New York Press, Albany

© 1997 State University of New York

Production by Susan Geraghty
Marketing by Bernadette LaManna

Printed in the United States of America

For information, address State University of New York
Press, State University Plaza, Albany, N.Y., 12246

Library of Congress Cataloging-in-Publication Data

Baum, Howell S.
    The organization of hope : communities planning themselves /
Howell S. Baum.
        p.   cm.
    Includes bibliographical references and index.
    ISBN 0-7914-3193-2 (hardcover : acid-free paper). — ISBN
0-7914-3194-0 (pbk. : acid-free paper)
    1. Community—Case studies. 2. Community organization—Case
studies. 3. Community organization—Maryland—Baltimore. 4. Jews-
-Maryland—Baltimore. I. Title.
HM131.B3754 1997   96-5109
                                                              CIP

10 9 8 7 6 5 4 3 2 1

To Madelyn, Elena, and Maya
In the hope they belong to communities that strengthen them

CONTENTS

PREFACE

Since childhood I have wrestled with questions of community. What group or groups outside the family was I part of? Where did my ancestors' immigration from Lithuania and Hungary place me in American society? To what groups could I turn for intimacy, sociability, and support, and who might look similarly to me?

In recent years I have become most actively a member of two intellectual communities, one concerned with planning, the other with organizations. These communities were born of shared interests. They have no basis in geography; indeed, members live expensively far apart. Some have common ethnic backgrounds, but ethnicity per se has nothing to do with these communities, which are held together by common ways of seeing things and personal affection. Such communities, one reads, are the way of the future. Yet their discontinuity is frustrating. It is important to see and touch others close up, often.

These personal experiences have shaped my intellectual interests. In studying planners, I have tried to understand how they can address problems in ways that are at once rational and responsive to community interests. In looking at organizations, I have been concerned with how individuals become members. Here I am again interested in membership, with a focus on communities, and with questions about how community membership influences problem solving.

The communities I have studied are nearby, not like the intellectual communities to which I belong, but entities more proximate, one based in geography, the other dependent on enough closeness for daily interaction. I am interested in these communities because they offer members identity, caring, and power. I have watched my city decompose, splitting racially and economically, to the point where few, not even elected officials, feel loyalty to groups larger than their immediate friends. For this reason, too, I hope such "anachronistic" communities persist, and can connect people who are different but must live together. Finally, my daughters' reaching school age forced me to think seriously about the kind of community I wanted them to find a place in.

As a planner, I want communities to be able to address their conditions with passion tempered by reason, thinking deliberately about their future and acting instrumentally to shape it. Yet communities are deeply conservative, preferring familiar habits and conditions to change. And, often despite their best intentions, they are as likely to follow fantasy as to embrace reality. Thus the ties and traditions of community can oppose the reasons of planning.

Serendipitously, about five years ago I heard that The Associated: Jewish Community Federation of Baltimore was engaged in strategic planning for its community, and shortly after I learned that the South East Community Organization would develop a plan for its largely working-class white ethnic area. I decided to study the two community planning processes for what they might tell about community and planning. Each offered the opportunity to hear people talk about what held their community together at a time when communities were eroding. Each process involved sophisticated leaders who were interested in reasoned planning.

I am a member of the Baltimore Jewish community. However, before this project I had little contact with The Associated, and I knew nothing about its strategic planning. I identify differently with the community than many who speak in this book. Hearing them has been a moving experience. Yet contrasts between their positions and those of others with whom I am more familiar have led me to consider how much difference a community can contain and how a community can contain differences.

I have had a long intermittent interest in Southeast Baltimore. I came to the City toward the end of the neo-ethic revival, and Southeast seemed excitingly urban. SECO was in its heyday, and it epitomized the possibilities of grassroots organizing. Still, I only occasionally visited Southeast and had no contact with SECO before this study. Now encountering the area more closely, I found waning ethnicity, differences of geography, race, and class, and no self-evident core identity. As the Southeast Planning Council began its work, these conditions led me to consider how much and what kind of similarity a community requires.

Whenever I have described this study to others in Baltimore, they have raised their eyebrows, perhaps offered a sympathetic comment on the project's exotic nature, and noted that the two communities are incomparable. I have insisted on thinking about them together, as instances of a common phenomenon, to see what we might learn about the reasons people associate with one another at the end of the twentieth century.

Just as I expected to find this "community talk" expressed in planning, I assumed success of the planning processes would depend on finding ways to reach agreement not just about problems and programs, but also about the communities' character. Thus I hoped to find planning models that were not just intellectually rational, but also socially and psychologically sensitive and meaningful. As the reader will quickly see, the stories of these two communities, their organizations, and their planning processes have complex parallels and contrasts and offer rich lessons.

There is a footnote about Southeast Baltimore. From mid-1991 until early 1994 I was an observer of Southeast planning. Then the U.S. Department of Education invited proposals for Urban Community Services grants, whereby university faculty and students would assist community groups in addressing their problems. Impressed by the Southeast Community Plan, in collaboration with Southeast Planning Council members, I helped put together a proposal for several University of Maryland colleagues and students to work with the Council to implement the plan. The proposal was funded in the fall of 1994, and in this process I shifted from observer to advocate and stakeholder. I wrote most of the book in my first role, but its observations about community and planning reflect, as well, a year as activist.

In both communities, I have been impressed by how personally people identify with their community and how actively they work at serving and improving it. Admitting an observer is not unlike taking in a house guest, and I am grateful for expansive hospitality in both places. This study would not have been possible without the cooperation of the two community organizations. At The Associated, Marshall Levin was a generous host, and Darrell Friedman, William Bernstein, Nancy Kutler, and Chaim Botwinick all freely shared their time and understanding. exemplifying the giving of which the federation is proud. At SECO and the Southeast Planning Council, Robert Giloth unhesitatingly invited me into the planning process, and John Papagni, Barbara Ruland, Carolyn Boitnott, Bobby English, and David Casey all graciously shared their time and ideas, showing the openness Southeast activists take as their premise.

Between the two communities, seventy-five people participated in at least one interview each. These conversations were a gift, not just because everyone was busy, but also because people were willing to tell community stories to someone they did not know. Their generosity, too, was essential to this study. Each talk offered surprises and insights, and the accounts here build on all of them. It was disorienting, stimulating, and a privilege to speak at once with traditional Orthodox rabbis, public housing residents, wealthy philanthropists, and grassroots activists. I doubt these are typical experiences anywhere.

The Aspen Institute's Nonprofit Sector Research Fund, directed by Elizabeth Boris, provided financial assistance for an essential part of this study. Aspen's support during the summer of 1994 and a fall 1994 sabbatical made it possible to interview people in the communities about their assessments of the planning processes, as well as to do much of the writing in a timely manner.

Nusrat Mannan provided valuable assistance in interviewing fifteen Southeast residents. Kui Zhao, with the University of Maryland

Urban Studies and Planning Program's mapping project, created the book's two maps.

Many people offered helpful ideas along the way. I enjoyed periodic talks with John Seeley, who has done exemplary research on community and philanthropy. He told many wonderful stories and offered insights and encouragement. Charles Hoch brought a sophistication about community and planning to reading early drafts. Howard Stein lent a psychoanalytic anthropological sensibility to understanding the case material. Paul Ephross read the chapters on the Jewish community and made many good factual and interpretive comments. Robert Giloth did the same for Southeast Baltimore chapters. In addition, Seth Allcorn, Michael Diamond, John Forester, Seymour Mandelbaum, Paula Singer, and Gary Tobin read parts of the manuscript and raised good questions about how to make sense of and write about these communities.

Stephen Blum, a fellow doctoral student in planning at the University of California at Berkeley twenty-five years ago, used to speak of planning as "the organization of hope." I did not catch the full meaning of this phrase until I began watching the two community planning processes here. Thus the book's title is his.

Yitzhak Rabin was killed as I was finishing the manuscript. As were many, I was surprised at how much I felt personally wounded. My grief was a measure of the ties of a community. In addition, Rabin personified the struggle to create community from groups that cannot yet see common reasons for being together, and his murder shows the uncomprehending passions that work against community. Rabin's death represents all the reasons why we should listen closely to both communities here and seek answers to the questions with which they struggle.

PART 1

The Question of Community

CHAPTER 1

Introduction

"Community" is a modern watchword. Those who speak it call for new attachments, and they respond to a sense that things have come apart.

Social theorists worry that people live individualistically, seeing their actions as private, not informed by or related to any public concern or common good (Bellah et al. 1985; Etzioni 1993; Selznick 1992; Sullivan 1982). Conservatives and ethnic activists are distressed that people live as if they had no group history or obligations to a shared past (Bloom 1987; Lasch 1978, 1984, and 1995; Nisbet 1962; Stein and Hill 1977). Religious observers are concerned that both individuals and groups act without reference to transcendent principles (Bellah 1975; Bellah et al. 1991; Berger 1977; Buber 1958, 1992; Douglas and Tipton 1983). Political scientists are troubled that people do not see one another as citizens of the same polity, sharing common ground rules, committed to making decisions that reflect and create common interests (Barber 1984; Mansbridge 1983).[1]

Although these observers do not agree on all points, they converge on ascribing social, political, and psychological virtues to communitarian attachments. Community, as they see it, can be a vehicle for enabling individuals to satisfy submerged longings for deep social attachments, revitalizing society, and restoring democracy.

People work at creating community in many ways. Much of the time they do so tacitly in their everyday affairs, making choices about whose views to consider in defining themselves and their desires, what to expect of others, and whom to associate with and how. Occasionally, people try more formally and explicitly to create community, through activities we call planning. Though intended to be more deliberate and rational, these efforts, as we shall see, always respond to ordinary wishes for and anxieties about attachments.

COMMUNITY AND THE CITY

This book is concerned with the loss and possibilities of community in contemporary cities. Traditionally, communities mediated between individuals and cities, to the benefit of both (Berger and Neuhaus 1977).

People have lived in cities through communities; their experience of the city has been that of the community. In cities of hundreds of thousands or millions of residents, communities have offered a focus for personal identity at a meaningful scale. In recent history most often framed in ethnic and/or religious terms, communities have helped individuals define who they are by offering a sense of identity more specific and special than one citizen among a multitude.

At the same time, local society has reinforced this identity by allowing members to be important and powerful. Community organizations and political institutions have enabled members to exercise control over not only the community but also part of the city. Communities and their institutions supplied the psychological and political conditions for transforming individuals into loyal citizens who had stakes in the city because they had stakes in their community. Thus, community organizations made cities governable: cities could be governed by governing communities.

However, conditions that once contributed to more or less coherent communities have changed. Social, economic, and geographic mobility, often part of a deliberate effort to assimilate into American society, has dissolved ethnically homogeneous, concentrated communities. Many metropolitan areas have become racial donuts, where whites who could afford to move departed for the suburbs, replaced in the center by African-Americans and other racial minorities. Older European ethnics and their descendants who remain, because they are too poor, too old, or too settled to move, encounter African-American neighbors with uncertainty about what they have in common. New immigrants still further mix the urban population. Not only do their encounters make people wonder whether they can form a community with many others at all, but cultural and linguistic differences often frustrate even the simplest of understandings.

Both cities and their residents have stakes in communities. Yet, because few act on behalf of cities, those most motivated to rediscover or create urban communities are individuals. Some turn to those with whom they share geography and problems, perhaps looking through these circumstances for a compelling positive collectivity. Some take strength from living near others who have similar jobs or occupy a similar moment in the life cycle. Some form communities whose members may be neighbors but whose attachment rests on more specific, and demanding, solidarity, such as religious or sexual orientation (FitzGerald 1987). Still others try to revitalize, redefine, or re-create communities that once gave comfort. They may reconsider the ethnic communities in which they grew up, looking for contemporary meanings and directions in old traditions.

These people struggle with the question of what shared identity could form a contemporary basis for community. They experiment with institutions and norms that may, by bringing psychological and social order to cities, make them meaningful and governable.

TWO COMMUNITIES

This book joins this exploration by examining the activities of two groups that have been communities and seek to articulate durable future identities. Both, through community organizations, have engaged in community planning to serve the needs of community members and to work through an identity that might sustain community. The stories of these groups address several questions. First, what principles, premises, purposes, or feelings attach significant numbers of people to one another today? What are viable bases for community? What do people who feel they are members of a community believe they are together to be or do? How do assumptions about community affect what members do when they organize to plan for themselves? And how do a community's premises shape relations with the city?

These communities' stories focus on their organizations' efforts to plan for the future. In "planning for a community," an organization does everything this ambiguous phrase implies. It provides a service to an existing community, and it creates the community anew. Every act of planning embodies assumptions about a community and relationships in it. Each planful act enacts a community. Thus, even though the formal planning processes of community organizations are only a small part of a community's life, they reveal a great deal about a community. Planning offers a pragmatic view of a community in action.

The two communities presented here do not exhaust the possibilities for contemporary urban communities, but they illustrate significant variations. The Associated: Jewish Community Federation of Baltimore is an organization of Jews in the Baltimore, Maryland metropolitan area. It has much in common with other American Jewish communities. More than that, even though its members speak in Jewish and often religious language, it resembles many other communities that traditionally defined themselves ethnically or religiously and ponder whether they are still a community.

Although there are poor people in this community, many of its members are well-to-do. In this respect, the community is similar to others that are professional and upper-middle-class. Many families and the community as a whole are socially and economically self-sufficient. They have the freedom to separate themselves from the city, and many are turned toward the suburbs. Geographically and psychologically poised on the city boundary, they confront basic choices about whether to participate in and re-create the city.

The South East Community Organization (SECO) represents Southeast Baltimore, a heterogeneous area where residents, their parents, or their grandparents immigrated from Europe. Ethnicity and religion once defined a number of communities, whose families shared a connection to work in local industries. However, ethnicity and religion have lost salience, and many blue-collar jobs are gone. When SECO helped organize a Southeast Planning Council, it confronted a question many in American cities face: What could hold together tenuously working-class descendants of white ethnics whose neighbors include a growing number of African-Americans, Latinos, Asians, and Native Americans?

Southeast residents have limited income and formal education. Individually and collectively, they have difficulty supporting themselves. They depend on outsiders—government, developers, firms, and foundations. Many choose to stay in the only place they have lived. Some who can move to the suburbs for schools that work and more consistent feelings of security. Others remain because they must.

It would do violence to the stories of these communities to link them to single views of community, but each sits close to a particular perspective. The Associated encourages Baltimore Jews to act on the principles Bellah and his colleagues (1985) espouse. The organization nurtures Jews in feeling they are part of a single, deep community. Many work, attend school, pray, and/or socialize with one another, and The Associated urges them to see their relations as expressions of a shared tradition and a commitment to a common future. The organization encourages and reinforces philanthropy and volunteerism as expressions of community members' caring about and for one another. Drawing on a rich religious tradition, The Associated promulgates what Bellah and his colleagues call a "second language" of community reciprocity and responsibility.

Southeast activists do not deny the value of such social attachments, but many participate in SECO and the Planning Council for more immediate reasons. Gans (1988) argues that "middle Americans" live and want to live differently than Bellah advocates. They are individualistic, and they find intimacy and identity in family, friendships, and informal proximate relations, rather than the broader, more heterogeneous groupings Bellah urges. What they need is not more extensive social involvement, but political power and economic security. More useful than recruiting working-class individualists to participate in societal institutions, Gans argues, is reforming institutions to fit middle Americans' limited tastes for participation and to produce employment and income.

In this view, the attachments that matter are not so much cultural and emotional as political. People should form a political community, in which they organize to act collectively. Sometimes they will promote common interests; other times, they will simply support a vehicle through which participants can satisfy individual interests. Consistently, SECO has framed the community identity largely in political and economic terms, while leaving social and cultural concerns to other organizations.

The debate between Bellah and Gans is a disagreement about America and Americans. Bellah and his colleagues argue that early American communitarian concerns place a moral obligation on contemporary Americans to live and act together. Moreover, they believe these communitarian impulses survive in a collective unconscious. If people could recover the language to articulate these yearnings, they would attach themselves to their contemporaries and reconnect with the past.

Gans emphasizes the opposite strand in American intellectual and emotional history, what Tocqueville (1945 [1862]) first called "individualism." Whether it has moral priority or not, through ideas and institutions it has, as Bellah and his colleagues concede (1991), effectively shaped Americans' desires and practices. To call these wishes a misunderstanding is to misunderstand them. For better or worse, many Americans have fewer communitarian tastes than Bellah and his colleagues would prefer. At the least, Gans asserts in drawing a class line, working-class Americans are likely to live in a world that is more individualistic and more local than that of upper-middle-class professionals and businesspeople.

There is no reason to bind each of these communities to one side in this debate, but the argument alerts us to look for certain themes in the juxtaposition of the stories. The Associated may be considered to have a more ambitious communitarian program, while the Southeast Planning Council program may be seen as more individualistic. Still, it should be kept in mind that the Planning Council is a coalition of community organizations that themselves carry burdens of cohesion in the Southeast. At the least, we ought to read the stories of The Associated and the Baltimore Jewish community with an eye to the ways individualism limits community. And we ought to look in the stories of SECO and the Southeast for indications of the ties necessary for even individualistic communities to act.

Further, class matters. Wealth brings an ability to control parts of the world and muster remedies for problems. It also lends confidence that one can with little risk extend oneself and connect to others who are different. It is not in itself sufficient for community, but it provides emotional, social, and economic resources that support community and organization. It would be reductionistic to see the two communities as different only in class; significantly, the Southeast is more diverse as well. Nevertheless, one ought to examine the stories for what they reveal about the effects of class on desires for and possibilities of community.

In addition to telling us about contemporary beliefs and feelings about community, the stories show how the dynamics of real communities shape their organizations. The Associated and the Southeast Planning Council are different not simply because they inherit different organizational traditions—Jewish federations and grassroots community organizations, respectively—but also because they respond to different interests in and impulses toward community action.

The persistence of these organizations indicates they fit their communities, and yet the interesting questions concern how they fit, where they do not fit very well, and how the nature of the fit affects the actions of the organizations. Community dynamics—relations among groups within a community—influence, for example, which issues come to a community planning agenda, how the issues are addressed, and what is decided. Thus, the stories can be read for models or, at least, principles of community organization that fit different types of communities.

Finally, these episodes in community planning offer lessons for designing planning processes that accommodate community dynamics. Planning is the pretentious effort to shape human events with deliberate concern about the future. It is an attempt to impose a rationality of choices upon the turbulent sea of human activities. The stories repeatedly show how planners rationalized the course the sea set for itself. At the same time, the stories suggest what planners must know and do about social and psychological dynamics to plan with a community—to be blunt, to plan at all.

LISTENING TO COMMUNITIES

This book focuses on two planning processes: The Associated's strategic planning and the Southeast Planning Council's community planning for Southeast Baltimore. I became interested in these projects because they were deliberate efforts to plan for communities, and they seemed likely to reveal something about how people think about community. I began with general questions about how beliefs and feelings about community influence planning efforts.

In proceeding, I had to learn to listen to a community. Literally, of course, a community does not speak. However, individuals may give voice to broadly shared sentiments, and an observer must learn to whom and when to listen for these expressions. Further, as the saying goes, actions speak louder than words. Anthropologists in particular have sought to identify formal rituals or informal patterns of activity that say something about a community. Even conflicts within a community, divisions that might suggest nothing holds people together, can represent shared concerns.

I have been doubly challenged to understand what people in these communities have said. First, I have tried to understand what they mean by what they say. For example, people in both speak of "community" but do not necessarily mean something specific or unambiguous. They may use the term to describe current social relations, but they may just as well utter it to express a wish that people lived more intimately and supportively than they do.

The word may also designate several groups simultaneously. For instance, during my first months at The Associated, I assumed "community" meant for speakers what it would have meant for me: all 92,000 Baltimore area Jews. In fact, people often reserved the term for a much smaller group: those contributing to, volunteering with, or working for The Associated or its agencies. Still, my confusion partly reflected ambiguous usage of the word to refer to the activists and the 92,000, both designating the activists an essential group and expressing the ambition of bringing all 92,000 into the fold.

Entering Southeast after a year in the Baltimore Jewish community, I mistakenly assumed "community" would mean in the second community much of what it meant in the first. Around The Associated, "community" connoted social and emotional intimacy, and people in Southeast seemed to be using the term inaccurately, to describe less intricate, more distant relations. Instead, while sharing some Associated wishes for closeness, the speakers often thought and spoke in terms of common political interests.

My efforts to understand the word "community" were prototypical of my attempt to learn two new languages. One other example illustrates the complexity of this project. At The Associated "fundraising" refers to members' financial investment in the organization, but it also measures how much people invest emotionally in the community. In Southeast Baltimore, homeowners have economic stakes in a place and are likely to stay there for a while, but "homeownership" also signifies community stability. "Fundraising" and "homeownership" have no etymological relationship, but they are cognates in referring to individual commitments to communities.

My second challenge in understanding what people said was to determine when they spoke for themselves and when they spoke for a community. This is more than a matter of learning who has knowledge of what many people think and thus makes a good informant. It involves, as well, discerning when someone's actions consciously or, often, unconsciously represent, give voice to, an opinion, emotion, or interest shared by many people by virtue of their being members of a community.

The most striking example was the years of seemingly endless debate I heard about and saw at The Associated regarding Jewish education. For a long time I wondered how people could speak of a single Jewish community when heated conflict between Orthodox and non-Orthodox not only divided people but blocked planning. Some I talked with offered a definitional answer, and one describing their experience: all Jews, whatever their differences, are one people, one community. Still, I wanted a more encompassing sociological or psychological explanation.

At some point, I "flipped" my interpretation of the years of planning stalemate. In addition to seeing it as a failure in coming to agreement, I saw it as a success of sorts in keeping Orthodox and non-Orthodox together. They related through conflict. As I listened to how the parties talked about their relationship, I came to attend more to the *persistence* of the conflict than the persistence of the *conflict*. I looked more at how the conflict expressed mutual dependencies between Orthodox and non-Orthodox and how these relations reflected and defined the community. And I learned how many impassioned arguments about education planning expressed community anxiety about whether it could survive.

TELLING STORIES OF COMMUNITIES PLANNING

The story of a planning process may be told in various ways. The usual approach is chronological, beginning when the idea of planning emerged and continuing through efforts to implement plans.[2] This narrative seems logical. It assumes that what precedes causes what follows and that the meanings of later events derive from what has gone before. However, certain characteristics of planning would lead in the opposite direction.

On the one hand, problematic experiences motivate people to plan, and these experiences may be said to cause or give meaning to planning. But planning is the effort to create unanticipated, even unlikely, futures by imagining desired states and designing strategies to bring them about. In this frame, the end gives cause and meaning to actions that precede it, although, strictly speaking, contemporary thoughts and feelings about a possible future motivate and give reason to actions to realize it.

And yet planning, like other human experience, is more complicated than even this version. Even if a past problem motivated planning to enact a more desirable future, more often than not, formulating the alternative helps define the problem and leads to redefining it. In other words, today's efforts to solve the problem that bothered us yesterday cause us to rethink the meaning of the problem. It would be fair to say today's planning activities caused yesterday's problem in the sense of creating a definition of the problem that now motivates us to respond.

More generally, planning processes have a characteristic some have likened to a "garbage can" (Cohen, March, and Olsen 1972; Cohen and March 1986). Planning activities, whatever motivated them, become a "container" into which people may place problems that concern them and programs they want implemented. These additional problems and possibilities become available for redefining the original condition and reconsidering solutions for it. Deliberations and actions may continue more or less coherently, but their focus may shift markedly over time.

We may say later that at last we understand the problem that first bothered us, or we may comment that we had to play with several designs before we could figure out what we really needed. Although planning documents may be clear and compelling, they only vaguely reflect the thinking and interactions that preceded them. They offer a version of things that is true at the time of writing, but other truths preceded that, and, presumably, others will follow.

In short, situations have no single "objective" definition. People define and redefine them. Although convention tells us a problem is solved when it is eliminated in the external world, in fact, a problem is solved when we believe it is solved. We may decide the world has changed, or we may simply have reconceived it. This does not mean external realities do not matter, but, rather, they matter in ways we assign to them.

In short, the intuitive argument for telling a planning story chronologically is not decisive. Indeed, it might make more sense to begin with the final events, and then tell what preceded them, now understood in terms of where they ended up.

Even if one were to try to construct a chronological version, there remains the historian's prototypical problem: Which events should be included? How does one decide whether something is relevant to the story? The answer depends partly on one's conceptual framework. For example, an economic determinist would assume economic forces are the most powerful influences on whatever happens, whereas a cultural determinist would assume beliefs most strongly affect social conditions.

The economist and the culturalist would each consider different events relevant to any story. They would disagree about what a planning process is "about." Is it about money? about culture? We could ask whether the story might not be about both, but this would force us to consider, then, how many things the story could be about. Is it also about personalities? political power? And if we decide several influences or meanings are important, how do we decide their relative importance, and how do we decide when something is sufficiently unimportant as not to warrant attention? The economist and the culturalist might disagree even about when the story started and when it is over. Our frameworks guide what we see, consider important, and accept as explanation.

I have tried to write the stories of these communities planning in ways that reflect the meanings to participants. This does not mean I have told the same stories they would have written (for those, see Giloth 1993, 1994; Levin and Bernstein 1991). Rather, I have aimed to understand planning activities as an expression of community dynamics. Further, I have tried to understand these dynamics in terms of both their explicit meanings to community members and their tacit, often unconscious meanings.

I have begun each history with a chronology of planning events, but the accounts do not always follow sequentially. One reason concerns the planning processes, where several parallel groups met simultaneously, some starting or ending before others, and where, consequently, a purely chronological narrative would distort the conduct of work. The other reason is that meanings and reasons neither conform to organizational structures nor follow the calendar. I have organized the histories in terms of basic challenges communities confront, and I have examined the medley of responses in relation to each.

As a result, the stories do not provide a complete record of planning activities. Nor do they give a full account of the outcomes. For one thing, not all proposals are equally important. Moreover, the formal outcomes of planning processes are often not really the end of planning, and an evaluation must move toward later, often less definitely formed events. Finally, I have focused on matters that concern community. As a result, some activities in which people invested much time and energy get less than proportionate attention.

THE RESEARCH APPROACH

I studied both community planning processes as an observer. I approached the director of community planning and budgeting at The Associated and the executive director of the South East Community Organization and asked each if I could study their planning process. I explained I was interested in the issues of community I have described here and wanted to look at planning as a situation where community members talked with one another about their community. I wanted to attend meetings, read documents, and interview participants.

I had no prior relationship with The Associated, though a former student was assistant to the planning director. The planning director and another staff member interviewed me about my interests, and the planning director asked for a formal proposal, including provisions for protecting confidentiality. After he consulted the president and talked with me again several times, he offered entry with a generous willingness to help. He was proud of his work and wanted recognition for it.

At SECO, I had begun to get to know the executive director at the time he was starting a community planning process, and I asked if I could observe. I offered an outline of research questions, but with little formality he simply invited me to come to meetings. Our initial relationship, as well as his openness to questioning and publicity, influenced his decision.

I began at The Associated in the summer of 1991. By this time, strategic planning participants had produced a plan, and task forces had taken steps to implement recommendations. I set out to reconstruct a history of planning to that point by reading meeting minutes and other archival documents and interviewing a sample of participants. I began to sit in on meetings of the Commission on Jewish Education and, later, the Joint Commission on Associated-Synagogue Relations. I continued to attend Joint Commission meetings until its cessation near the end of 1993, and I stayed with the Commission on Jewish Education and its successor, the Center for the Advancement of Jewish Education, through the spring of 1994. I have developed an account of the core strategic planning process from others' reports and records, while observing firsthand planning for Jewish education and relations between synagogues and the federation. I have written more generally of issues and interests with respect to the first part, while I have used meeting discussions more specifically to understand ways of addressing issues in the second part.

I began studying Southeast planning when the process started in the spring of 1992. I attended meetings, examined documents, and interviewed a sample of participants about past history and contemporary events. I have attended meetings of the Planning Council, its Coordinating Committee, and work groups since then. Thus, the account of the Southeast, which goes through the fall of 1995, is based on the firsthand observations that characterize the second period of Associated planning.

Associated staff allowed me to study strategic planning on the condition that I not identify participants by name or in other ways. Consistently, I have used pseudonyms for speakers at meetings, and I have characterized others generally as staff members, rabbis, or community leaders. No such condition was discussed in connection with my entry into Southeast community planning, but I have followed the same convention there, largely for consistency, but partly also to protect certain individuals who probably would not want to be named.

The result, perhaps especially in the more open Southeast culture, is sometimes awkward. In fact, several staff and community members played essential planning roles in each case, and this version obscures their responsibility. On the other hand, the cases are meant to tell the stories of two communities, where individuals are less important than the dynamics they represent. The convention serves that purpose.

PLAN OF THE BOOK

Part 1 introduces issues and the settings and provides a conceptual framework for analyzing the case studies.

The next four parts each focus on a specific task communities and their organizations must manage. These sections juxtapose the case studies, creating a tacit dialogue between the communities. In each case, the material first analyzes community dynamics with respect to the focal task and then examines how those dynamics influenced planning. The parts conclude with generalizations from the communities.

Part 2 looks at how the communities set their boundaries. Part 3 examines how they defined good community membership. Part 4 analyzes how they managed resources. Part 5 looks at how the communities tried to continue themselves.

Part 6 draws conclusions about community identities, community organizations, planning for communities, and cities.

CHAPTER 2

The Baltimore Jewish Community,
The Associated, and Strategic Planning

INTRODUCTION: THE TWO COMMUNITIES
BRIEFLY CONTRASTED

A Baltimorean persuaded to think about the Jewish community and Southeast Baltimore together would probably start talking about their differences. To begin with, they live in opposite corners of Baltimore, where geography corresponds to class, race, and ethnicity. The City's central core is home to its poorest residents, in addition to some professionals and well-to-do who have moved near the Inner Harbor. Incomes generally increase as one moves north in the City. Jews live largely in the Northwest, while the Northeast is mainly Protestant and Catholic. Most of the 59 percent of the population that is African American live in a pie-shaped wedge moving westward from the center of the City and in a corridor extending north from a concentration just east of the center to the City line. (Figure 1 shows the location of the Jewish community and Southeast Baltimore.)

Thus Baltimoreans interpret the geographic distance between the Northwest Jewish community and the Southeast in terms of social distance. For the most part, their members do occupy contrasting class positions, as measured by income, education, and occupation.

A 1985 study found 91,700 persons in greater Baltimore who were Jewish or related to someone Jewish living in 36,000 households. Their median annual household income was $36,000, with 28 percent earning more than $75,000 and only 8 percent earning less than $10,000 (Tobin 1986).[1] The 1990 Census found 76,861 persons in 30,450 households in the 26 Census tracts comprising the Southeast planning area. The highest median annual household income in any of the tracts was $32,857. Sixteen of the tracts had median incomes below the City median of $24,045, and three were below $13,200 (Baltimore City Department of Planning 1992a, 1992b).[2]

The Jews have significantly more formal education. Forty-nine percent of adults have at least a college degree, and 23 percent have a grad-

FIGURE 1
The Baltimore Jewish Community and Southeast Baltimore

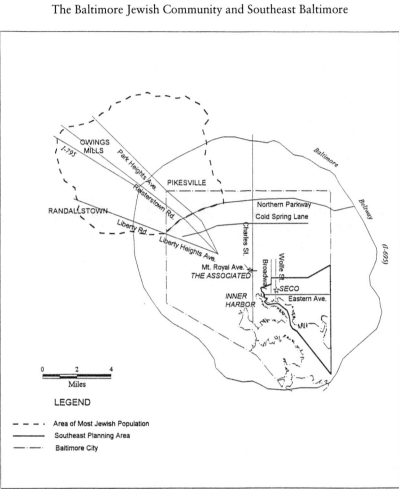

Produced by Urban Studies and Planning Program, University of Maryland at College Park, 1995

uate degree. In contrast, only 11 percent of the Southeast population over age 25 are college graduates, and only 50 percent are even high school graduates. Again, Southeast compares poorly with Baltimore City overall, where 15 percent have college degrees and 61 percent graduated from high school.

Workers in the two populations have different occupations. In the Jewish community, 46 percent are professionals, managers, or proprietors; 34 percent are in technical, sales, or clerical positions. The rest are in blue-collar, service, or other work. In Southeast Baltimore, only 21 percent are professionals, managers, or proprietors; 32 percent are in technical, sales, or clerical positions. Nearly half the labor force work in manufacturing or services. The Southeast labor force resembles Baltimore City in these respects, though the City has slightly more higher skill and higher status positions—24 percent in professional, managerial, and proprietary positions, and 33 percent in technical, sales, and clerical.

These class differences, however, only begin to describe the two communities. For one thing, they refer to individuals, not collectivities. They contribute to a picture of resources individuals can put into a community, and hint, with respect to Southeast, at some of the problems a community may face. And yet the statistics do not touch on some important personal characteristics and assets, nor do they say anything directly about relations among persons that constitute the social, cultural, and emotional realities of communities. With regard to the latter, they suggest bases for class identifications, but whether being professional or blue-collar is an important part of either community's identity depends on more than statistical homogeneity.

There is much more to each community's story. Both have considered ethnicity and religion central to their identity, and now they confront a world where ethnicity moves them less strongly, transcendence is elusive, and community is a question. In each, not everyone cares whether "the community" has a future, and many who do care wonder what might hold them together, give them purpose, and move them toward better, more meaningful times.

To understand these communities, the next two chapters examine the history of each, introduce its community organization, and summarize community planning events. The accounts reveal contrasts, some related to class differences, but also similar strivings toward the future.

A BRIEF SOCIAL HISTORY

Beginnings

"The proprietary charter establishing the colony of 'Mary-Land,' named after Henrietta Maria, the wife of King Charles I, was a mixture of business and religion" (Fein 1971:4).[3] So begins the most comprehensive published history of the Baltimore Jewish community. The account makes clear that, while Maryland was open to entrepreneurs, the founders assumed they would be Christians. The 1632 proprietary charter invokes "zeal for the propagation of the Christian faith" and concludes that the charter will always be interpreted in terms of "God's Holy and Truly Christian religion" (Charter of Maryland, secs. I and XXI; cited in Fein 1971:4).

The next few years saw growing tension between Protestants and Catholics, and in 1649 the colonial legislature passed the Act Concerning Religion, known as the "Toleration Act." While declaring tolerance for Christians, it declared,

> Whatsoever pson or psons within this Province . . . [who] shall . . . deny our Saviour Jesus Christ to bee the sonne of God, or shall deny the holy Trinity . . . shalbe punished with death and confiscacon or forfeiture of all of his or her lands and goods to the Lord Proprietary and his heires ("Act of Assembly of the 21st of April 1649," *Maryland Archives*, I:244–47; cited in Fein 1971:6).

The next section of the history book introduces "the first known Jew in Maryland," Jacob Lumbrozo, a healer, farmer, innkeeper, businessman, and Indian trader who became known, simply, as "the Jew Doctor." In February 1658 two men testified that Lumbrozo, about a year earlier, had expressed the view that Jesus' resurrection might be the product of necromancy or sorcery. Lumbrozo was sentenced to death for blasphemy under the Toleration Act. Fortuitously, ten days after his arrest, he was freed under a general amnesty in honor of Richard Cromwell's accession as lord protector of England.

After Lumbrozo was released, he changed his name from Jacob to John and acquired residency papers by giving the standard Christian oath, though he did not evidently convert to Christianity. Nevertheless, the account continues, "After Lumbrozo's death in 1666, no Jews appeared in Maryland for one hundred years" (Fein 1971:8).

The history recognizes Benjamin Levy, a merchant who came from Philadelphia in 1773, as "the first permanent Jewish settler" (Fein 1971:9). Twenty years later, Solomon Etting also moved to Baltimore from Philadelphia, going into business and shortly afterwards establishing a city water company. He later became a director of the Baltimore and Ohio Railroad. Jacob Cohen, Jr., a German, came to Baltimore in the early 1800s. He, too, became a director of the B&O and served many years as secretary-treasurer of the City's school board (Fein 1971:13–25).

Even so, the history next turns to "the struggle for equality." The Maryland constitution, adopted in 1776, declared

> It is the duty of every man to worship God in such manner as he thinks most acceptable to Him: all persons professing the Christian religion are equally entitled to protection in their religious liberty. . . . No other test or qualification ought to be required on admission to any office of trust or profit than such oath of support and fidelity to the State . . . and a declaration of belief in the Christian religion (Maryland Constitution, sec. 33 & art. 35; cited in Fein 1971:25–26).

Thus Jews were forbidden to hold elected office or practice law.

Beginning in 1797, Etting and others petitioned the Maryland Assembly to repeal these provisions. Jews were becoming city residents and active businessmen. Yet not until 1826 did the state legislature, after much heated argument, pass what became known as "the Jew Bill," which declared that

> every citizen . . . professing the Jewish Religion and . . . hereafter . . . appointed to any office of public trust under the state of Maryland shall in addition to the oath required to be taken by the Constitution and laws of the State or the United States, make and subscribe a declaration of his belief in a future state of rewards and punishments, in the stead of the declaration now required by the constitution and form of government of this state (Constitution of Maryland, art. 70, sec. 9; cited in Fein 1971:35).

The account concludes by heralding "the rise of Jews in government service" with the victories of Etting and Cohen in the next City Council elections (Fein 1971:36).

This story of the first two hundred years of Baltimore Jewish life contains the basic themes that shape modern accounts of the local Jewish community. First, the Baltimore Jewish community is old. Second, Jews were active in local economic and civic life. However, the first words of this history establish another theme: anti-Jewish prejudice. Pride in deep roots is balanced by caution about neighbors.

Immigration and Settlement

Jews came to America as part of a broader European immigration. They wanted economic opportunities, along with political and religious freedom. Reprisals for involvement in the abortive 1848 revolution and the Russian pogroms in the 1880s each gave the Jews especial reasons to leave Europe.

The first big wave of immigration came from Germany starting in the 1840s. Jews, as other European newcomers to Baltimore, settled in Southeast Baltimore. Some who went into the clothing business began to prosper as the City became a garment center. The invention of the sewing machine in the 1850s and Civil War demand for uniforms boosted the industry. The Jewish population grew from two hundred families in 1840 to ten thousand Jews by 1880.

Yet differences between a small, wealthy elite and the mass of workers began to divide the Jews (Fein 1971:76–81). Gradually, the more successful moved from the Southeast toward the west and north and, following the Civil War, established themselves in the northwest corner of the City, the start of a century-long movement away from the City.

From the beginning of mass immigration, Jewish leaders established charitable organizations to care for the less successful. In 1834 they organized the United Hebrew Benevolent Society, a mutual aid society. Nine years later they created the Hebrew Assistance Society, reorganized in 1856 as the Hebrew Benevolent Society, to provide for relief of the Jewish destitute.[4] Like later charitable enterprises, it was financed by subscription. The Hebrew Ladies Sewing Society was established in 1856 to sew clothes for the needy, as well as to allow indigent women to earn money by sewing. In 1863 the Hebrew Benevolent Society established the Hebrew Hospital and Asylum in response to various problems: kosher food was not available in other hospitals, dying Jewish patients in those hospitals were being besieged by proselytizers, and Jewish doctors faced barriers in practicing elsewhere.

Thus wealthier community members established the first of many charitable institutions. In the remainder of the century, German Jews created such organizations as the Jewish Education Alliance, the Hebrew Free Burial Society, the Council Milk and Ice Fund, and the Jewish Home for Consumptives.

In the years following the Civil War, as persecution, epidemic, and famine struck Eastern Europe, a second wave of immigrants, including many Jews, came to Baltimore. The German Jews called them all "Russians," in acknowledgment of the czar's dominion over Poland, Lithuania, the Ukraine, and other once independent countries. During the 1880s, 24,095 Jews landed in Baltimore; 20,000 more arrived in the 1890s; and 25,000 more between 1900 and 1905 (Fein 1971:149).

Numerically, the immigrants overwhelmed the Jews already living in Baltimore. Some also saw them as a social threat. A German Jewish elite led the Jewish community and represented it to outsiders. Now they confronted tens of thousands of Russians who not only came from another culture, but acted in lower-class ways many Germans feared would arouse anti-Jewish feelings. On the one hand, the Germans regarded the Russians as fellow Jews and wanted to help them; on the other, they worried about the dangers of associating with the Russians.

These national differences took on economic meanings. Most of the Russians came from cities, and most had occupations tied to the growing industrial economy. For example, 38 percent had been employed in manufacturing or as artisans, and 32 percent had worked in commerce (Steinberg 1989:95). Probably because of their involvement in urban industry and commerce, two-thirds of Russian men were literate (Steinberg 1989:101). In Baltimore, many went to work in the shops and factories of German businessmen. Russian Jewish life in Southeast Baltimore featured the conditions of poverty found in many American cities of the period. Russian workers organized unions and struck against German factory owners. These conditions did not encourage German charitable concern for the Russians.

Increasingly, Germans and Russians lived in separate societies. As the Germans moved toward the Northwest, they became known as the Uptown Jews, in contrast with the Downtown Russians who remained in the Southeast. These geographic labels connoted status differences. Germans and Russians socialized and prayed separately. The Russians created their own charitable institutions, often in obstinate parallel to German institutions, beginning in 1890 with the Friendly Inn, providing shelter to new immigrants. In 1903 came the Hebrew Immigrant Protective Society, later the Hebrew Immigrant Aid Society, followed by the Jewish Free Burial Society and the Hebrew Free Loan Association.

As charities proliferated, contributors wanted assurance money was solicited honestly and for worthwhile causes. Hence in 1906 the German agencies were joined into the Federated Jewish Charities. Two years later, the Russian charities, including the Jewish Court of Arbitration and the Baltimore Talmud Torah Society, formed the United Hebrew Charities.

In the next decade, both groups added new charities, including some allied with both, and philanthropists pushed for consolidation. In 1921 the two groups merged into the Associated Jewish Charities, the predecessor to today's Associated, described below (Cahn 1970:1–10). However, although it included both German and Russian charities, the German elite would dominate for nearly half a century.

During the 1920s the Russian community prospered, with some children of sweatshop workers and peddlers becoming businessmen and professionals. The Downtown population, too, began to move northwesterly, toward the Park Heights–Reisterstown Road area, while their Uptown predecessors moved farther, toward City boundaries and the suburbs. Still, while both groups left the area of original settlement, they continued to live pretty much separately through midcentury.

This chapter in Baltimore Jewish history reveals two dynamics. On the one hand, feelings of unity nurtured a social welfare tradition in which the better off took care of the less fortunate. At the same time, differences in nationality, wealth, and status divided the community. Russians' resentment of Germans' condescension encouraged the Russians to develop their own institutions. Differences between the groups involved more than simply economic disparities, but that conflict expressed the shame and resentment some of the poor have felt toward the wealthy. Although older generations today can still identify people as German or Russian, the Russians' economic success and German-Russian intermarriage have blurred lines and diminished the importance of national differences. Yet one outgrowth of German-Russian differences continues to matter a great deal.

Taking an Identity in the Modern World

Jewish immigrants coming to the United States confronted the question of how to think of their identity. Were they a religious group or an ethnic group? If religion played any part in their identity, what kind of religion, and what part?

In medieval Europe, Jewish communities, or *kehillot*, were geographically defined and self-contained, a reflection of both traditional Jewish concepts of community and external hostility (Elazar 1971:808–54). Rabbis exercised considerable religious and civil authority; more accurately, religious and civil authority were largely indistinguishable.

As the Enlightenment and emancipation of minorities accompanied the development of the nation-state beginning in the eighteenth century, Jews followed the customs of their lands in defining themselves. In Germany these forces eroded the autonomous Jewish community and made Jews individual citizens of Prussia. Following German traditions, Jews thought of themselves as a religious group, in parallel with Protestants and Catholics. At the same time, the Enlightenment discouraged religion in favor of science and humanism. Thus those Jews who continued to think of themselves religiously developed liberal practices adapted to modern knowledge and social and economic life.

Eastern Europe, in contrast, was more an amalgam of national groups. Nation-states emerged slower and later. Although the Russian government, for example, oppressed the Jews, both sides understood the Jews to be a national, or ethnic, group, and separate Jewish communities persisted into the twentieth century. Consistent with life in Eastern Europe, Jewish religious practice followed traditions of several centuries. At the same time, in contrast with the Germans, religion was not the primary element in their Jewish identity (see Elazar 1971, 5:808–54; Liebman 1973).

America offered German and Russian Jewish immigrants free choice in defining themselves. As the Germans arrived in the mid-nineteenth century, they established what became known as Reform congregations, featuring liberal practices and patterns of worship adapted to American customs. The first Reform congregation in the United States was Baltimore's Har Sinai, founded in 1842.

Russian and other Eastern European immigrants arriving later in the century, by and large, preferred to stay with more traditional religious practices, even while they identified themselves more by nationality than religion. They joined and formed what came to be called Orthodox congregations, religiously and socially like the institutions of small East European Jewish settlements.

Over time, as the Eastern Europeans tried to assimilate into American society, many wanted a more "American" form of worship, a compromise between Orthodoxy and modernity. These interests supported the creation of Conservative Judaism, situated between Orthodoxy and Reform. Although Conservatism emerged in Philadelphia and New York around the turn of the century, Baltimore Conservative congregations grew during suburbanization following World War II.

Reform, Conservative, and Orthodox Jews are arrayed roughly from left to right along a continuum of religious practices and social views. The Reform are most modern and liberal religiously and socially, while the Orthodox are most traditional religiously and among the most conservative socially. However, boundaries are fuzzy. Although traditional, "ultra-," Orthodox are most rigorously observant, more liberal "modern" Orthodox may be indistinguishable from "right-wing" Conservatives, and "left-wing" Conservatives may resemble the Reform. In addition, Reconstructionists, a small group who moved from Conservatism, are often like the Reform. Differences in formal liturgy exaggerate differences in individual belief and practice.

The 1985 survey of the Baltimore Jewish community found 20 percent of its members to be Orthodox, 35 percent Conservative, 29 percent Reform, and 12 percent other (including Reconstructionist) (Tobin 1986). These groups are no longer consistently associated with German and Eastern European backgrounds and have their own dynamics. The most significant differences divide the Orthodox (particularly the traditional Orthodox) from the non-Orthodox. Baltimore has the highest proportion of Orthodox of any American Jewish community, and the number is continually growing because Baltimore enjoys a reputation as a city with a wide range of Jewish institutions and a low cost of living. Most of the growth represents immigration from New York City. Geographically, the Orthodox and non-Orthodox tend to live separately, with the traditional Orthodox in the Park Heights area and most Reform and Conservative Jews in the adjacent northwest suburbs.[5]

While, as this survey shows, most Baltimore Jews identify with a religious denomination, they vary in the importance they give religion in their identity and attachment to a Jewish community. Today, the Orthodox are most likely to emphasize religious identity, while the Reform are particularly likely to emphasize ethnicity.

These later chapters in Baltimore Jewish history contribute to a dynamic tension that has influenced community life, The Associated, and strategic planning. On the one hand, a long shared world and local history, punctuated by persecution, draws Baltimore Jews together as members of a community who worship similarly, if not identically, do business and socialize with one another, and care for mutual needs. Yet differences in worship and articles of faith, relative emphasis on religion and ethnicity, economic success, and involvement in community institutions divide the Jews, leading some to question whether they comprise a single community.

THE ASSOCIATED:
JEWISH COMMUNITY FEDERATION OF BALTIMORE

As charitable institutions multiplied in the late nineteenth century, contributors looked for ways to ensure their money went efficiently to good causes. In 1895 the Boston Federation of Jewish Charities became the first fundraiser that coordinated allocations to service agencies (Elazar 1976). Baltimore's Associated Jewish Charities was formed in 1921. The Associated is now one of about two hundred local Jewish federations in the United States and Canada. Because of the amount of money The Associated raises, it is known as one of the "big 16" federations.

Associated staff and lay community leaders[6] emphasize The Associated's fundraising functions. It conducts annual campaigns and solicits endowments to support local agencies and national and international Jewish organizations. The seventeen Baltimore agencies include education, housing, recreation, vocational, counseling, health, refugee resettlement, and geriatric programs. Occasionally, The Associated organizes a special campaign, such as operations to bring Soviet Jews to Baltimore. Prominent among international contributions are funds for Israel.

The Associated, or federation, can be seen as a community organization that exercises certain governance functions. Activists call The Associated the Jewish community's "central address." Contributions are like a voluntary "tax" community members pay to provide services. The Associated, as one of the most centralized federations, exercises great control over local service agencies as a result of an agreement whereby, in return for federation funding, they do not raise money independently. The Associated occasionally mediates conflicts between Jewish groups or institutions. It sometimes speaks for the Jewish community on public issues.

Anyone contributing $25 to the annual campaign is a member, with voting rights at the annual meeting. However, a few hundred families contribute most of The Associated's funds. The 1993 annual campaign raised $22.5 million from 17,000 gifts, but half the money came from fewer than 75 gifts, and three-fourths from about 300. The annual budget is approximately $30 million.

The Associated board consists mostly of big contributors and agency board presidents, with power concentrated in an Executive Committee. A professional staff of forty-five is headed by a president, a vice president for finance and operations, a vice president for community development, an assistant vice president, directors of the campaign, finance, marketing, and the Women's Department, and an executive vice chairman for legacy and endowment. The president, some top managers, and a small group of lay leaders centered in the Executive Committee make most major decisions.

The Associated has a reputation in the federation world for its fundraising success, staff competence, and contributions to national and international Jewish leadership. Staff speak proudly of Baltimore as the "Jerusalem" of Jewish communities. The longevity of Jewish families, their commitment to the federation, and the broad range of Jewish institutions, they say, make it the most desirable place in America to work in Jewish communal service. They boast of the willingness of community leaders to "come together at one table" to set directions and resolve differences as distinguishing Baltimore from other Jewish communities. Community members and staff call attention to many Baltimoreans who have moved from The Associated to leadership in national and international Jewish organizations.

From its origins, the federation has been an association of people who feel proprietary responsibility for their community. Board members have represented families whose economic success has entitled them to community political leadership. Leaders in The Associated have been active in the larger Baltimore and Maryland professional and business communities. For example, the Council of Jewish Federations, comprising all North American federations, held its annual meeting in Baltimore in 1992, and William Donald Schaefer, governor of Maryland and former mayor of Baltimore, began his address to the conference by declaring how impressed he was to recognize so many business leaders in one place.

Business defines much of Associated culture. Lay leaders and staff wear corporate attire. Consistent with the federation's fundraising focus, people talk a great deal about money, and monetary metaphors run through discussions. It is common to speak, for example, of "buying into" a decision. That double meaning is deliberate: political endorsement is presumed to lead to financial support. In the early 1980s, the title of the chief executive officer was changed from executive vice president (the top lay leader was president) to president (with the lay leader redesignated chairman), to command desired respect from corporate leaders.

Decorum and style are important at The Associated. Public meetings are carefully planned; staff members draft scripts for lay conveners. The organization aims at harmonious agreement. Participants speak respectfully, avoiding anger as well as overt aggression. People may refer to their conflicts with others but are expected not to rehearse them or seek to resolve them publicly. Indeed, people at meetings grow anxious whenever discussion approaches conflict or disagreeable topics. In these instances, speakers may be told to save their concerns for a later meeting or private conference.[7]

Men founded The Associated and have dominated it. Traditionally, women were relegated to a Women's Division (now the Women's Department; Rosenberg 1976). The president and four of the seven vice presidents or directors are men. Only two of forty-one top lay leaders (originally presidents, later chairmen) have been women, the first in 1983. Only in 1992 did a woman head the annual campaign. In 1994 sixty-eight of 101 board members were men.

The strategic planning committees described next included more women, but, even so, two-thirds of formal decision makers were men. Even though the first woman president headed the Strategic Planning Committee, Associated tradition designated her "chairman."

STRATEGIC PLANNING AT THE ASSOCIATED

Origins of Strategic Planning

In the late 1980s, despite continuing fundraising success, The Associated faced two challenges. One was growing agency requests for funds, particularly for repairs and renovations to old facilities in the City. Federation leaders felt they lacked guidelines for spending. Further, requests for capital funds for old facilities raised a policy question: Should The Associated maintain its institutions in the City, or should it more deliberately build in suburban Owings Mills? On the one hand, Jews were increasingly moving to the suburbs, but, on the other, any precipitous Associated move would jeopardize the value of other Jewish institutions in the City, including several large synagogues near the agencies.

A second challenge was more gradual, not yet urgent. The federation continued to raise more funds each year, sometimes impressively supplementing the annual campaign with special campaigns, even as the recession deepened. But The Associated was relying on a contracting number of families to sustain contributions. While it was succeeding in fundraising, it was losing community involvement. As time went on, particularly after the 1991 publication of the National Jewish Population Survey (Kosmin et al. 1991), the second problem became more broadly defined as declining identification with the Jewish community as a result of intermarriage, assimilation, and apathy.

In 1986 Associated leaders hired a new president, whom they expected to raise and allocate money with clear priorities. One of his first acts was to initiate a strategic planning process that formally began in January 1988. Reasons for and purposes of strategic planning can be understood in several ways. One, simply, is that the new executive wanted to put his mark on the organization. The federation had never engaged in strategic planning. A growing number of nonprofit organizations were doing it for reasons that made it attractive to the new president and lay leaders who had hired him: "strategic planning" connoted fiscal accountability and profitability associated with the corporate sector (Bryce 1992; Bryson 1988; Espy 1986; Miller 1989; Nutt and Backoff 1992).

The president presented strategic planning as an effort to think creatively about what the federation should be doing and set rational community-wide priorities for allocating funds. At least retrospectively, some agency executives interpreted the interest in priority setting differently. Although they did not object in principle, they saw the federation using it to consolidate control over agencies. Adding centralized priorities to centralized budgeting could further weaken agencies. To some agency executives, this was the hidden agenda.

The other side of setting spending priorities was strategizing more systematically to raise money, particularly among wealthy Jewish families that gave the federation nothing or less than they seemed able to afford. Both the substance and process of strategic planning aimed to address this concern. Seventy persons served on the main strategic planning committees; by the end of implementation, the number of participants was close to three hundred. The Associated gave priority to including representatives of wealthy families, so they would "buy into" planning recommendations.

Some people, among both participants and nonparticipants, viewed strategic planning as less important for rendering a plan with specific text than for involving the wealthy in discussions that would renew their investment in the federation. It would immerse them in the excitement of planning for the future of the Jewish community, acquaint them with a vast array of community needs while showing them the good work of agencies in addressing these needs, and give them new reasons to contribute. As a description of typical fundraising activities, this view does not contradict the depth to which the wealthy felt responsibility for their community. They wanted to feel good in solving problems, and strategic planning would show them a way.

It is important to look at how this planning process related to the community. Strictly speaking, the federation was engaging in strategic planning to set organizational directions and priorities. This was not to be a community-wide planning process open to anyone interested. Still, when several hundred people who knew of strategic planning wanted to take part, federation leaders tried to include as many as possible while getting persons who identified with each of the denominational groups, major synagogues, and agencies.

Significantly, as noted earlier, people at The Associated use the word "community" to refer to the families that contribute to the federation. Thus federation leaders could argue that strategic planning for the organization was also community planning. Members of this community participated in planning, and some were among the recipients of services for which priorities were to be set. Nevertheless, meetings were not publicly announced, they were not open to the general Jewish public, and records of them were not published. In these respects, planning was tied to organizational interests.

Still, the relationship between strategic organizational planning and the community was ambiguous. On the one hand, federation leaders made clear they were planning for the allocation of funds they raised. The Associated would take a reading on community sentiments through the voices of planning committee members, either in representing the interests of a constituency or in reporting their impressions of others' needs.

At the same time, emerging research on increasing intermarriage gradually congealed "Jewish continuity" as a focal issue. In federation terms, this meant potential contributors were less involved in Jewish communal life. Pointedly, leaders in some of the wealthiest families saw their children not only marrying non-Jews, but losing interest in philanthropy or else directing their charitable concerns toward such secular issues as homelessness and child abuse (Mayer 1988).

Eventually, during implementation of the strategic plan, federation leaders made explicit an issue that may have underlain strategic planning all along: the challenge to give the federation a religious meaning. Many in the Jewish federation world, including some at The Associated, speak of federations as the embodiment of a "civil religion," practices that are not intrinsically religious but that contribute to feelings of connection to something transcendent (Woocher 1986; see also Bellah 1967, 1975; Bellah and Hammond 1980). Some considered work in the federation not only their primary Jewish social activity, but also the emotional equivalent of traditional worship. However, many in the broader Jewish community found such civil religion pallid and unappealing, not satisfying any longings for faith or spirituality. Particularly, but not only, the younger generation could not understand why they should be concerned about the federation. Ultimately, this loss of authority was the most serious challenge to The Associated, and federation leaders eventually turned to the synagogues and invited them to join in promoting "Jewish continuity."

A Brief Chronology

The Executive Committee of The Associated Board approved a strategic planning process in September 1987. It created a Strategic Planning Committee to work as a subgroup of its Executive Committee, and it decided to engage a consultant to guide the planning process. In January 1988 the Strategic Planning Committee convened. The thirty members included representatives of leading families, two rabbis, and others active in the federation. The committee included persons identified with each of the denominations, though, overall, it reflected the traditional distance between the federation and the Orthodox. Nineteen (63%) of the members were men.

The Strategic Planning Committee authorized three working subcommittees. Their members included persons from the Strategic Planning Committee, as well as others with special expertise or interest. The Service Delivery Subcommittee was established to determine what services The Associated should fund, by considering what community members needed, setting priorities among needs, and deciding who could most effectively provide the services where. Reflecting women's interests and involvement in social services, this subcommittee had the highest proportion of women (42%—8 of 19 members). One member was a rabbi.

The Relationships Subcommittee was charged to examine and improve relations among groups and organizations within the Jewish community, between the Jewish community and the larger Baltimore community, and between the local Jewish community and national and international Jewish communities and organizations. This subcommittee was the largest, to include people involved in the many relationships under scrutiny. Four of the thirty members were rabbis; eleven (37%) were women.

The Financing Subcommittee was established to analyze revenue needs and establish goals and strategies for raising funds. Most of the members were from wealthy families, no rabbis were members, and the subcommittee had the highest proportion of men (71%—17 of 24).

Overall, seventy persons participated in the Strategic Planning Committee and its subcommittees. This group resembled The Associated generally in being largely male (67 percent, or 47 persons). Yet, significantly, as noted, the Strategic Planning Committee chair was the first woman elected head of the Associated Board. Those who selected her valued her ability to bring together disparate community interests.

The three subcommittees began meeting in late March or early April and continued working through the end of 1988, when they delivered draft reports for their sections of what would become the strategic plan. The consultant and staff revised the drafts and produced *Building a Stronger Community: Toward the Year 2000* in June 1989 (Strategic Planning Committee 1989, vol. 1; hereafter, Plan 1989). The Executive Committee accepted the plan and created a Strategic Planning Implementation Council to put the plan into effect.

The Strategic Planning Implementation Council first met in July 1989, and designated six task forces to formulate actions to implement clusters of recommendations. The task forces involved Services; Administration, Budget, and Decision Making Process; Facilities; Communications, Image-Building, and Community Relations; Human Resources Development; and Financial Resources Development. They included Strategic Planning Committee members and others.

Task forces met for different periods of time, depending on how long it took to dispatch their responsibilities. By the middle of 1990, all task forces had either ended or been superseded by permanent structures.

The Services Task Force took up Jewish education issues from the Service Delivery Subcommittee. However, by 1990, Associated leadership, along with other federations, began to focus on Jewish education as a means of encouraging Jewish identity and promoting Jewish continuity. As a result, the Board created a Commission on Jewish Education to develop a strategic plan for Jewish education and to serve as the Board's standing committee on Jewish education. In the fall of 1993 the Commission became part of a Center for the Advancement of Jewish Education.

The Communications, Image-Building, and Community Relations Task Force took up the Relationships Subcommittee's recommendation that the federation seek a shared vision of mutual responsibility with synagogues. Associated leaders decided improving relations with synagogues should be a high priority, and the Board created a Joint Commission on Associated-Synagogue Relations at the end of 1991. That group met through the fall of 1993.

CHAPTER 3

Southeast Baltimore, the South East Community Organization, and Southeast Community Planning

A BRIEF SOCIAL HISTORY

Origins

Southeast Baltimore is "different" from the rest of Baltimore City. The area reflects the beginnings of the City and its neighborhoods remain virtually unchanged since they were first developed during the early, middle and late 19th century. . . . Baltimore City is really a big industrial "town" . . . Baltimore City developed as a collection of neighborhoods and continues to remain a city of neighborhoods. Baltimore is also a port city with a heavy concentration of industry around the harbor. . . . Due to the concentration of industry near the port activities, East Baltimore was planned as a community of small row houses designed and priced for the working man. . . . Due to the settlement of immigrants from eastern and southern Europe, the southeast area has become a mosaic of the various nationalities. . . . Other sections of the City tend to be described through the use of "class" terms such as: poor, affluent, or middle-class (Truelove 1977b:5, 6).

Thus begins the official history of the South East Community Organization, written during its heyday. The description combines historical fact with deliberate image making. The history commences in 1726, when Edward Fell settled in what would become Southeast Baltimore and began to accumulate land, which he called Fell's Point. Fell's Point was one of three separate towns in the area, along with Baltimore Town and Jones Town. Its asset was the deep channel that made it a port. In 1773 the Maryland provincial assembly joined these towns to create Baltimore City. Maritime activity expanded in Fell's Point, and it was primarily responsible for Maryland's becoming the second largest shipbuilding center in America (Olson 1980; Truelove 1977b:Appendix D). Figure 2 shows Southeast Baltimore today.

In 1780 John O'Donnell, a Far East trader, settled and began to accumulate property east of Fell's Point. In 1830, three New York

FIGURE 2
Southeast Baltimore

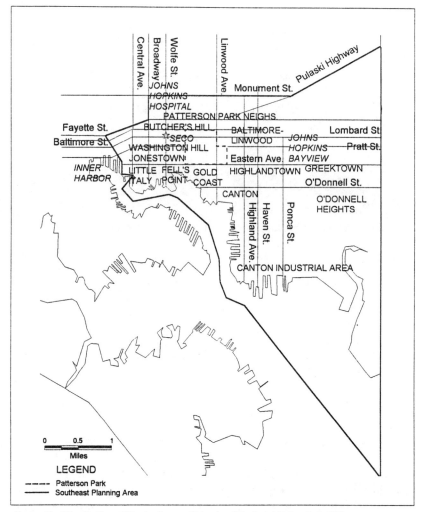

Produced by Urban Studies and Planning Program, University of Maryland at College Park, 1995

entrepreneurs purchased his family's holdings and consolidated them into the Canton Company, anticipating prosperity that would come with railroad expansion through the City. The land formed an area one-third the size of Baltimore and became "probably the nation's earliest, largest, and most successful industrial park" (Olson 1980:77). Brewing, a cotton mill, copper smelting, and canning were the first of many Canton industries.

The expansion of American railroads and canals attracted poor men from England and Ireland beginning in the 1830s. Soon after, German immigration started, bolstered by steamship connections between Baltimore and Bremen. However, the poverty that drove immigrants to America made their new lives in the City difficult. They could not afford decent housing and lived under poor sanitary conditions. Churches and other ethnic institutions responded with health care, welfare, and schooling for the immigrants (Olson 1980).

As a group, the Germans were particularly successful. The high point of German life in Baltimore was the 1860s and 1870s, with 12,000 Germans arriving in Baltimore in 1868. The German community established not only cultural institutions, but also welfare organizations, including the German Workingmen's Relief Association, St. Joseph's Hospital, and the Hebrew Benevolent Association. Churches, synagogues, and schools were German or bilingual. In 1872 the City government responded by creating public German-English schools (Olson 1980:179–83).

Southeast Baltimore grew in the late nineteenth and early twentieth centuries as a result of massive industrialization and immigration. Canton remained the industrial center, adding a railroad, copper and brass works, a Standard Oil refinery, and Western Electric and General Motors plants. Meat packing, more breweries, Crown Cork and Seal, and Crosse and Blackwell were established in Highlandtown, to the east. Sparrows Point, Bethlehem Steel's largest plant, was built nearby in Baltimore County (Giloth 1993; Reutter 1988; Truelove 1977b:Appendix C). As Southeast Baltimore grew into the City's shipping and manufacturing center, most families settling there directly or indirectly depended on industry for their income.

European events of the 1870s and 1880s sent more people to America. Minorities fled Bismarck's rule in the Austro-Hungarian Empire. Bavarian, Polish, and Bohemian Catholics began coming to America in the 1870s. Russian pogroms following the assassination of Czar Alexander II in 1881 drove thousands of Jews to America (Fein 1971; Olson 1980). Later came Italians, Greeks, Ukrainians, and Finns. An early-twentieth-century school survey identified thirty-seven nationalities in Highlandtown (Truelove 1977b:Appendix E). By and large, residential patterns followed nationality and religion.

The Catholic Church served as religious, educational, and welfare institution for Catholics. It responded to immigrants' diversity by modifying its practice of organizing parishes geographically and establishing national, or ethnic, parishes, including, eventually, priests who came from parishioners' cultures and spoke their language. At St. Leo's in Little Italy, in 1880 an Italian priest succeeded a series of Irish. The Redemptorists recruited German, Bohemian, and Polish priests for other Baltimore communities (Burke 1978; Olson 1980:179; Truelove 1977b:Appendix F).

Ethnicity

The lines from SECO's official history capture central themes in Southeasterners' identity. Southeast Baltimore goes back to the City's origins and grew with the City. The port and much of the industry that built the City's economy developed in Southeast. Many who worked the plants and the port were European immigrants who settled in Southeast, where they established ethnic neighborhoods and institutions.

The SECO account reflects a resurgence of white ethnic pride in the 1970s. It reports:

> the southeast area has become a mosaic of the various nationalities. . . . Southeast Baltimore today contains a population of approximately 94,000 people of which 10% are black Americans and 1,500 (less than 2%) are American Indians; the majority comprise the white ethnic constituency. The area is a patch-work quilt containing identifiable neighborhoods of Polish, Greek, Italian, Ukrainian, German, Finnish, Irish, Czech, Black, Appalachian, and Lumbee Indian immigrants (Truelove 1977b:6).

A 1976 *New York Times Magazine* article enthusiastically lauded SECO's "Ethnic Renewal." The author articulated the views of Monsignor Geno Baroni, whose National Center for Urban Ethnic Affairs sponsored SECO projects:

> Baroni's gospel is that ethnic cohesiveness is a legitimate and powerful force that should be mobilized to preserve neighborhoods. If working-class ethnics have their own turf, Baroni argues, they can make common cause with their black neighbors (Kuttner 1976:4).

"Ethnic Renewal" played on Southeast whites' simultaneous rehabilitation of housing and identity, but it raised without answering the question of what "renewed" ethnicity was. Immigrants had naturally continued ways of life they had practiced in Europe. Their grandchildren were American, and ethnicity, rather than the core of everyday affairs, was more likely symbolic activity, such as holiday meals, music, or festivals.

"Ethnic mosaics" and "patch-work quilts," common metaphors among "new ethnics" in the 1970s, hinted at these changes in their contrast with an earlier metaphor, the "melting pot." The melting pot is a bubbling cauldron, where immigrants actively mix and change. Mosaics and quilts are static patterns. Although the fixity of the pieces might suggest their strength and integrity, a mosaic is a fragile design, to be viewed but not touched.

Moreover, the unmetaphorical argument about tensions with blacks hinted at some of the meaning of renewed ethnic identification. At a time of black pride, many working-class whites, anxious about black militancy and resentful about their limited economic success, sought new status by appealing to their own special ancestry (Gans 1979; Goering 1971; Stein and Hill 1977). The SECO account emphasizes white ethnicity in a way that glosses over, perhaps means to obscure, racial differences in Southeast. Before one can give much attention to the 10 percent who are black or the Indians, who, the text notes, are less than 2 percent of the population, the account emphasizes the majority are white ethnics. Even if one were to think about blacks or Lumbees, the next sentence lumps them together with Czechs and Ukrainians as only two more immigrant groups.

In fact, the ethnic and racial composition of Southeast was changing even during the 1970s. Though, as the history noted, only 12 percent of Southeast were not white in 1970, by 1980 that proportion nearly doubled to 23 percent. In 1990, 28 percent of Southeast residents were not white. Twenty-five percent were African-American, 1 percent Native American, 1 percent Asian, and 2 percent Hispanic[1] (Baltimore City Department of Planning 1992b[2]).

These data open a place for other histories. For example, Baltimore's free black population in the mid-nineteenth century included many stevedores, dock workers, and caulkers, among them Frederick Douglass, who worked in Fell's Point. They often competed with whites and suffered periodic violence at their hands. A small black population continued to live in Fell's Point and the area just north of it later called Washington Hill. Baltimore's black population grew with urban migrations in the twentieth century.

While West Baltimore became the geographic, as well as social and political, center for the black population, many blacks moved, as well, into the area of East Baltimore around the Johns Hopkins Medical Institutions. In the 1950s, closer to downtown and the water, in what had been Jones Town, the City government built Lafayette Courts, the first of several area public housing projects. It became the home for a predominantly black low-income population. In recent years, more blacks have moved into the area around Johns Hopkins.

Lumbee Indians migrated to Baltimore from North Carolina in the early 1940s in search of industrial work. Today about two thousand live in Southeast Baltimore, most in Fell's Point. Some move between Baltimore and North Carolina, while others stay in Baltimore, many with plans to return South after they retire. A great majority (75%) continue to hold blue-collar jobs. The Baltimore American Indian Center, started in Fell's Point in 1968, sponsors cultural activities and provides services for Lumbees and a few Indians from other tribes (Dial and Eliades 1975; Makofsky 1971; Urban Planning Workshop 1980).

Decline

The image of Southeast Baltimore as a place of ethnic neighborhoods had several meanings. Above all, it conveyed a proud picture of the people of Southeast. They built the economy, and yet they lived by rich traditions that gave their lives meanings beyond the wages they earned.

In addition, the ethnic image of Southeast carried a subtler message—that, in fact, something held all Southeast together. "Southeast Baltimore" existed as more than lines on a map. While Polish, Italians, Greeks, Irish, Ukrainians, and Germans followed different customs, they shared a history of immigrating from Europe and struggling to establish families in America.

Further, as the fleeting references to blacks and American Indians suggest, the positive image of ethnicity served to distract people from worrisome signs of change. As all of Baltimore, Southeast was changing racially. In addition, the City and Southeast were changing economically. Corporations were investing overseas, closing some American plants and relocating others in suburban or rural areas. Sparrows Point, once the world's largest steel mill, shrank from 29,000 workers in 1957 to 8,000 in 1987 (Reutter 1988). American Can closed; Western Electric and General Motors were cutting back.

As jobs left the City, workers went with them. The SECO history, acknowledging the City had lost 100,000 of one million residents since 1950, insists, hopefully, "the population seems to be stabilizing near the 900,000 mark" (Truelove 1977b:5). In fact, the City's population continued falling, to 787,000 in 1980 and to 736,000 by 1990.

Reasons people moved out of Southeast Baltimore changed the population profile. When jobs left, families with working adults followed. The departure of employers and workers took tax revenues and reduced the quality of City services for an increasingly poor population. Education suffered greatly: many parents lost confidence in public schools, and a growing number of families left the City when children reached school age. During the 1980s the Southeast school-age population dropped slightly from 26 percent to 25 percent. The elderly, many of them original occupants of their homes, largely stayed. Some felt committed to the area; others could not afford to move or had nowhere to go. While between 1980 and 1990 the number of residents 65 and older stayed around 12,000, their percentage increased slightly from 15 percent to 16 percent. Most owned homes, but few had much income. They represented 37 percent of homeowners; 19 percent lived in poverty.

These trends raised questions about Southeast's continuity. It was losing people and jobs. Young families moving out often sold family homes to strangers, who were unrelated to those who stayed. These changes raised questions about Southeast's identity: Was it anything more than a piece of land? Did culture or social relations hold it together?

Southeast's history frames dynamics in tension. On the one hand, a traditional image of working-class white ethnicity draws at least white community members together. Yet increasingly the lines of race, class, position in the life cycle, and geography pull Southeasterners in separate directions.

THE SOUTH EAST COMMUNITY ORGANIZATION

In the late 1960s working-class white ethnics and gentrifying urban pioneers joined forces to stop the proposed demolition of hundreds of Southeast homes for construction of an expressway. They described the defeat of "The Road" as a triumph for ethnic blue-collar families. From this victory they went on to examine a variety of problems they found they shared, and in 1971 they formed the South East Community Organization.

In 1974 SECO created Southeast Development, Incorporated (SDI), a nonprofit corporation, to implement economic development projects. In a few years SECO became not only a forceful representative of Southeast interests to City government, but also an effective quasi-government of Southeast. Civic leaders reflected that SECO had, in fact, operated as a de facto extension of City government (Truelove 1977b).

SECO has developed a national reputation as a neighborhood organization that has successfully promoted community social and economic development. In its early years, the National Center for Urban Ethnic Affairs supported SECO and SDI as an example of what could be done to regenerate ethnic communities. The Ford Foundation has funded organizing and economic development projects. Books and articles on neighborhoods and community organization have praised SECO's work (Cassidy 1979; Clay and Hollister 1983; Cunningham and Kotler 1983; Kuttner 1976).

Today SECO is an umbrella organization supporting neighborhood associations representing many of the 77,000 residents of Southeast Baltimore. It has moved from its original emphasis on community organization—which neighborhood associations, many of which SECO helped build, themselves do—toward social programs and economic development. While SECO continues to organize residents on issues such as library closings and development threats, SECO and SDI have sponsored adult literacy, Head Start, and elderly housing programs, recycling, a coalition against lead poisoning, a project to promote racial harmony, and various housing and development projects. The director at the time of Southeast community planning characterized SECO as an "issue umbrella" that could help neighborhood associations and residents act on issues of common concern.

Because Southeast Baltimore comprises diverse neighborhoods, SECO does not draw authority from an overarching community solidarity, as The Associated does. While SECO helps organizations address their problems, it does not attempt to mediate group conflicts. In 1992 fewer than 150 persons contributed money to the organization, and not all lived in Southeast. In contrast with The Associated, SECO serves Southeast residents but does not claim to represent them.

SECO and SDI have separate boards but a common executive, who is executive director of SECO and executive vice president of SDI. SECO and SDI together have about twenty-five professional and support staff members. The organizations have tried to diversify their boards racially and economically, as well as geographically. The boards are changing, but members are still mostly middle-class white professionals.

Participation at SECO and SDI is open to anyone. In contrast with The Associated, these organizations face a paucity of people with interest and time. Wealth would be considered an illegitimate claim for power, but no one contributes so much even to raise the issue. Virtually all the annual combined SECO and SDI budgets of about $1 million comes from outside Southeast, mainly in the form of grants.

Anyone who lives or works in Southeast may vote for board members at the SECO annual meeting. In addition, staff involve residents in program decisions. Citizen participation is part of organizational ideology and gives projects legitimacy. In addition, volunteers, often bringing considerable expertise, vitally supplement small staffs.

SECO's culture reflects its origins. The acronym for the organization that resisted the highway, Southeast Council Against the Road (SCAR), expressed a deep sense of violation by government. SECO has often represented Southeast residents' sense of facing a hostile world, such as a government that either cares only about business and the wealthy or is incompetent, or developers intent on plundering the area. Most around SECO consider themselves honest, hard-working, blue-collar people or their allies. They work with City government and other major institutions expediently and cautiously. Many Southeast residents proudly see themselves as members of the opposition.

Stories of SECO's origins portray the first activists as colorful characters, mythologized as much for their eccentricity and courage as for their insight and leadership (Truelove 1977a, 1977b). When a personnel committee interviewed the candidate who became SECO's first director, they took him to a popular bar, where they publicly engaged him in an into-the-late-night beery conversation about his past and dreams, and they decided to hire him. The outcome of this ostentatiously déclassé interview was proclaimed in the title of the 1977 official SECO history: "The Director Wears Blue Jeans" (Truelove 1977a).

SECO is no longer the loose place it was in the aftermath of the 1960s. The director at the time of Southeast planning pushed staff to think creatively and rigorously about problems and programs. Southeast community planning followed a number of organizational strategic planning exercises and was as carefully prepared as Associated strategic planning. At the same time, SECO continues to respect and encourage individuality and openness. Dress and demeanor are informal.

These conditions produce discussion that both resembles and contrasts with that at The Associated. Because SECO, like The Associated, is a voluntary association, staff try to accept ideas from as many as possible. Although in the early days SECO was split by intense conflicts—most prominently, between advocates of grassroots organizing and advocates of development programs—discussion is now relatively harmonious. One reason is that leaders try to recognize and respond to as many interests as possible and find issues and programs that transcend racial or class differences. Another is that SECO does not attract social conservatives from traditional ethnic communities and avoids the conflicts they would raise with liberals who dominate the organization. Those aggrieved about blacks, welfare, and public housing take their concerns elsewhere, such as neighborhood associations and the police community relations council.

Women's issues have been part of SECO discussions. Although in the early years women spoke up mainly to say they felt neglected by male leaders, ensuing debates recognized gender as a legitimate basis of interests. The executive director is a man, but women manage many projects. SECO has had women presidents. The 1993 SECO board included thirteen women (counting the president) and eleven men. Women were active in the Southeast planning process as well. Two of four Coordinating Committee members were women, as were thirty of sixty Southeast Planning Council members.

The arithmetic is less important than the taken-for-granted role of women in community organization and planning at SECO. Although this reflects the egalitarian ideology of SECO's origins at the end of the 1960s, it also represents women's role as community leaders. That goes back to when most women stayed home while their husbands worked, and it expresses women's concerns about taking care of people in a community as an extension of the household and family.

SOUTHEAST COMMUNITY PLANNING

Southeast Planning and Associated Planning

The Southeast Planning Council, representing 78,000 Baltimoreans, and The Associated, representing 92,000, engaged in community planning in overlapping years, and yet one might safely guess no more than a handful in the two communities combined were aware of both efforts.

Part of the explanation is that the Southeast Planning Council was new, unfamiliar even to many in Southeast. Associated strategic planning, in turn, was mainly for organizational activists, and it was little known outside federation circles. But most of the explanation reflects Baltimore's religious and economic segregation. Groups living in opposite corners are unlikely to be aware of or curious about one another.

Still, there were links between The Associated and Southeast planning. When Southeast activists struggled to create a community organization in the early 1970s, the Baltimore chapter of the American Jewish Committee contributed $5,000 toward a first-year budget of $20,000.[3] Federation activists responsible for that donation still recall it proudly.

Twenty years later, SECO, now an established organization, looking for support for a Southeast community planning process, applied to the local Morris Goldseker Foundation. Grant decisions are made by a three-member committee: the presidents of the Johns Hopkins University, Morgan State University, and The Associated. They are advised, in turn, by a subcommittee of one representative from each of their institutions. Thus The Associated was integral to decisions that gave SECO $76,000 for Southeast planning.

However, aside from these important but exceptional contacts, planning in the two communities proceeded independently. The fact that neither knew what the other was doing meant that neither could learn from the other. As much as this says about the two communities, it tells still more about the culture of the City.

Origins of Southeast Planning

With a sense of irony, some Southeast activists reflect that SECO's original success two decades earlier set in motion the developments that pushed them to create a community plan. When Southeasterners stopped demolition for the expressway, they saved the residential character of the waterfront—but not just for themselves. Inadvertently, they facilitated the construction of the "Gold Coast" in the 1980s. Past the east end of Baltimore's Inner Harbor, expensive housing and boat slips lured wealthy outsiders into what had been working-class communities.

Long-time Southeasterners regarded the new condominiums and apartments as an intrusion. Physically, they blocked views of the water. Residents felt they were losing not just an invaluable amenity but a visual experience that held their community together. Moreover, people with modest incomes resented those with money who moved in because of the view and proximity to downtown but had no interest in the community. And Gold Coast developments raised property taxes and associated housing costs, making it harder for old-timers to stay.

In 1987 Southeast activists organized the Waterfront Coalition to limit development and promote preservation. Two years later, SECO helped organize and staff the Southeast Linkage Group to promote policies to tie development to community benefits (Giloth 1993). The group drafted legislation to assess impact fees on development. Although the City Council did not pass the bill, a Council task force recommended Southeast prepare a community plan to articulate its interests. In 1992 SECO provided staff to create the Southeast Planning Council and support it in producing a Southeast Community Plan.

Like The Associated, SECO had two purposes in planning. Substantively, specific issues demanded consideration. The Gold Coast directly threatened a traditional way of life. More broadly, it forced attention on the community's weaknesses: jobs were leaving, those who could afford to go were following, and the City apparently could get along without the people of Southeast Baltimore.

Thus Southeast planning was an effort to articulate directions that would revitalize the area. Housing, jobs, shopping, and transportation were obvious issues, but the larger challenge was to create a coherent positive image of a community and bring it to life. At the same time, Gold Coast development dramatized Southeast's vulnerabilities to and dependence on outside forces. The Council linkage bill use was an effort to change that relationship. Consistently, Southeast planning would try to involve government and other outside actors in addressing community concerns.

The second broad purpose of Southeast planning was to redefine and strengthen SECO's relationships with neighborhood associations. When SECO was created in 1971, ninety organizations sent representatives to the Founding Congress, and one thousand people turned out in the rain to hear Ralph Nader speak (Truelove 1977b:38). The first director actively worked with residents, and SECO staff helped neighborhoods organize and develop programs. Yet SECO's organizing success gave rise to tensions: as neighborhood organizations grew, they asserted their independence from SECO, particularly where conservative working-class groups saw SECO staff as unacceptably radical. The dynamic first director was followed by an uneven group of successors.

By the time a new director joined SECO in 1988, the organization was quiet and hardly related to neighborhood associations. He moved to redefine SECO as a resource for neighborhood organizations to collaborate on common concerns, such as lead paint, illiteracy, and recycling. In this context, Southeast community planning was an opportunity to renew relations with all neighborhood associations by creating a forum where they could work collectively on community-wide issues. The two purposes of Southeast planning were inseparable: because economic and political resources were scarce, addressing substantive issues depended on organizing community participation, and vice versa.

Two characteristics of Southeast community planning that distinguished it from Associated strategic planning would shape the planning process. First, although the federation's strategic planning was much more systematic and comprehensive than anything the organization had ever done, it was an extension of normal planning activities. In contrast, though the current SECO director had initiated strategic planning exercises, such practices were still relatively new. Hence nurturing and institutionalizing the practice of planning were crucial.

Second, the federation's strategic planning was primarily organizational, not community, planning, though participants represented community constituencies. Southeast planning would be open to all interested community members. Although both planning processes depended on community support for legitimacy, The Associated had well-exercised norms of participation, whereas Southeast planning would have to establish some.

Practically, The Associated had staff who could—and did—draft a sophisticated plan after meeting with community members. SECO and the Planning Council, in contrast, depended on knowledgeable participants for some research and writing. Thus both the novelty and its broad dependence on community participation gave it a distinct character.

Largely for these reasons, participation in Southeast planning was more fluid than at The Associated. The Southeast Planning Council had approximately sixty members, but not all attended meetings. After initial information gathering in workshops, much of the activity that led to plan recommendations took place in three task forces. They were open to anyone interested, decision making deferentially sought consensus, and influence generally followed participation. The published plan listed nearly three hundred participants, including Southeast residents, SECO and SDI staff, City agency staff, elected officials, and outside advisors or experts. The residents were diverse, though the most active were likely to be middle-class, white, and originally from elsewhere.

Such open participation led to long lists of issues and proposals. Emotionally, they elaborated themes of loss and regeneration. Southeast had lost so much: jobs, businesses, young families, generational continuity, intimacy, and, above all, faith in itself. People wanted to find a way, as the plan's subtitle later put it, "towards a future of hope and opportunity" (Southeast Planning Council 1993; hereafter, Plan 1993). The prerequisite was to define enough of a shared identity to support and give coherence to planning proposals.

Traditionally, ethnicity and religion had bound large groups, and for some still did, but newcomers did not share old ethnic loyalties. Many who worked in the factories or the port once felt joined to others of the same class, but it was unclear that being part of a working class strongly tied Southeast residents anymore. Moreover, nonwhite "new ethnics" now lived among "old ethnics." Many newcomers, particularly "gentrifiers," had come in search of urban livability; they liked what they called the area's "diversity." Yet they were outsiders observing "diverse" communities whose members increasingly worried about "stability"—defense against modern incursions. Many shared the same problems, but this negative condition did not lead directly to a positive identity encompassing 77,000 people.

Thus, as much as Southeast planning was a search for a positive program, it was also a quest to define a Southeast community that would both benefit from the program and enact it. Ideally, new life for the Southeast would mean new life for those now living in Southeast, but that was a question, not a certainty.

A Brief Chronology

In late 1991 and early 1992 community activists in the Southeast Linkage Group and SECO staff worked out the basic outlines of the Southeast planning process. They delineated planning boundaries and divided the domain into four geographic "clusters." They established a Southeast Planning Council and invited members. Four of the core group became the Council's Coordinating Committee. The Council first met in March 1992.

Over the next four months, each cluster had a workshop to discuss local issues. Attendance averaged between fifteen and twenty, including some Council members, other cluster residents, city planners, elected officials or their representatives, and SECO staff. With slight variations, the groups at cluster meetings resembled both the Planning Council and the Coordinating Committee in having equal representation of men and women.

In the fall, the Council brought together residents and experts in six development opportunity workshops, focusing on sites that cluster workshop participants saw as urgent problems or attractive opportunities. The most elaborate, and exceptionally adversarial, were two workshops on environmental and design issues on the chromium-polluted Allied Chemical site.

In early 1993 the Council created task forces on Housing, Industry, and Community Services and Infrastructure to synthesize discussions in the cluster and development opportunity workshops. About fifty residents and experts participated. Each group did additional research and developed recommendations. In June, the Planning Council approved a plan draft. The Council invited residents to a Community Assembly in July, where the plan was presented and discussed; about sixty people consensually accepted it, subject to suggested modifications.

During the fall, Coordinating Committee members and two SECO staff members fleshed out the plan, crafting language and adding detailed descriptions of each recommendation, including implementation requirements. The plan was released in December.

Implementation began once the Community Assembly accepted the plan. In the fall of 1993 Coordinating Committee members aproached a foundation for funds to implement certain recommendations. Coordinating Committee members began lobbying the Mayor's Office and City departments to endorse or implement the plan or parts of it.

The Planning Council authorized an enlarged Coordinating Committee to meet on an ongoing basis to oversee implementation and future planning. That Committee, consisting of about ten members, began to meet monthly in February 1994. It was authorized to convene the Council and arrange workshops as appropriate.

SIMILARITIES AMONG DIFFERENCES

One who saw only the obvious differences between these communities and organizations might imagine Associated community planning would involve comfortable decisions by leaders of a successful community, whereas Southeast community planning would involve repeated struggles among diverse groups to find a shared identity, set a common direction, and identify goals they had any chance of getting implemented. There is something to these images, but they miss important aspects of communities. They overestimate the association between financial success in the Jewish community and social coherence and clarity and depth of personal identification with the community. They underestimate the extent to which Southeast residents of different neighborhoods and ethnicities feel a common bond.

Although the two organizations stated their reasons for planning differently, both proceeded from a sense their community had lost cohesion and energy. Both confronted the declining pulls of ethnicity and religion in defining American communities. Both regarded planning and community organization as inseparable. Both came to reckon with the fragility of individuals' ties to the communities the organizations aimed and claimed to represent. Despite differences in economic circumstances, members of both regarded the outside world with anxiety and struggled to find a basis for identity that would hold many within.

CHAPTER 4

Community, Identity, and Planning

Before turning to the stories of these communities planning, we look at why people belong to communities, how communities regulate themselves, and how community planning affects relations between communities and their members.

INDIVIDUALS AND COMMUNITIES: COMMUNITY MEMBERSHIP AND IDENTITY

A community is both a social and a psychological entity. Socially, it is constituted by a web of relationships through which members interact frequently, for various purposes, and as whole persons. Psychologically, it is a sense of unity shared by persons who identify themselves with some combination of real and idealized aspects of the collectivity created by these relationships. Individuals are attached to communities by

> a framework of shared beliefs, interests, and commitments . . . bonds that establish a common *faith* or fate, a personal *identity*, a sense of *belonging*, and a supportive structure of activities and relationships (Selznick 1992:358–59; emphasis added).[1]

People join a community when they have *faith* in it as something greater than the routines of everyday life, something justifying a group loyalty that may conflict with but will take priority over mundane responsibilities. That faith justifies including the community in their personal identity. They define who they are in terms of what the community is. They come to think of themselves as somehow the same as it.

Identifying with a community is a delicate psychological act. A group must see something sufficiently the same among themselves to justify considering their aggregate a community. Moreover, they must see something sufficiently special in the community—so idealize it—to feel it is worth identifying with and to take its obligations as superior to mundane affairs. Yet they must see sufficient differences among themselves to retain personal autonomy. And they must see similarities and differences realistically enough to appraise themselves accurately and act effectively in and on the community.

This tension between sameness and difference, unity and individuality creates the ambiguous experience of *"belonging"* to a community: members have a place in it that is theirs; at the same time, it possesses them.

At one extreme, the political and psychological risk of totalitarianism is that people completely idealize a community and identify wholly with it. They will enjoy the pleasures of feeling at one with a powerful, perfect, good, loving social body,[2] but they will lose their autonomy and efficacy. Alternatively, people may so "realistically" analyze society into minute details that everything seems separate and unique, and nothing transcendent justifies identifying with or caring for a community. Not only will people have impoverished personal lives, but social and political domains will suffer from lack of reciprocity and public concern.

When people can temper their desire for the ideal with realism and find reality good enough, they may identify with a community. However, when social reality resists their ideals, they must find a way to reconcile the two if they are to identify with a community.

One approach is to take the ideals as guiding images in changing reality. This, after all, is the aim of community planning. When a community organization such as SECO or The Associated engages in community planning, it only does more formally and with more focus what people are doing all the time—shaping the institutions of a community to fit their needs. This is why the dynamics of a community—relations among its members—influence and constrain organized planning efforts.

Problems arise when reality resists the ideals. If reality is obdurate or ideals demand too much, people may simply imagine the real is the ideal. Fantasizing may take the place of strategizing. Planners who confront social conditions that seem unalterable or dangerous may unconsciously retreat from realistic intervention by working on an elaborate document, imagining the tremendous effort itself will change the world.[3] What looks like planning may be soothing but illusory.

PLANNING FOR COMMUNITY

Because community is a social and psychological entity, community planning has social and psychological functions. The social aims and consequences of planning are most readily apparent. Yet they are often motivated by elusive psychological considerations. To understand the stories of community planning, we must be prepared to read them as accounts of simultaneous psychological and social intervention.

We look at four purposes of community planning. Each represents an inherent interest of community members. Each tacitly organizes members' activities such that, whether they recognize it or not, groups of people are continually trying to order social relations in ways that serve these purposes. As a result, these interests and activities implicitly shape formal community planning agendas and decisions.

Each of these purposes may be understood as posing a question. Occasionally the answer is an explicit, formal statement. More often, because communities rarely reflect on themselves, an answer is tacitly incorporated into a policy, program, or response to a problem. Because a community consists of people, the answer frequently involves how a group in the community is treated.

Sometimes a community does not have a single or unambiguous answer. Especially then, the community may speak in several voices. Groups paired with one another may argue different sides of an ambivalence in the community mind, and the community's response lies in their confrontation, not either side alone.

Setting Boundaries: How Can the Community Be Made to Contain the Most Good?

Communities must have boundaries to distinguish members from outsiders. Socially, boundaries enable people to know whom they should care about and whom they may rely on. Psychologically, boundaries draw moral lines between good or special insiders and bad or ordinary outsiders. Communities need to control their boundaries to get and keep things of value inside. Members must perceive more rewards from being part of the community than from leaving, and the community must give members a valuable object with which to identify.

Community boundaries may be geographic (including territory), social (including those who participate in certain groupings), or cultural (including those who follow more specific, extensive, and complex norms of activity). These boundaries differ in the extent to which they can be expanded (to include more members or other objects), what they can be expanded to include (things of more or less value), and the degree to which the community can control them (to attract and hold valued things in or keep worthless or noxious things out). Communities, in turn, have varying choice about where and how to draw boundaries and varying ability to maintain them.

Geographic boundaries are easiest to manipulate but require no commitment from those inside and are highly permeable.

Social boundaries, such as organizational membership or participation, give a community asymmetrical control: it can keep undesirables out, but it must create incentives for desirables to join. Those who do join bring greater commitment than those simply enclosed in geographic boundaries.

Cultural boundaries, such as conformity to a moral code or pattern of religious observance, are harder to extend but may be easier to enforce. A community will have difficulty attracting or keeping members if behavioral norms call for socially or psychologically costly compromises with life outside. However, those who firmly commit themselves to the culture are likely to stay. Moreover, a community can keep out undesirables by concealing norms or blocking access to settings where they are enacted.

Southeast Baltimore and the Baltimore Jewish community inherited different boundaries and had different power to choose new ones, but both wanted to bound their communities more securely around many members and things of value.

Defining Good Membership: What Should Members Do to Make the Community the (Socially, Emotionally, and Morally) Best Possible?

Inside community boundaries, members give value to the community, and communities need as much as members can contribute. Members offer resources, such as effort and money, which enable a community to act. Members interact with and support one another. Members bring status that reflects on the community.

In addition to contributing instrumentally, members give moral and emotional value to a community. Their actions reflect on and embody it. To encourage others to identify with and contribute to it, members must epitomize something ideal. Then people will see and sense something transcendent in those with whom they interact.

Communities hold different values and set different standards in defining themselves and establishing criteria for good membership. Purely geographic standards, such as living within a territory, ask little. Social standards, such as membership or participation in groups or organizations, call for more. Cultural standards, prescribing patterns of behavior, demand the most. In general, the more exacting a standard, the more value community members believe it contributes.

Definitions of good membership not only idealize a community but also unify it, draw the loyal attachment of people who strongly identify with it, and thus empower it, to the degree they are consensually accepted. A single, specific, broadly legitimate definition is most beneficial in these ways.

Where significant groups define good membership differently, equal legitimacy for the standards is necessary for widespread loyalty to the community, though pluralism contributes less to social interaction, cohesion, and idealization. Where groups hold conflicting and competing definitions of good membership, interaction, cohesion, loyalty, and idealization suffer, and the existence of the community may come into question.

Because definitions of good membership are so important, communities have difficulty discussing or making deliberate choices about them. As part of culture, they define what is normal and make it hard to consider alternatives. Further, the longer a group's history, the more complex and demanding the norms of goodness, the more likely they are deeply, and often unconsciously, embedded in everyday practices. It is difficult even to delineate the norms, for they are pervasive and seem only natural. And it is this taken-for-granted-ness that makes them seem transcendent. Considering them open to reflection and choice degrades them.

Definitions of good membership have a paradoxical quality. The more they demand actions that differ from or conflict with the requirements for everyday success outside the community, the more they make it possible to idealize the community, but the more they raise questions about the community's continuity in the world. Hence communities must balance norms that idealize the community with practical strategies for maintaining it.

The Baltimore Jewish community and Southeast Baltimore traditionally defined good membership differently, but both faced questions whether the old definitions could be maintained and, if not, whether there were acceptable alternatives.

Managing Resources: How Should the Community Raise and Allocate Resources So as to Reinforce Its Goodness?

A community must have economic resources to support collective activities and make them more attractive than life elsewhere. However, these activities must reinforce concepts of good membership, so that people can idealize, identify with, and attach themselves to the community. These ends require, in addition, that the ways resources are raised and allocated strengthen, or at least not weaken, boundaries and affirm, or at least not conflict with, definitions of good membership.

In general, a community is better off raising resources from its members than relying on outsiders. However, because no community is economically autonomous, this distinction is not straightforward. What matters are the conditions under which money enters the community, who controls it, and whether it is sufficient for community purposes.

A community has obvious advantages if a number of members earn enough to make significant donations. However, extreme dependence on a few wealthy members, if it makes others feel superfluous, can work against cohesion. If some get prestige for their wealth, and if wealth is not part of the definition of good membership, their status may challenge membership norms, make it harder to idealize the community, and diminish cohesion. Alternatively, dependence on consistent, generous, unquestioning outside benefactors can give a community value and contribute to unity by transmitting others' appreciation.

Allocation of resources helps idealize the community and hold it together when it extends boundaries to include more of value, when it supports activities that enable people to act as good members, and when it allows the community to maintain itself. An insufficiency of resources or an allocation that reduces community value or promotes conflicting membership norms has the opposite effects.

Southeast Baltimore and the Baltimore Jewish community had access to different amounts of resources from different sources, but they faced similar questions about which activities to support to maintain the community instrumentally and morally.

Continuing the Community: What Should the Community Do to Ensure It and Its Goodness Continue in the Future?

Because members value a community, they want it to continue. What that means depends on how the community is defined. Geographically, territorial boundaries simply need to be filled. Social and cultural standards set progressively more exacting requirements. They are harder to satisfy quantitatively, but those who meet them will maintain the community qualitatively.

Normal ways of continuing a community include biological reproduction and adoption, immigration, recruitment, and education. However, continuity becomes a question when it seems unlikely without extraordinary action. Hence it calls community members to reconsider traditional answers to the other three questions. Boundaries may be adjusted to include more, and perhaps different persons or things, of value or to exclude undesirables. Good membership may be redefined to permit more, and different, people to idealize, identify with, and attach themselves to the community. New resources may be raised and/or resources differently allocated to implement these changes, to sustain the future community, or both.

People facing such questions feel like mourners, grieving the possible demise of both the community and that valued part of themselves they identify with it. They confront the possibilities that their community may simply die or that it may go on in ways that do not resemble the community they live in and love. They may find that the future members they could get would define the community and themselves in new ways (see Marris 1975).

This is the moment when community members measure their ideals and reality, to see which must yield and how. A changing reality that overwhelms ideals leads to the end of the community. Unblinking affirmation of ideals in the face of new realities leads to triumph in fantasy but decline in reality. Finding a balance between the two is the condition for planning that is realistic and potentially successful in continuing important aspects of the community.

The Baltimore Jewish community and Southeast Baltimore, with different traditions and resources, faced similar questions about whether what followed them would resemble them and, if not completely, what was the minimum they would accept and work for.

PART 2

Setting Community Boundaries

CHAPTER 5

Setting Jewish Community Boundaries: The Affiliated and the Unaffiliated

Community planning depends on secure community boundaries. Planners must be able to identify constituents and beneficiaries. Community members must know whom they should identify with and care about. And they must be able to demarcate limits to caring: where to draw the line before others who are different, who may be objects of indifference. Those outsiders help community members define what they are not.

"The unaffiliated" are the one Jewish group other Jews can say they do not care about. Indeed, some do not consider them community members. This indifference is puzzling in the context of The Associated slogan "We are one," as well as Jews' historic concerns about unity. Moreover, when community leaders are anxious about "Jewish continuity," it seems strange to disregard anyone. The key to this riddle lies in how community members use "the unaffiliated" to define community boundaries.

A clue comes from the ambiguous way Baltimore Jews speak of "the community." Sometimes it comprises all 92,000 Jews. Other times it includes only a third to half that many, just those who affiliate with Jewish institutions by joining, contributing, or volunteering.[1] In part, these two views reflect The Associated's roles. As a community organization, it claims to represent all Jews. As a fundraising organization, it serves donors. More generally, ambiguity about "the community" expresses ambivalence about "the unaffiliated." These mixed feelings reflect psychologically complicated efforts to define and protect community boundaries.

We first analyze the organizational and psychological relations between the affiliated and unaffiliated. Then we examine how these dynamics influenced strategic planning.

THE AFFILIATED, THE UNAFFILIATED, AND THE COMMUNITY

Baltimore Jews differ in many ways. They belong to different denominations, are from different generations, live in different geographic areas, claim different places of origin, and earn different incomes. The division between the affiliated and unaffiliated, like these others, raises the question whether Baltimore Jews should be considered one community or several.

Asked about the implications of such differences, an Associated staff member described the thinking of strategic planning participants:[2]

> There was agreement by everybody that there is one community. There were elements of different communities. But absolutely there is one community. In Baltimore it is one community. There is central giving and participation. Everyone from every segment is involved with The Associated, the organized Jewish community. Except for the unaffiliated. "Community" is used in the singular because of the concept of people-hood. It is inclusionary. The Law of Return [in Israel, which grants Israeli citizenship to anyone with at least one Jewish grandparent]. Every member of the Jewish people is a member of the Jewish community in whatever area he resides. That is a geographic definition. Even the unaffiliated are members of the Jewish community.

In this complicated view, there are "different communities," but "absolutely there is one community," although "the unaffiliated" do not belong to it. And yet "even the unaffiliated are members of the Jewish community." "Community" takes three meanings here. The "different communities" are social groupings—people who are similar and may interact with one another. Common examples are "the Orthodox community," "the German Jewish community," "the Park Heights community," and "the religious community."

The "one community" is "The Associated, the organized Jewish community." Federation leaders call their organization the "one community" for two reasons. First, it dominates local Jewish fundraising[3] and is the only general community organization. Contributing to the federation can be considered an indicator of individual commitment to the community. Equating the community with the organization also is a political stance, claiming for The Associated the legitimacy of being the sole Jewish community organization. It asserts Jews can become full community members only by giving to the federation.

The Associated subsumes the "different communities" into the "one community" by treating them as "constituencies." Although one might call denominations, age cohorts, genders, or client populations "interest groups," this term is not used, and "factions" is explicitly eschewed. Either term would imply separateness and independence. In contrast, "constituencies" constitute—make up, are part of—a larger whole, in this case the Associated community.

The one group apparently remaining outside are the unaffiliated, and yet "the Jewish community" includes them. This is the community of the Jewish people, comprising everyone who may be considered Jewish according to halacha, Jewish law:[4] either the child of a Jewish mother or a convert.[5] This time-honored concept of the Jewish community reflects millennia of recorded history (Elazar 1971, 5:808–53; Kaplan 1981 [1934]). Especially for older generations, it reflects shared experience. It also expresses a wish all Jews could make up a cohesive, caring, strong community. In contrast to the "different communities" and "one community," this "Jewish community" is abstract. It does not depend on social contact or institutional participation. It exists by definition, when people think of it.

People around The Associated speak most ambiguously about the "community" when they mix the federation's fundraising and community organization roles. Claiming to be "the central address" of a unitary community, they must include the peoplehood definition with the narrower institutional definition. One implication of this usage is to affiliate the unaffiliated, to get tens of thousands more involved with the federation.

No one believes this would be easy, but there are two reasons The Associated might recruit the unaffiliated. First, they represent untapped financial, social, and political assets. Second, their nonaffiliation challenges the economic and emotional commitments of the affiliated by implying institutional membership is not necessary for belonging to the community.

Yet there are other consequences of taking peoplehood as the basis for the federation community. One is the financial cost of engaging and serving thousands of people who would be unlikely to give much to The Associated. Practically, as a fundraiser, the federation does best by concentrating on its committed contributors and others with significant wealth.

In addition, recruiting the unaffiliated would force Associated participants to look at why others choose neither to give money to the federation nor to join other Jewish institutions, and they might recognize others' doubts or resistances in themselves. The affiliated risk weakening their commitment. Moreover, if the affiliated redoubled their investment but failed to win over many of the unaffiliated, the affiliated would have committed themselves to supporting others who gave nothing in return. The unaffiliated become financial and psychological free riders.

It might be safer to avoid possible resentment by holding to an institutional definition of the community, excluding the unaffiliated. And yet it could be hard to avoid feeling guilty for caring less about any Jews than others. How could people choose between guilt and resentment? And if they could choose neither, what else could they do? Let us listen to what planning participants say about the unaffiliated.

AMBIVALENCE TOWARD THE UNAFFILIATED

Affiliation as a Social Act: Interest in the Unaffiliated

Different attitudes toward the unaffiliated are associated with different beliefs about why people affiliate. On the surface, more or less sympathetic interpretations of why people do not affiliate lead to greater or less interest in reaching out to them. However, the affiliated seem to choose interpretations that rationalize their attitudes toward the unaffiliated.

For many whose main Jewish activity is participation in The Associated, affiliation, to oversimplify, is as simple as writing a check. Anyone who wants to affiliate with the community can contribute to the federation. Religious knowledge, observance, and faith are not necessary for federation membership. Those who take this view see affiliation mainly in social terms, as organizational membership.

Many in this group extend "affiliation" to any organized Jewish group. They include not only federation donors, but also synagogue members, Jewish Community Center (JCC) members, those who join Jewish social or political organizations, and purchasers of Israel bonds. Such a definition might include a little over half of the Jews. An Associated leader represents this view:

> I am not sure what [unaffiliated] means. . . . I guess someone who has nothing to do with the Jewish community but is Jewish. If they belong to the JCC but don't contribute to The Associated, don't belong to a synagogue, don't belong to ZOA [Zionist Organization of America], don't buy Israel bonds—is that person unaffiliated? I don't know. I guess they are affiliated. {*Interviewer*: The Orthodox follow halacha and have strict rules about what one should do and how one should affiliate. You aren't emphasizing any strict rules.} But it isn't important what I think. {Why?} I don't think it is important whether a person is Jewish, Catholic, or Protestant. I happened to be born Jewish, and so I participate in the Jewish community.

Those who see affiliation as a social act also interpret the decision to affiliate in terms of social, external influences. They see the unaffiliated reacting to circumstances rather than acting on inner beliefs. When conditions change, the unaffiliated will affiliate. For example, when young adults become financially secure, they will be able to afford synagogue membership or Associated gifts. When couples have children, they will see the importance of synagogues for giving their children an identity. Some have disaffiliated after an unpleasant experience with a federation solicitor or agency staff member, and they would rejoin if properly welcomed.

An Associated leader expresses this view in talking about efforts to reach out:

> One reason we developed a marketing plan was to reach these people and let them make a decision. We are conducting many focus groups with young people. My son just had one at his house. They are nice Jewish kids, but they don't do anything, don't give to The Associated. {What did they say?} They don't know [what The Associated does]. They have been turned off by a poor solicitor. People don't want to be just asked for money. They want to be invited in to do something. Surprisingly, a large number have never been asked. {Why not?} A kid goes to college for four years, to the University of Pennsylvania. When he comes back, he might live in South Baltimore, on Montgomery Street [a non-Jewish area]. He is struggling to get himself a job. What we are interested in is finding these kids and rekindling their interests. Or people moving in from out of town, and nobody knows them. For example, a guy who goes to work with Black and Decker [where he meets few Jews] and lives out in Ruxton [another non-Jewish area].

Those who see affiliation this way are optimistic about increasing it and encourage "outreach" from the affiliated to the unaffiliated. Strategically, they emphasize how The Associated can change conditions affecting affiliation. Staff can contact the unaffiliated and represent the federation as an accessible, rewarding place. Or synagogues can lower the costs of membership for families with limited incomes.

Affiliation as a Psychological Act: Indifference to the Unaffiliated

Those who think of the Jewish community primarily in religious terms think differently of affiliation and the unaffiliated. For them, the primary institution with which to affiliate is the synagogue. Moreover, synagogue membership should reflect and strengthen Jewish observance, knowledge, and faith. Affiliation for them is a psychological, internally motivated act. For the Orthodox particularly, the synagogue or the shtiebel (small house of ultra-Orthodox worship, usually organized by and centered around a single rabbi) matters institutionally mainly as a way of supporting personal religiosity. In other words, social affiliation is only a sign of and support for adherence to elaborate cultural norms.

These people see affiliation differently from the first group in two ways. First, they consider it a reflection of inner belief, demanding more than crossing an organizational threshold. At the same time, this group expects belief as a matter of course. For them, being Jewish is not a choice. Though they sympathize with those who find it hard to gain Jewish knowledge and observe rituals, they are unsympathetic toward those who do not try.

As Associated leader active in his synagogue expresses this view:

> The strategic plan differentiated between the unaffiliated and the unaf-
> filiable. We determined the community should not spend time and
> resources chasing the unaffiliable. They don't want to be part of it for
> any reason. [I am willing to approach them,] but if they don't want a
> two-way street, there are others with whom you can make inroads.

Because even synagogue members need support to learn and observe
more, this group emphasizes "inreach" to those who have social affiliation but need stronger psychological affiliation.

This point of view unites rabbis across denominational lines. A liberal
takes a position other rabbis would endorse:

> The synagogues ask, Are there too many resources concentrated on the
> unaffiliated? We are struggling with the affiliated. . . . I am concerned
> about the number of members of this congregation whose parents pay
> their dues. People in their late thirties and forties, making a good living.
> Their parents pay because they are afraid they wouldn't join on their
> own. This is the next generation. . . . For a significant part of our com-
> munity, there is an I-don't-care attitude. We have spent too much time
> on the unaffiliated.

Another liberal rabbi observes,

> Synagogues are not concerned about the unaffiliated. We are concerned
> about deepening the commitment of those who are affiliated.

A more conservative non-Orthodox rabbi concludes:

> I have a concern that outreach to the nonaffiliated will weaken the syn-
> agogue. It will take money. It will weaken synagogue education [by
> introducing children without family religious interests]. . . . Whatever
> one thinks of outreach, once you define it . . . if you are successful,
> how is this going to change the community you bring them into? For
> example, the JCC. If one-third of the membership, one-half of the mem-
> bership don't believe in anything[, in what way is it a Jewish institution]?

In other words, just formally affiliating people who believe in little will
not engender belief and will only encourage unbelievers to continue as
they are. The rabbis speak for most who see affiliation psychologically in
arguing it is more reasonable to begin with those who somehow made it
into the synagogue and try to deepen their knowledge, belief, and faith.

The Unaffiliated and Community Boundaries: Emotional and Institutional Choices

The language of "affiliation" is dichotomous. Few who think of themselves as affiliated describe the unaffiliated unambiguously as part of the

community. Those who view affiliation socially are most sympathetic to the unaffiliated, but even they use language that sets the unaffiliated outside the community. In The Associated culture, federation contributors and activists comprise "the community," and the unaffiliated are contacted through "outreach." Many who think of affiliation psychologically and religiously would agree with a conservative rabbi who, though speaking of "the community" more broadly, still concludes, "They are not really part of the community."

Ambiguity about whether the unaffiliated are in the community reflects not simply conflicting definitions of the community, but also mixed emotions toward those who do not want to be active members. Many affiliated resent the unaffiliated for being free riders. Without reciprocity or appreciation, federation leaders give time and money for them, and the religious observe and believe for them. Because affiliation may be seen as psychological or social, the affiliated can define their relationship with the unaffiliated, and manage any ambivalence about them, in a psychological framework, an institutional one, or both.

Psychologically, many affiliated are uncomfortable resenting the unaffiliated. Though feeling let down, they also feel guilty about anger against other Jews. They might avoid this feeling by drawing community boundaries that clearly put the unaffiliated on the outside, beyond the requirements of caring. However, many would only feel more guilty for abandoning fellow Jews. Exchanging one kind of guilt for another is not a bargain.

However, the unaffiliated also seem dangerous because they are so close to the community boundary. Though part of the community, they cannot be fully trusted to keep what the community values from the outsiders with whom they have contact. Those on the boundary unsettlingly remind insiders of their own temptations to rebel against the demands of membership. For many, the unaffiliated unconsciously represent the Gentiles, non-Jews. They seductively model a life without the discipline of the Jewish community.

For example, the rabbi commenting on the consequences of recruiting those without serious Jewish interests to community institutions worries how they will affect others. They offer an easy, effortless model of being Jewish, one that could subvert others' commitments of time, money, or, worse, belief. The unaffiliated encourage the affiliated to doubt their social or religious commitments. Do they believe enough to warrant their investments in Jewish institutions and practices? Symbolically posing this question, the unaffiliated put the community at risk.

Older Jews have two images of the outside world. A hostile view is symbolized most dramatically by the Holocaust but also draws on persecution and discrimination in Maryland history. Closer at hand, many remember the exclusion of Jews from Baltimore neighborhoods, private schools, and other institutions. One leader recalls "No Jews and dogs wanted" signs.

In contrast, many contemporary images are benign, but unsettlingly so. The rising intermarriage rate[6] reflects and symbolizes increasing social contact between Jews and Gentiles, as well as Gentiles' greater acceptance of Jews. Many who affiliate with the Jewish community regard the growing ease of assimilation, paradoxically, as a more insidious danger than overt hostility. In part, recalling German Jews' misplaced confidence in their assimilation in the 1930s, they still mistrust the motives of outsiders. In part, they simply worry about the loss of committed Jews.

Some may hold both ideas simultaneously, as expressed in the Jewish philosopher Emil Fackenheim's "614th commandment" (his supplement to the 613 in halacha): "the authentic Jew of today is forbidden to hand Hitler yet another, posthumous victory" by ending the Jewish people through assimilation (1967:272). In this formulation, assimilation is equated with genocidal atrocities, killing not only the assimilator, but the entire Jewish community.

Assimilation may be tempting, but the thought stirs up guilt and anxiety. One way to avoid anxiety over urges to flee community discipline is to deny them, to insist that only those on the boundary have them, and, finally, to push the latter out of the community, thus symbolically expelling dangerous impulses. This is the phenomenon of scapegoating, portrayed in Jewish tradition by the scapegoat for Azazel, on which the Jews in the desert placed their sins and which they then banished (see Baum 1987; Eagle and Newton 1981; Frazer 1940; Girard 1977; Taylor and Rey 1953; Toker 1972).

This psychological process shapes how the affiliated think of the unaffiliated. By not affiliating, they start the slippery slide toward assimilation, becoming the threatening outsiders. To avoid the temptation to follow and potential betrayal, unconsciously the affiliated may expel the unaffiliated, as unworthy of caring about.[7]

In this vein, one federation leader, asked about the unaffiliated, remarks, "I know an unaffiliated person. It ['unaffiliated'] sounds like an outcast." It is as if, she implies, the affiliated, shunned by the unaffiliated, have retaliated by casting them out. A federation leader from a wealthy family who argues repeatedly for including the poor in Associated decisions, when asked whether she cares about the unaffiliated, says, simply, "I don't."

This is a psychological resolution of ambivalence toward the unaffiliated. And yet it is troubling to accept personal responsibility for not caring about other Jews. It is safer to couch this position in institutional terms.

Synagogue members can conclude that limited resources force them to choose whom to serve and that priority must go to current members. Associated leaders can decide that, if the unaffiliated do not want federation services, there are not enough resources for services specifically for the unaffiliated. Federation policy makers can conclude that efforts to get contributions from the unaffiliated would not be repaid in new gifts. They can emphasize The Associated is a fundraising organization.

These are realistic considerations, though they rest on an absolute dichotomy between affiliated and unaffiliated. Psychologically, they have the virtue of placing responsibility for difficult decisions on external constraints. Thus institutional calculations may overlay or rationalize psychological ones.

STRATEGIC PLANNING AND THE UNAFFILIATED

Associated activists who felt ambivalent about the unaffiliated treated them ambiguously in strategic planning, voicing concern but not backing it up programmatically.

The question of the unaffiliated was assigned to the Strategic Planning Committee's Relationships Subcommittee. It began by distinguishing groups of Jews. The first was "donors," who affiliate at least by giving to The Associated. The second was "affiliated non-donors," "persons who identify themselves as Jewish and participate in the life of the Jewish community but do not normally support the Associated" (Relationships Subcommittee, Strategic Planning Committee, vol. 2, 1989:6; hereafter, Relationships Report). They belonged to synagogues or the Jewish Community Center, for example.

The "unaffiliated" were divided in two on the basis of likely affiliation:

> Experience shows that attempts to draw back into the Jewish community persons who wish to ignore or reject their Jewish identity are rarely effective. . . . But many persons—especially newcomers to the area, college students, and young married people—may be unaffiliated without intending to reject a connection to the Jewish community (Relationships Report 1989:11).

The latter group was the "affiliable," the former the "unaffiliable." The "affiliable" were good unaffiliated in two respects. First, they might be persuaded to affiliate. Second, their deviance was only social, not psychological or religious, as with the "unaffiliable," who rejected Jewish identity.

Consistently, the Subcommittee's first plan draft recommended "that no special measures be taken with respect to the unaffiliated generally." "But," it continued, the Associated should encourage its agencies, and other organizations in the Jewish community, to reach out to the "affiliable"—Jewish newcomers, college students, and other persons who may be unaffiliated because of temporary circumstance rather than settled preference (Relationships Report 1989:12).

The draft proposed to "Treat the 'affiliable' as a client-group" (Relationships Report 1989:12). This did not mean engaging the thought processes that led people from the organized community, but, rather, offering "services oriented particularly to their situations and needs—for day care, for example," to attract them into it (Relationships Report 1989:11).

The strategic plan retained this language with two changes. No longer distinguishing the "affiliable," it referred to all "unaffiliated," and it added synagogues to those who should reach out. Anticipating changes in budgeting procedures, it urged,

> If . . . the Associated reviews service agency budgets in terms of how fully they meet the needs of particular client-groups, then unaffiliated persons should be treated as one group (Plan 1989:13).

Nevertheless, when recommendations were turned over to implementation task forces, no action was taken on this one. When budgeting was reorganized, the unaffiliated were not identified as a constituency.

Joint Commission on Associated-Synagogue Relations

Two implementation bodies, the Commission on Jewish Education and the Joint Commission on Associated-Synagogue Relations, occasionally discussed the unaffiliated, but neither made a commitment to outreach. The Joint Commission was set up in 1991 to implement a recommendation that the federation and synagogues "Seek a shared vision of mutual responsibilities, and improve communication" (Plan 1989:14). Because of the participation of rabbis and synagogue members, when the Commission discussed affiliation, it usually focused on synagogue membership. Some lay members advocated outreach.

Several rabbis, of widely ranging religious views, disagreed. A liberal stated his case simply:

> Jewish life is in the stages of decline. We talk about outreach, to the unaffiliated, to other groups. But we need to focus on our core.

A traditional rabbi said, similarly, "We should focus on the currently affiliated. . . . Inreach should be a high ranking." Another rabbi, summarizing discussion by a group of rabbis, reported the consensus was "focus on people with some connection with the Jewish community . . . possibly write off the unaffiliated."

When the Joint Commission's Jewish Continuity Subcommittee later discussed a proposal for a family camp to promote community continuity, a lay leader raised questions about who should be the target population:

> It is like in baseball, addressing the season ticket holders. . . . They are already there. There are a lot of people who are not committed that you are trying to reach. Even though they are not involved in Jewishness or Judaism.

The next few speakers picked up the theme by agreeing about what one called the "transformational" potential of a camp. Then one member, a high Associated leader, turned the discussion around:

> I want to say something in terms of participants. We are the Joint Commission on Associated-*Synagogue* Relations. So obviously we are targeting people affiliated with synagogues. But further down the line we should invite unaffiliated people, and have a group of rabbis there.

The comment closed discussion and carried the day.

Disagreement was based not on the possible effects of a family camp on participants' religious practices or personal identities, but on who deserved to be considered part of the community. The questioner spoke inclusively, but his respondent insisted on equating the community with the affiliated: institutions should be self-serving, aiding those who had already paid their way.

Although "further down the line" designated the unaffiliated for a later agenda, it was not inconsistent with "writ[ing] off the unaffiliated."

Commission on Jewish Education

The Commission on Jewish Education was set up in 1990 to develop a strategic plan for Jewish education. Initial work was assigned to four subcommittees, each focused on one type of program: Jewish Day School Education (religious day school), Congregation and Communal Religious School Education (afterschool and Sunday religious and Hebrew instruction), Higher Jewish Education (university and adult education), and Informal Jewish Education (informal educational experiences).

The Day School Subcommittee report emphasized challenges in educating those so affiliated as to want day schooling. In varying ways, the other three subcommittees referred to affiliation as an issue and the unaffiliated as a group.

The Congregational and Communal School Subcommittee included affiliation among educational goals. It wanted graduates to be adults who "Have a strong concept of oneself as a Jew," "Belong to Jewish communal organizations and participate actively in them," "Become actively involved in synagogue life," "Support Jewish causes and actively become involved in Jewish philanthropy," and "Are actively participating in Jewish communal life" (Subcommittee on Congregational and Communal Religious School Education 1991:3; hereafter, Congregational and Communal School Report). The report did not mention the unaffiliated but recommended "develop[ing] a comprehensive outreach campaign in order to attract school-age children who are not currently enrolled in a Jewish school" (Congregational and Communal School Report 1991:18).

The Informal Jewish Education Subcommittee, comprising the strongest advocates for affiliating the unaffiliated, declared,

> Outreach should extend to a wider segment of our community. Creative new approaches must be identified to address the Jewish needs of the vast numbers of Jews who are marginally affiliated with or are not participating in existing Jewish institutions and their programs.

Linking affiliation to social opportunities, the report urged,

> THE ASSOCIATED, in collaboration with service providers, must utilize its marketing resources to determine the desired needs of various population groups and to inform people about available programs. Often, many individuals are non-participants because they are not aware of existing programs or because services are not oriented to their particular situations and needs (Subcommittee on Informal Jewish Education Subcommittee 1991:7; hereafter, Informal Jewish Education Report).

"Target constituencies" included groups especially likely to be unaffiliated: single-parent families, college youth, and singles (Informal Jewish Education Report 1991:7–8).

The report on higher education indirectly reinforced this position by focusing attention on client groups that included those likely to be unaffiliated. "Singles," it noted, "constitute the group with the lowest rates of Jewish observance and participation" (Ukeles Associates 1993:13). "Parents with young children" were interested in Jewish education for their children, but some lacked time or money to enroll or otherwise affiliate. "Mixed married couples" often did not affiliate with synagogues or other Jewish institutions.

When the Higher Education Subcommittee set priorities, however, it emphasized the affiliated. First priorities included programs for parents of young children, but also professional Jewish educators, lay leadership in Jewish organizations, and professional staff in Jewish organizations. Singles and mixed married couples were a second priority (Ukeles Associates 1993:29–33).

The subcommittees thus were split on the unaffiliated, and the Commission had to reconcile positions. Staff drafted a plan outline and introduction. Recommendations were listed in order of votes on earlier balloting, and at the top of program initiative recommendations, with eighteen of twenty votes, was

> Develop a *comprehensive outreach* campaign to marginally affiliated populations who are not currently participating in existing Jewish institutions and their programs (Conceptual outline, n.d.:15).

However, the introduction suggested that, although nonaffiliation was a problem, outreach might be unnecessary. It characterized Jewish education as "a lifelong enterprise" following a "'start-stop-and-start' pattern interrupted by spans of many years," following "diverse stages in [people's] lives." Sporadic affiliation was a manifestation of this pattern:

> Nearly every demographic study undertaken to date in North America indicates that while the number of affiliated and actively identified Jews may be decreasing, (1) a significant proportion of Jewish children in North America receive a Jewish education at some point in their lives, and (2) a significant proportion of Jewish families in North America do affiliate with a synagogue or temple (Draft introduction, n.d.:4).

Although nonaffiliation was a problem, action might not be necessary.

The Strategic Plan for Jewish Education included the recommendation on outreach. Implementation and further planning were turned over to a new Center for the Advancement of Jewish Education. Through FY96, however, no education programs focused on the unaffiliated.

ANALYSIS

These episodes show how formal planning activities reflect and are an effort to manage community dynamics. Institutional actions mirror complicated social, cultural, and psychological relationships. We can read the texts of reports and plans as an account of the communal and institutional meanings of these relationships. Moreover, we see in successive drafts a record of collective thought processes. For example, where something in an earlier draft is revised or absent later, we see "changes of mind," some simply efforts to think more reasonably, but others calculated attempts to forget and repress, analogous to individual efforts to push dangerous thoughts into the unconscious. And yet earlier thoughts often remain, invisibly but definitely shaping such overt outcomes as documentary text, group decisions, and program design or implementation.

Affiliation matters in the Jewish community because its boundaries are social and cultural. Community members are concerned about the unaffiliated because their numbers are increasing. But many community members are ambivalent toward the unaffiliated, wanting them to be part of the community but resenting their autonomy and seeming ingratitude, perhaps envying their freedom but also feeling guilty about being angry at them. Associated activists resolve the psychological conflict by appealing to institutional "realities": the unaffiliated are a bad investment of scarce funds. Symbolically putting the unaffiliated outside the community, those who reason this way are free of guilt.

Thus Associated planners strengthen community boundaries around a valued core by casting out the bad unaffiliated and keeping the good affiliated. The remaining challenge in continuing the community, unfolding in later chapters, is to make what is inside valuable enough to hold members.

CHAPTER 6

Permeable Southeast Boundaries: Dumping, Loss, and the Decline of Ethnicity

Southeasterners similarly hope to secure community boundaries around valued members, but two conditions frame this challenge differently. First, Southeast Baltimore is geographically defined. In contrast with the Jewish community, members and planners face no ambiguity drawing lines to distinguish members from outsiders. However, because lines on a map neither offer rewards nor exact obligations, members easily come and go.

Second, in contrast with claims, desires, and realities of unity in the Jewish community, Southeast Baltimore is pluralistic. Neighborhood associations prize their autonomy. SECO is the umbrella group, but no one considers it a "central address" or grants it authority over civic activity. Government agencies administer most services, and public officials have the most legitimacy to speak for area residents as a whole. Culturally, rather than one deep, broad tradition, Southeast residents appeal to diverse heritages, some recent, some narrow.

Thus, to continue the community, Southeasterners must create social incentives and promulgate cultural norms to encourage people to engage in valued activities that are located or have significant effects inside lines on a map. This chapter looks at how Southeasterners think about the permeability of geographic boundaries; the next chapter looks at how planning participants responded by investing in the boundaries.

PERMEABLE BOUNDARIES

Southeast boundaries are highly permeable. The firmest line is the eastern edge, the border between Baltimore City and Baltimore County. The City's property tax rate is nearly $6 per $100 assessed value, while the County's is less than half that. County homes are more expensive than comparable City homes; one factor is that County schools are considered better. At any rate, though this boundary matters, Southeast residents sit on its disadvantaged side and have no control over it.

The planning area is part of two City Council districts. Most lies in the First, except for a strip along the northern edge that is the south end of the Second. The First District was traditional turf of the East Baltimore Democratic machine. It is largely white. In fact, when the City Council redrew boundaries after the 1990 Census, it put part of South Baltimore's Democratic machine territory into the First, to make it the only majority-white district (79% white, 19% black, 2% other). The Southeast Baltimore blocks in the Second District are predominantly black and help give that district a 68 percent black majority (29% white, 3% other; Thompson 1991:10). To white residents of Southeast, this redistricting is a sign they have lost power to outsiders.

Railroad tracks, streets, and interstate highways traverse Southeast. Tolls are collected on the interstate, but revenues go to the State, which maintains the roads and tunnels. Much of the freight and most of the passengers are simply passing through. When trucks try to avoid tolls or inspections on the tunnel routes, they take to the streets through Southeast, creating noise and pollution, damaging roads built for lighter traffic, shaking buildings, endangering the lives of pedestrians, and destroying the tranquility normally associated with being at home or conducting business. These disturbances are another sign Southeast cannot control its boundaries.

Dumping

The trucks are emblematic of many difficulties. The noise they make, the exhaust they put into the air, the rubble that falls off when they hit bumps, and the piles of material they leave at certain destinations—all literally and symbolically represent the many ways Southeast residents feel dumped on. Being dumped on means being forced to take someone else's garbage.[1]

Cluster D includes Southeast's industrial area. When community leaders prepared an agenda for its cluster workshop, dumping was a central theme. A Coordinating Committee member asked what a bus tour should see. She mentioned "dirt piles." A staff member added suggestions she had heard from residents, including a funeral home, a dump, toxic drums, and a car recycling junkyard. Civic association leaders continued:[2]

DAVID BENTON: The Esso at Boston and Interstate is going to be closed down; now it is a dumping ground. . . .

JACK WAYLAND: The problem is, the street construction project funnels down at Ponca, and it prevents turning left, north at Ponca. . . .

ANDREA TAFT: The project will cut out parking spaces proposed from one hundred to sixty. . . .

JOHN MARATSOS: Parking is an issue.

BENTON: Air pollutants from the Fabco factory are killing plants. My wife says her plants are not doing as well as they used to.

TAFT: My plants are doing as well as they always did.

HAROLD MARTIN: The dirt piles are a problem. It is contaminated with petroleum from gas stations. There is also dirt hidden in warehouses. And if dirt has to be hidden in warehouses, there is something wrong with it.

WAYLAND: We are becoming a dumping ground.

ELAINE SCOTT [COORDINATING COMMITTEE MEMBER]: . . . Incinerators to burn the dirt [a reference to a businessman's storing toxic dirt in piles while hoping to get permission to build an incinerator to burn it in Baltimore County].

MARATSOS: The present City Council persons are on my side; not like the old group, and the Governor, the old dictator. I read that the Governor is going to set up a task force to see what causes all the cancer. He has caused a lot of it. Those who live in the community know best what is good for the community. It's us versus outsiders. They don't want government to work. We are number one in cancer in Maryland, number three in the USA.

WAYLAND: We are considered the industrial district. In fifty years you will have a dead First District.

Here dumping is a literal problem. The neighborhood has dumps for dirt, toxic chemicals, and junked cars. Not only are these places unsightly, but they invisibly kill plants and people. Although incinerators might burn the toxic dirt, they, too, pollute and are ugly. The reference to the street construction project only apparently involved a different subject. It illustrated how outside planners and politicians decide to reconfigure roads without regard to local residents, how they dump cars into neighborhoods, leaving commuters to park in front of people's homes.

Waterfront development was the stimulus for Southeast planning, and the plan was supposed to articulate residents' goals so community representatives could negotiate authoritatively with developers. An exercise at cluster workshops involved asking participants what they would or would not want developers to do. People at another cluster workshop listed many types of dumping as they set forth development rules:

- No red light district businesses
- No more bars or liquor stores
- No illegal billboards
- No building that blocks the view of the harbor
- No truck routes
- No more incinerators
- No halfway houses

- No addition to the parking burden
- No more citywide drug treatment centers
- No development which turns its back to the rest of the neighborhood—enclaves we don't feel welcome in

Red-light businesses were a sore topic. The City Council was considering a bill to break up the adult entertainment "Block" and disperse businesses to industrially zoned parts of the City. Large sections of Southeast were being discussed as relocation areas. A city councilman commented at the workshop,

> The motivation for this bill is that foreign developers built Commerce Place next to the Block and now can't rent it. . . . They ought to have checked things out before they built, rather than push the problems onto the community.

Bars and liquor stores encourage public drunkenness, and residents complain about fights in the middle of the night when the bars close. People feel the Liquor Board grants and transfers licenses without regard for neighborhood concerns. Halfway houses and drug treatment centers are examples of undesirables coming into the community.

Another city councilman reported,

> We are being inundated by developers in the office. The Allied site [a huge tract polluted by more than a century of chromium production, where the owners were proposing massive development] . . . I told them to go to the community. But next spring may be too late for us to develop a plan to stop development there.

One reason residents might not have time to respond, some said, was the City was trying to grease the skids for developers.

For many, Southeast is the victim of a triumvirate of outside dumpers: private businesses, developers, and City government (especially the Mayor; in contrast, many approve of the three First District councilmen). A long-time community activist asked her neighbors at one meeting, "Do we need to make a decision now that we do or do not trust our elected officials?" The chair shunted the question aside, but the issue was clear: a community that cannot depend on city government to protect it is vulnerable to all kinds of dumping.

Loss

The other side of being powerless to control boundaries is being unable to prevent valued things from leaving. Southeast mourns a seemingly unending stream of losses.

Almost always the first thing any resident mentions when talking about how the area has changed over the years is loss of jobs and industry. "Twenty years ago," one reflects,

> you found the City made things or sold things or designed things by local people in Baltimore, and it's all being bought up. This is part of an international market. . . .

Outside firms have purchased local banks. Railroad cars are no longer manufactured in the home of the Baltimore and Ohio Railroad. "So," he concludes, "you lose a lot of industries."

A blue-collar worker makes this discussion more concrete:

> It seems like we are losing more and more of the industries. They are closing down and moving elsewhere or just going out of business: Western Electric . . . the shipyard down in Sparrows Point. The steel mill down there at one time, I think, employed about thirty thousand people; now they are down to maybe five or six. As far as businesses in the area, a lot of the area, a lot of the major manufacturing places have really gone by the wayside, even Crown Cork and Seal. Some of the breweries in Highlandtown, they are no longer there. . . .
>
> You know, everybody used to be able to work in their own neighborhoods; now you don't find that as much. I myself, I work for Seagram's down here [not in Southeast]. . . . There was a Four Roses plant down here over at Willow Spring Road. I worked there for about four, five years, and they closed up about a year or two ago. So I say that's how it's changed.

The decline of Sparrows Point is economically and symbolically the biggest change in the local economy. In 1887 the Pennsylvania Steel Company, later part of Bethlehem Steel, began construction on a plant in southeast Baltimore County just outside the City. The first steel rolled out in 1891. The company built a town for workers, with houses laid out in a hierarchy of sizes and types corresponding to the occupants' ranks and races. Sparrows Point grew, boosted by munitions orders during World War I. The mill made tin plate for the cans that revolutionized the food and retailing industries. The American Can Company, headquartered in Baltimore, and Campbell's were among the first customers. Sparrows Point made steel for cars; it built ships. Through acquisitions and mergers Bethlehem Steel became one-third the size of U.S. Steel in the 1920s. Sparrows Point grew with America.

Although the Depression hurt Sparrows Point, perfection of a technology for putting beer in cans in the 1930s and ship and aircraft construction during World War II boosted Bethlehem Steel and the plant. Even with intense labor conflict and unionization, the Point rode through a postwar economic boom to a heyday that lasted into the late 1950s. At its peak in 1957, Sparrows Point, with the world's largest steel mill, employed 29,000 people.

Aluminum was the greatest challenge to Bethlehem Steel, and complacent management was not equal to it. Foreign steel production, union militancy, and recessions further reduced Bethlehem Steel's primacy, and Sparrows Point began to decline. By 1987, its centenary, employment had dropped to eight thousand and was continuing to fall (Reutter 1988).

The Point was not just a place to work; it was a way of life. Those who lived there never left its sights, sounds, or smells. It was a place of employment for new immigrants. Families that spoke different languages at home shared the experience of working there. Sons worked alongside fathers. During World War II, women joined the ranks. Even when workers unionized and fought management, they took pride in building what mattered in the world: ships, cars, plate for cans.

The loss of more than twenty thousand jobs in one firm alone must have a devastating effect on a community. General Motors, Western Electric, Esskay Meat, American Can, Lever Brothers, Proctor and Gamble, Crown Cork and Seal, Crosse and Blackwell—the list of firms that cut their workforce or left over the years goes on and on. The tens of thousands of families whose blue-collar breadwinners were forced to look for other work lost not only their incomes, but the faith they could depend on the economy to support them.

And many of them did what the distillery worker above did: they commuted to suburban jobs, or they moved near the jobs. Southeast Baltimore, like the rest of the City, began to lose population. A member of the Coordinating Committee summarized what happened between 1970 and 1990 with a slide presentation at one of the cluster workshops:

> losing population, but slowing rate of decrease . . . losing households . . . different from Baltimore City . . . lost 1/2 person per household, going from 3 to 2-1/2 . . . Southeast Baltimore gained children under 5 . . . gained people 65 and older . . . lost school-age children and their parents . . . 37 percent of household owners are 65 or older . . . race is more diverse . . . whites went from 78 percent to 72 percent, other from 3 to 4 percent, and blacks from 19 to 25 percent . . . number of owner-occupied households went down very slightly from 58 percent to 56 percent . . . vacants are 11 percent in Southeast Baltimore, 9 percent in Baltimore, and 14 percent in Cluster A.

Not all these changes occurred at once, nor did they stem from the same causes, but the loss of industrial jobs was a prime mover. Young men took their families to the suburbs, often leaving parents or grandparents in Southeast to get old alone. An accumulation of dependent people in the City, compounded by the growing impoverishment of the

City and the federal abandonment of cities in the 1980s, challenged City government's ability to provide services, including, prominently, schooling. If employment did not pull young families to the suburbs, the decline of City schools pushed, accelerating the exodus.

A simple measure illustrates school performance. On tests where 50 represents the national mean, in 1990–91 Southeast children scored 41 in math and 39 in reading, below even the Baltimore City averages of 42 and 41, respectively. Nevertheless, 90 percent of students were promoted at year's end (Baltimore City Department of Planning 1992b). "Until the schools become good," a community leader argues,

> you are never going to keep them here, the young families, which means the children won't grow up in the neighborhood. Or the only thing you are going to keep here are the people who can afford to send their children to private school or are too poor to leave the neighborhood. That's not good for a community like Southeast and definitely not good for Baltimore, and we are seeing a lot of that. . . . There's still a lot of flight to suburbia. We are losing our black middle class now because of it.

These trends contributed to the growing number of vacant houses. Housing in Southeast Baltimore was traditionally passed down in families, or at least within the ethnic community. Now when a grandparent dies, a suburban child or grandchild might try to keep the home in the family— not moving back into it, but not selling it either. They might try to rent it, without experience in managing property, and find their tenants have run down the house to the point where it is not worth taking care of. Outside investors might buy up properties, rent them as profitably as possible, and abandon them when expedient. A resident sums up these properties as "lost housing."

The loss of jobs, people, schools, and housing engenders still more losses. A minister observes,

> You have the old community lamenting what has been lost, finding a few around that are still neighbors that they can still count on, but pretty well ignoring the new people except to complain. And the new people may be kind of rootless and rudderless, and so they don't share the old values. . . . What is happening is that the old-timers could control the people who might have moved in and that they are no longer able to do that, and that sense of closeness . . . it has gone from a closed community to a divided community.

A young man who moved his family out of that community concludes, "People have that sense of loss of control." As social attachments have weakened, moral authority and community have declined, and Southeast ceases to be either safe or familiar.

ETHNICITY

There is in all this still another loss. Southeast Baltimore is no longer the cluster of ethnic communities it once was. In a way, this is what immigrants hoped for. They wanted American freedom, opportunity, and success. They could not help acting as if they still lived in Europe, and many tried to maintain their customs, but they also wanted their sons and daughters to become good Americans.

Many children feverishly threw off their parents' old country ways, to make it as, simply, Americans. And yet a number later concluded they had struck a poor bargain. They had assimilated, and yet America had not made them rich. Resentful at their limited success, guilty about how quickly they had rejected their parents, they and, still more, their unquestionably American children began to resurrect their ethnicity (see Hansen 1964 [1940]). In the 1970s black pride gave an added push to whites' interests in ethnicity.

However, what it meant to be Italian, German, or Polish in late-twentieth-century America, many decades after the first arrival, was anything but clear. For one thing, the original immigrants were more likely to have identified with a region or a town than a modern nation-state. But, more than that, life in that town, if it still existed after World War II, probably bore little resemblance to conditions when the first generation left. If the third generation were motivated to reclaim aspects of their grandparents' lives, they were forced to choose between conditions that no longer existed and conditions that their forebears would not recognize.

Thus ethnicity had different meanings for different generations. Survivors from the first generation might remember how they had lived in Europe. Some of the institutions they had created in Southeast Baltimore still existed, but these had lost most of their founders and much of their vitality. For their children and grandchildren, ethnicity was part inheritance and, especially for the third generation, part invention.

Not only might the third generation identify less strongly than the first with some place in Europe, but the content of the identification was different. The third generation had grown up in America; it provided the primary meanings for their lives. Most who thought of themselves as, say, Italian or Polish, meant much less by it than their grandparents. For the latter, ethnicity was part of a coherent culture. For the grandchildren, isolated symbols, such as foods or words, were more likely to carry the burden of ethnic identity (Alba 1990; Gans 1979; Waters 1990). The ethnicity of the third and fourth generations, an observer wrote, emphasized "concern with identity, with the feeling of being Jewish or Italian," rather than deep involvement in ethnic culture or institutions (Gans 1979:1).

A Story about Ethnicity

A forty-year old man of Italian descent who grew up in Highlandtown portrays typical changes in ethnicity in the story of his life. He describes the neighborhood of his youth:

> Highlandtown was an enclave for Italians. Before that, the Jews lived there. On Lombard, at Haven, there were shopping areas. There were Jewish shopkeepers. Then there was a German influx. Next came the Italians. As the Germans and Italians moved in, the Jewish people moved out. I don't know where they went. . . . Near Our Lady of Pompeii you found a lot of Italians. The Italian population there was larger than Little Italy. Our Lady of Pompeii had a far larger Italian population than Little Italy. It was an enclave for Italian people around there. . . .
>
> I am kind of surprised at how outsiders assess it [when they speak of "diversity"]. The people who live there and grew up there, we can cut it like a pie. It is not diverse. Highlandtown was almost all white—predominantly Italian, German, Polish, a few Jews. It had a handful of blacks. . . .
>
> Schools were not a major issue back then. There were three groups. There was a high Catholic population, and they went to Catholic schools. Pompeii. Holy Rosary. St. Elizabeth's. Little Flower was farther up on the other side of Belair Road. St. Stanislaus. Each had its own ethnic population. St. Stanislaus was Polish. Pompeii was Italian. St. Elizabeth's was Hungarian, some Polish. I know them all because we played all of them in a league.

This is a picture of a world of familiar, ethnically shaped institutions. It was a small world, where "everybody knew everybody," where "one bunch of people" sat together in class for years, and where, if he hit his brother on the way to school, his mother would hear about it before he got home. It was a coherent world where the older generation watched out for the younger.

As he grew up, his parents encouraged him to be ambitious. "My parents said to me, 'You are going to do better than we did; you are going to college.'" Because of their urging, he was one of the few students in his high school class who went to college, and "In my generation, I am only the second to go to college, and the first to graduate from a professional school."

He married and bought a rowhouse near where he grew up. He had children and enrolled them in Catholic school, but raising a family in the old neighborhood proved difficult:

> Property values had become stagnant, but the City kept on increasing the tax assessment. You could hear more sirens. But you often couldn't hear them because of all the noise from people getting out of the bars at two in the morning.

One night I looked out my window at two in the morning and saw someone hit someone on the head with a baseball bat. I had the phone in my hand and called 911. An hour and a half later a policeman knocked on the door and asked what the problem was. I didn't mean to be smart, but I told him he was an hour and a half late, that someone was splitting someone's skull with a baseball bat in the middle of the intersection an hour and a half earlier. He said they had gotten a number of calls on that. But I didn't see anyone come out. One night I saw people being handcuffed on my front steps. This was three in the morning. I asked the policeman what the problem was, and he told me it was none of my business.

By this time, people from the neighborhood were moving to the suburbs: "Then you had people not living [in the city] saying, Why are you living there?" And now he

had friends who didn't live in the City, who had individual houses. That is what everyone wants, an individual house. It is the American Dream—a little bit of ground. . . . It doesn't matter where it is, even in the City, but it is something they want. But high taxes make it hard to buy in the City.

His children wanted a dog, and his yard was too small. One day he visited a friend who had moved to the suburbs:

I thought how wonderful it was—a green carpet, being able to hear the birds. And they had a swing for their children. I felt I was cheating my children by not having a swing.

And so he bought a detached house in the suburbs and moved. His yard is large, he gets a good tax deduction, and his neighborhood is one of the safest in the metropolitan area.

His parents urged him to succeed in American terms, and his community gave him the strength to do so. He moved from the old neighborhood because it had changed, and he felt he could not properly raise a family there. He moved out, too, because he had changed, wanting more than his parents had and able to afford it.

Yet his individual success, he believes, carries the cost of ethnic solidarity. "I have thirty-seven first cousins," he explains.

We have a large family. . . . My cousin Frankie was one of the first to move out, and he moved to Cape St. Claire [a suburb on the Chesapeake Bay]. People said, "He thinks he's too good for us." Then his son had problems, and they said the reason was that he moved to Cape St. Claire.

In his next words, somehow continuing that story, he explains, "I am very proud of being Italian, but we assimilate into American society. We don't try to change it. We just try to learn it." He was proud to be

Italian, but it seemed inevitable that, as an Italian-American, he, too, would end up in a suburb.

He immediately goes on to reminisce about one of the first people he knew who made the move:

> Someone I knew moved out. He felt ashamed. That he had turned his back on the neighborhood. I feel the same. There is a part of me that feels I turned my back on them.

So goes ethnicity.

Talking about Ethnicity

In 1990 Southeast still had a higher proportion of foreign-born residents (5%) than Baltimore as a whole (3%). English was the household language in fewer homes in Southeast (85%) than in the City (90%). Where household members spoke another language, it was most likely a non-Spanish continental European language (13%, compared to 7%).[3] Foreign-born speakers of European languages were particularly likely to live in traditional ethnic areas in the eastern part of the Southeast.

Southeast residents, especially those who have come from elsewhere, frequently mention "ethnic diversity" as an attraction of the area. A man who moved from another part of the city proclaims, "It's the only place where ethnicity even exists anymore in Baltimore in terms of people defining their neighborhoods." A Fell's Point businessman argues that restaurants, food stores, and antique shops "are here because of the ethnicity of the neighborhood."

Someone who has lived in Southeast nearly twenty years declares ethnicity

> is more important than you think. It's probably not so important to the new people who move in. It's so much who you are to the people who have always lived here, and it's part of the package. . . . It's just that what you are includes your nationality, and they are conscious about it. Not that anything is wrong with it, whatever nationality you are, but it's part of who you are. When I called Martha Hacker last week, I told her who I was, and the first thing she said was, "What nationality is that?"

However, as soon as people talk about ethnicity at any length, they tell a story of how it has been watered down. Those who moved to Southeast speak of being attracted to an apparently vital ethnic culture but either finding it to be less than they assumed or watching it wane. The following account moves from enthusiasm to simple appreciation to concern:

> I had come from living in Greenwich Village, New York, and loved that diversity. When I came and was looking around in Baltimore, I found that Washington Hill and Fell's Point really reminded me of the

Village, and I found it was much cheaper living here, too. But I liked the ethnic mix that was here, that there were American Indians, old Polish, Ukrainians, an Italian neighborhood. Especially at that time [1976], there were many ethnic mom-and-pop stores and bakeries and things like that. I like that, because that's really, truly American to have that kind of mix. . . .

East Baltimore, Southeast Baltimore, and that whole area of Fell's Point, Highlandtown, Greektown, Little Italy were culturally more diverse. . . . In New York . . . you can go to a Hungarian restaurant in one corner, walk three blocks, and you can walk to a Polish restaurant, walk six blocks, and you go to an Indian restaurant. I think some of that was happening here. I think this is a very ethnic town, but it never really played on it. So I think they lost some of their smaller ethnic areas, have never really built up on them. Like there's not a Ukrainian restaurant around here; there is a Ukrainian church, but there is really not a Ukrainian restaurant. There is a Russian Orthodox church here that has a festival, but you can't go and find Russian food in Baltimore. So they really never used a lot of that cultural mix that they had and really try to expand on it as a way of bringing money into a neighborhood . . . except for the Greeks and Italians.

Ethnic Southeast Baltimore communities have eroded since the 1970s, she reflects:

This neighborhood has lost some of that. Because there used to be a lot of little Polish bakeries, and there's still a couple of Polish sausage and butcher stores, but many of them have closed. There was a very nice little Ukrainian store that's no longer here. So I think that's something I have really missed, and I have seen that change, but it's not that people have left. . . . I think just the older people had left who were using those facilities. And I don't think in Baltimore a lot of the younger children, the second generation are keeping a lot of their ethnic functions, which is really sad, which people still do in New York. . . .

But I think if you drive through Southeast Baltimore, you can really see how ethnicity at one point was very important. Because if you look at the churches, it's not just a Catholic church, it's an Irish Catholic church, it's a Russian Orthodox church, Ukrainian church, or Polish church. . . . St. Michael's, which is changing from a German church to basically a Spanish church. The population in this area was basically German, and you had a lot of Lutheran churches because of that in this neighborhood. . . . Now, since the population has changed, it has a Spanish Mass and a large Spanish population. . . . I think that's the biggest change as far as the ethnic cultures that are coming into East Baltimore. We are beginning to have some new cultures coming in, Spanish and Korean. We have a Korean church in Highlandtown now.

When large numbers of ethnics moved to the suburbs, they left only the shells of community institutions:

So basically you are still seeing the biggest part of the population in churches are the people who originally went to that church and are now living in the suburbs and coming back, and that's definitely true with the Greek Orthodox, Russian Orthodox, and Ukrainian church. . . . If you look at the Ukrainian church . . . if you look at the neighborhood twenty-five years ago, everyone who lived around that church was Ukrainian, and up here at the Russian Orthodox church, a good percentage of people who lived in this community were Russian Orthodox, and most of those people have moved into the suburbs. They were able to successfully educate their children, and their children became professionals, and instead of living in the city, they have moved to the suburbs. I think that's the biggest thing that has happened here. Especially with the increase with the Asian and Spanish population. . . .

If you look at the area around the Ukrainian church, that neighborhood used to be all Ukrainian when I first moved here. If you went out on Saturday morning, every single woman in the area was scrubbing their steps to keep that marble. That marble had to be glittering. And the houses were immaculate on the side street side; you don't see that anymore. So there is not that pride of where you are, and it's really affecting the neighborhood. So if you don't have that pride, you don't have the neighborhood. You just live here, especially in older blue-collar white areas, except in Greek and Italian . . . but Ukrainians are not speaking Ukrainian, and Poles are not speaking Polish.

A social service professional who moved to Baltimore to work with Southeast residents believes ethnicity "is still strong for the older generation," but even there notices group differences. Although she sees "a strong identification and common experience" in the Greek community,

I don't sense the exact same thing in the Polish community. . . . For the Polish community it seems more like a camaraderie in the same culture. It is an identity that seems more generic. For the Greek community, it seems more cohesive. They are certainly cohesive politically. They pulled together to back Perry [Sfikas, elected to the City Council and State Senate]. Maybe the Polish community doesn't need to do that. They have [Cornell] Dypski [Delegate to the Maryland General Assembly] and the other politicians.

However, even older generation natives of Southeast Baltimore describe a decline of ethnically shaped practices and institutions. At the start, they can fill in elaborate details of ethnic community maps, as does, for example, a long-time Canton resident:

Most of the people have an ethnic background. We have German people, Polish, Italian. I think they take the majority of the ethnic backgrounds. We have others. We have Irish. And they came, and they built their parishes, like Sacred Heart was a German Parish, St. Casimir's was a Polish parish, and then St. Brigid's, I think, was more Irish. And then we have the Italian Lady of Pompeii, and like in Little Italy we have all kind of Italians there, and they had branches all from these churches. So the community was built around the churches. . . . The ethnic background, it keeps people together.

She tells stories of a grandmother who worked in a cannery and died of tuberculosis at age forty-two, leaving six or seven children, and others. Significantly, however, these stories of ethnicity refer to ethnic "background" and "the old days." Now, she continues but without noting any sharp break, ethnicity is something to consume:

I love the different ethnic festivals. I like to go to the Polish festival. I like the German festival. I like the Greek festival and the Ukrainian festival, Spanish. . . . I like them all, and I go to as many as I can.

A man whose German family lived in Highlandtown tells much the same story as the Italian man above, but with a German focus. A vivid history includes potato famine and hard work, but it ends with people, including himself, moving toward or into the suburbs. He finishes up much like the Canton woman, exalting ethnic diversity, but finding it mainly in occasional festivals:

[Ethnicity] is what makes us unique; we are different. We have got a little bit of everything. We have got Italians in Little Italy, Hispanics over at Fell's Point. We have some black populations throughout the area. Our area down here is mostly white. You know, we all have different neighborhoods and different things and different people. It's kind of nice in a way. If you got to a fair or something like that, you'd see all the different kinds. . . . One thing I used to like was all those city fairs they used to have, all the different ethnic fairs, and all the food and stuff like that, and we still see that in Southeast, whereas I don't think the rest of the City now, I don't think they are putting those on anymore. So we still see it in the neighborhood fairs, things like St. Nicholas every year. Some of the other neighborhoods. I think there is a German festival in Fell's Point, Hispanic festivals. . . .

Fairs offer a chance to taste food rarely eaten, hear and dance to music only occasionally played, and touch the trappings of a culture largely spent.

THE ETHNIC DILEMMA, BOUNDARIES, AND THE PLANNING CHALLENGE

A Baltimore native who has worked in the Southeast for twenty years summarizes what has happened:

Forty years ago this was the great American melting pot, and there was less emphasis on the diversity. . . . There have always been people who have wanted to preserve their heritage, but that was not the predominant focus in the community. The predominant focus was in working together and being American.

The decline of ethnicity shows the first generation's success. At the same time, it represents a loss—of roots, tradition, specialness, and transcendent meaning.

This loss shows the permeability of Southeast's boundaries. They could not contain the old ethnic communities. The Italian's story illustrates the forces no instrument of Southeast could control. It could not regulate the economy, neither the decisions of corporate managers nor those of suburban shopping center developers. It could not control the housing market, nor individuals renting out family homes, speculators, developers, or low- and moderate-income families seeking cheap housing. It could not command the public schools. It could not police the drug trade.

At the same time, the Southeast could not keep this man from changing. Although crime and bad schools pushed him out, he also came to want, and to be able to afford, things Southeast could not provide, such as an American Dream home with a lawn. The waning of ethnicity accompanies and represents the passing of many things that made Southeast life familiar, secure, rooted, and special. As Commerce Place shows, Southeast residents are part of a global economy, where decisions in other countries touch their lives. Neighborhoods can control less than even a generation ago.

A Southeast native sums up these changes in practical terms:

> We don't have power and strength in the cities anymore. We have lost too many of the rich, smart people. They have gone off to make their fortunes in the suburbs. There are not enough smart, hard-driving, rich people left.

These conditions frame the planning challenge for Southeast Baltimore: to make the boundaries matter, so it is more rewarding to live or do business in Southeast than elsewhere. A socially and culturally defined community can keep and attract members by promulgating norms promoting valued activities and creating incentives for people to engage in them. If individuals or institutions want better opportunities for interacting or freedom from external threats, often, as with the Jews, they can move. Southeasterners, however, must reckon with their place as it is, trying to modify it, change its inhabitants, or attract new ones. The next chapter examines efforts to define Southeast as a place of value and begin to make it one.

CHAPTER 7

Establishing the Boundaries: Investing and Regenerating

A sense of loss and a commitment to regeneration defined the mood of Southeast planning. The Southeast Community Plan begins with these words:

> Southeast Baltimore is at a crossroads. Over the past twenty years, southeast Baltimore neighborhoods have experienced changes in population, business and commercial areas, and housing. While many of these changes have had a positive impact on life in southeast Baltimore, there are many longer-term trends that threaten the continued vitality of southeast Baltimore's neighborhoods.

The first item on a list that follows is "48.5% loss of total jobs in the Canton Industrial District." Soon after comes "Shift from owner to renter occupancy in a number of neighborhoods." Following closely is "20,000 southeast residents who are functionally illiterate."

"While southeast Baltimore suffered these changes," the final paragraph on the first page explains,

> spending cuts reduced the capacity of local government to undertake the intensive planning effort needed to address them. Thus, the burden fell on southeast residents and communities to take the lead in planning for the future. The Southeast Community Plan makes recommendations intended to turn the tide of the above mentioned trends (Plan 1993:1).

Hence the plan's subtitle is "Towards a Future of Hope and Opportunity."

When the plan was released in December 1993, the Planning Council invited community members, elected officials, local planners, and the press to a reception in an old warehouse. It had once been a broom factory but now was a business incubator, a home for new small businesses that needed affordable space. Coordinating Committee members called the building's regeneration and its tenants' births symbols of the new life the plan would bring Southeast.

A Committee member introduced "community voices," Southeast residents who would read the plan's development principles. After each, he asked everyone to respond with a series of refrains. For the first few principles, the crowd chanted, "A future of hope and opportunity for the people and children of Southeast Baltimore." Following others, "A plan by the people for the people." Finally, "We are building a new beginning."

The broom factory offered an apt metaphor: Southeast was a structure that no longer fit its original uses, but it was available for new purposes. The challenge was to give the boundaries of Southeast Baltimore meaning by putting things of value within them, or else within the control of those living inside. Revitalizing Southeast depended on investing in it: committing money and passion to seed a greater future return, furnishing it with authority and control, infusing it with vitality, and arraying it with honor.

GETTING STARTED AND DEFINING SOUTHEAST

When the core activists and SECO staff met in January 1992 to design Southeast planning, they began to delineate a process and structure and to identify participants. As they talked, they increasingly realized they needed to define what it meant for Southeast residents to develop a plan for their community: What authority should and could they claim? What should a community plan be and do? How they answered these questions would define Southeast.

Selecting Participants

An introductory sentence on a "very preliminary list" of possible planning participants stated, "We need people who can work cooperatively for a community-wide purpose." This sentence encapsulated a dilemma and a constraint: on the one hand, to include people from throughout the community, but, at the same time, to include only those who could cooperate and to define the purview of planning so participants could agree on a common purpose. The core group wanted to include as many as possible, but they also wanted to produce a plan in a year.

They easily agreed they wanted a planning council that would represent all significant interests. They would ask neighborhood associations to send representatives. They would contact major institutions, such as Johns Hopkins Hospital and Francis Scott Key Medical Center. They wanted to include staff from the Department of Planning and the Department of Housing and Community Development, though they decided to ask them only for specific assistance. They identified clergy who could speak for important groups. Someone mentioned merchant associations, and another asked about realtors, but the group worried their interests might conflict with residents' and decided to include some in "key informant interviews" and to invite them to meetings as appropriate.

The list grew larger than an efficient work group. Those meeting moved to distinguish a larger representative planning council and smaller task groups. The council would bring authority to the effort, while task groups, including council members, would work on specific issues.

This decision returned people to considering whom to ask to serve on the planning council. The preliminary list included activists they knew. When they reviewed names in terms of representation, however, they saw most were white, many of them middle-class people who had moved to Southeast. They tried to identify blacks, Hispanics, and American Indians they could add and agreed to think further. Those who knew specific minority or low-income persons volunteered to contact them. In February, invitations went out to an expanded group of potential members.

Defining Southeast

Geographically, the core group had little difficulty defining Southeast. They took SECO's boundaries. More complicated was defining what kind of a thing Southeast Baltimore was: physical territory, an economy, a social network, a culture, or some combination of these? How Southeast was defined would affect which issues went on the agenda and, in turn, which community groups decided to participate.

At the least, the core group could consider Southeast a physical place. Yet such a view did not automatically elaborate itself. Land use is part of a physical area. Housing is physical, but it has social aspects, and both reflect a housing market beyond Southeast boundaries. Employment matters to Southeast residents, but people could work outside the area, and jobs respond to distant economic forces. Schools, trash, crime, and drugs are similarly complicated.

The group split between those who argued for restricting attention to physical and economic issues and those who advocated a broader view, including such social concerns as health, education, and day care. Several factors led to a decision to define Southeast as a physical and economic place.

Many in the core group came from the Waterfront Coalition, which was primarily concerned with physical development. SECO sponsored human service programs such as Head Start, adult literacy, and GED training and had organizing projects on education and racial harmony. Still, much of SECO/SDI's reputation and staff strengths involved physical and economic development. At the least, the group assumed, they would have difficulty analyzing social problems in only a year. Recognizing SECO/SDI's emphasis, they believed they could best get funding for physical and economic development recommendations.

SECO's role was also a consideration. Historically, it had helped build many neighborhood associations, which now jealously guarded their autonomy. Accordingly, the director had reframed SECO's role as helping community organizations do what they could best do and facilitating coalitions where useful. In this context, the core group decided that, although code enforcement, sanitation, and crime were often residents' biggest concerns, local associations should handle them.

The group decided not to take on residents' other major worry, schools, for several reasons. They felt neighborhood associations should see what they wanted and could do. At the same time, a citywide bureaucracy made school policy, and they doubted one community alone could have much impact. In addition, they recognized the complexity of educational issues and did not want to burden the new planning effort with them.

Finally, they assumed the most valuable things planning could bring into Southeast boundaries were jobs and good housing.

Four from this group became a Coordinating Committee and issued the following description of Southeast planning:

> The purpose of the Southeast Plan is to help define how future physical development in southeast Baltimore should take place so as to strengthen neighborhoods, minimize negative impacts from large-scale development, and increase the social, economic, and recreational opportunities of southeast residents and businesses. By physical development we mean new commercial and residential projects, commercial revitalization, new and renovated housing for seniors and families, preservation or re-use of public buildings and parklands, transportation improvements and parking, and economic development initiatives....
>
> The Southeast Planning Council, the community coalition sponsoring the Southeast Plan, realizes that there are important issues for southeast neighborhoods and citizens that the Plan will not directly address. These include crime, trash and sanitation, and schools. Many of these are best addressed by neighborhood associations and their members who have the experience, know-how, and long-term commitment to solve them with volunteer work and advocacy (Southeast Planning Council, "Southeast Community Plan: An Overview," February 14, 1992).

Claiming Authority for Planning

Yet whom could the Planning Council claim to act for, and what could it legitimately do? Two considerations required getting associations from all over Southeast to sign on to planning. One involved extending the Council's authority to Southeast's geographic boundaries, so it could claim to represent the whole community. In addition, each group that participated could promote its interests with the expectation the plan would recommend things it wanted. Thus broad involvement would enable the plan to propose putting things truly valued throughout the geographic Southeast.

Although the core group shared assumptions along these lines, their explicitness in inviting widespread involvement and defining the plan's purview contrasted with vagueness about authority. One reason was that few had thought about these issues. At the same time, they regarded the planning council as an experiment—to see not simply whether it could plan for the community, but also what authority it could get. The council might start with SECO's authority, but it had to be able to develop broader legitimacy of its own (see Giloth 1994).

VISUALIZING SOUTHEAST BALTIMORE

The challenge in Southeast planning was simultaneously to recognize the importance of different neighborhoods and to establish a salient common Southeast identity. By dividing Southeast into four clusters, the Coordinating Committee acknowledged neighborhood variations but limited differences and encouraged residents to think of themselves as members of a cluster, intermediate between their neighborhood and the entire Southeast. The Committee structured planning in several ways to create a shared vision of Southeast Baltimore, one significant enough to motivate community planning.

Actually, the Planning Council itself offered an image of the Southeast when it first met in March. It had fifty-one members, including the four-member Coordinating Committee. Most were white, though several blacks, American Indians, and Hispanics had been invited. Some minority persons who had agreed to serve never came to a meeting. The Coordinating Committee later expanded Council membership, partly to include more minorities, but it had little participation from minorities or the poor.

Elements of the first Council meeting, repeated in cluster workshops, encouraged people to think of themselves as having shared interests. Routinely, someone presented statistical summaries of Southeast conditions, sometimes with breakdowns for clusters, in comparison with the City as a whole, on such matters as population, household size, age, racial composition, and housing condition and tenure. Thus Southeast residents could begin to describe themselves as a unit.

In addition, the first Council and cluster meetings featured bus tours, to enable people literally to visualize the Southeast, its boundaries, and what they contained. Residents described their neighborhoods to fellow passengers. Repeatedly, riders expressed surprise at what they saw. They were impressed by Southeast's extent; often people did not know neighborhoods less than a mile from their homes. People were struck by the diversity of housing, churches, shopping, and industries.

The physical Southeast was most apparent on a tour, and Council members' first reactions set some directions for later planning. Much of what they said concerned vulnerability to outside influences. Vacant stores showed that shopping districts were losing customers to the suburbs. Many people were alarmed by environmental hazards, including contaminated dirt piles and an incinerator. People said they were surprised and concerned by the number of vacant houses and empty lots.

At the same time, they saw assets in the physical Southeast. Much of the housing was sound and moderately priced. In the right hands, even abandoned units could be returned to the housing market. Patterson Park, in the center of Southeast, was a grand city park. The waterfront, bounding the area on the south, was beautiful, visually unified the community, and, as some saw it, had been and might again be a place of employment.

People also talked about the social Southeast. They spoke of its people and their diversity as a prime strength. The many community organizations had an impressive capacity to mobilize people. Still, Southeast needed social development: the community ought to publicize ethnicities more, and disparate groups should learn to cooperate more. The social problems people identified emphasized their lack of control over boundaries. Many considered crime the top issue, and a number called for improving public schools.

In short, participants thought the Southeast had good, decent people, but the places they lived, shopped, and worked were threatened by the larger economy and political system. Rebuilding Southeast would depend on influencing those entities.

The Coordinating Committee encouraged the Planning Council to fantasize about the Southeast, to see it not as it was, but as it might be. Before the bus tours, a leader conducted visualization exercises, asking people to close their eyes and let their minds wander. On one occasion she explained,

> Just because we live in this area doesn't mean we know it. So we will take a tour. . . . We will follow our thought process and our feeling process. We have here people from different views, different cultures, different religions, different areas.

Another time she instructed people to "think about Southeast together," to take seriously their "dreams. . . . Wouldn't it be wonderful if we could . . . ?" The workshop aimed at creating "collective dreams," a concern for "the future—planning for a great future for Southeast." Those attending represented a "wonderful mix of races." In visualizing Southeast, they should all think about "the advantages and beautiful things about Southeast," about how to

> make a Southeast we really dream about . . . things we want to keep in place and increase . . . things we want to get rid of and keep from happening . . . beyond the nitty gritty daily irksome things . . . so you are dreaming. . . . What kind of a Southeast do you want to see happen?

In the world of dreams, anything is possible. If people dream together, they will see both their differences and their unity. Different cultures can make up a wonderful mix of races. By evoking fantasy, the leader invited Council members to see themselves as members of a good, powerful, unified Southeast.

In fact, as planning proceeded over a year and a half, strangers got to know one another as residents of a common Southeast. They shared information about neighborhoods, found joint concerns, and worked together. The bus rides became planning mythology. They were videotaped—not just what people might have seen outside the windows, but also what they said to one another as they rode. Excerpts were shown at meetings. Many might have seen the rides as a metaphor for their new relations with other Southeasterners: traveling together, trying to make sense of what everyone saw, anticipating a common destination.

Indeed, as publication of the plan neared, a long-time activist argued the process had succeeded in just those terms:

> The process had value, and whether the document produces any other kind of change, the fact that the process took place will allow change and will allow more power to communities. . . . I've seen people work together. I've seen people invest in this. . . . Each individual in the process has been strengthened, I think, by participating in the process. Just because they know it is there, and there is some document or somebody you can talk to. You know you can say that there are these other models for development, wait a minute, wait a minute, there are things that we want. And we actually know what they are, so we don't have to take six months to figure them out while you're trying to get your zoning permit through in the next twelve days.
>
> So I think that it has paid off already for the people who have participated, for the communities that they represent, just because the process took place and helped. Even if there was no Southeast plan, the fact that the clusters got together, and, you know, the guy from Graceland met the guy from St. Helena, who met the new community leader from Steelton, who was looking desperately for somebody who had some experience as a community leader to tell her she was doing a good

job and to give her a number that she could call if she didn't know how to handle rats and street lights and all the other typical problems, has been a positive effect. The fact that there has been a plan that can be presented to the rest of the world as a unified front.

INVESTING IN THE SOUTHEAST

The Dilemma

In aiming to be inclusive, Southeast planners faced the same dilemma as Associated planners: to recognize real differences, yet to produce reasons for, an image of, and the experience of unity. One strategy is to emphasize unity and subordinate group differences to abstract principles of identity. Another is to recognize differences and establish the unifying principle that every group will get something for its interests. The first approach treats the community as a psychological focus for personal identity; the second regards the community as a political system.

Associated planners took the first approach, consistent with federation rhetoric, considering all Baltimore Jews similar as Jews, though, as we shall see, when that position failed to produce agreements, The Associated turned to the second approach.

Southeast Baltimore, in contrast, had no ready unifying ideology. The admonition to dream and follow the feeling process encouraged fantasizing about abstract unity, but reality worked against it. "Ethnicity" had drawn people together in the 1970s but had less power in the 1990s because another generation had passed and because new nonwhite immigrants diluted a sense of commonality. At the same time, Southeast neighborhood associations treasured their autonomy and would resist endorsing a single principle or institution. Hence Southeast planning inclined toward an inclusiveness based on political pluralism.

Economic Development

The plan shows the fruits of this approach. It aimed to increase the value of Southeast Baltimore for as many groups as possible. Recommendations for economic development, housing, services, and transportation proposed to protect things of value and introduce new ones.

At the same time, each sector involved distinct problems with managing boundaries around benefits. Roads epitomized the difficulties of controlling design, funding, and use. Social services would aid mainly people living nearby, but they depended on outside funding. Better, affordable housing would benefit whoever lived in Southeast, but residential choices were shaped by a regional housing market, the economy, and schools.

Housing and social services will be examined later. Here we will look at boundary and investment issues related to economic development. Its place at the head of the plan reflected the premise that increasing the economic value of living in Southeast was crucial to the community's future. As in each part of the plan, some recommendations got priority, because problems were pressing, action was necessary or possible, or both.

These recommendations aimed to return economic activity to Southeast, to instill the area with a value all residents could appreciate. The economic development mission statement declared,

> Southeast Baltimore has its economic roots embedded in its industrial and commercial districts. With the loss or downsizing of major industrial plants, and with the growth of suburban malls, Southeast's economic base has been suffering. Between 1980–87, the Canton Industrial District lost nearly 50 percent of its total jobs. Southeast now has many vacant, under-utilized properties, displaced workers, and younger workers who can no longer find employment in their community.
>
> Future economic development in Southeast will build on our strengths: existing businesses, location, transportation, land, buildings, key health institutions[1] and people. We will pursue the development of clean industries that generate a minimum of negative impacts and that are linked to community residents through education, training, apprenticeship, and job placement. . . .
>
> Our ultimate goal is to restore economic opportunity to the list of advantages of living in Southeast (Plan 1993:16).

The first two priority recommendations aimed to attract modern industry to Southeast. Recommendation 1 would

> Create a state-of-the-art industrial park to stimulate employment and business development opportunities . . . for small and medium-sized businesses, port-related commerce, life science manufacturers, and health care suppliers (Plan 1993:17).

Recommendation 2 urged including the Canton industrial district in Baltimore's Empowerment Zone application.

Recommendation 4 advocated legislation to give local residents priority in any publicly assisted development jobs.

Three priority recommendations offered aid to new or struggling small businesses. Recommendation 3 would set up a Southeast Baltimore Community Development Loan Fund with local money to make capital available for business and affordable housing development. Recommendation 5 would

> Establish a Comprehensive Small Business Assistance Center in Southeast . . . providing loan packaging, technical assistance, entrepreneurial training, and advocacy for an array of retail, service, and industrial establishments (Plan 1993:21).

Recommendation 6 combined small business assistance with more comprehensive physical and economic development as means to revitalizing the Eastern Avenue "Main Street" in Highlandtown.

The final priority recommendation (7) aimed

> To complete planning and initiate development of [several identified] vacant and under-utilized strategic industrial and residential sites [to] provide employment and home ownership opportunities for southeast Baltimore residents while supporting the revitalization of southeast Baltimore neighborhoods (Plan 1993:23).

Other recommendations, left for later, longer-term efforts, filled out a picture of a renewed Southeast economy. One proposed a Southeast economic development marketing plan. Several concentrated on stimulating places of employment, including traditional port-related industries and new life sciences. The plan recommended upgrading workers' skills and increasing links between schools and businesses to ensure high school graduates were ready for work. A recommendation supported revitalizing neighborhood commercial districts.

These recommendations acknowledged Southeast Baltimore could not be economically self-sufficient. Yet one recommendation focused on managing the community boundary:

> Develop working relationships with Baltimore County to cooperate on economic development planning, promotion, and labor force development. The Eastern Baltimore Area Chamber of Commerce [with members mainly from the County] and Southeast Development, Inc. should participate in a market study of commercial and industrial areas within their service boundaries (Plan 1993:24).

The recommendations rested on the principle that a rising economic tide would lift all Southeast boats. Those who crafted the plan assumed everyone, especially the poor, would benefit from growth in employment and spending. If there was a group not specifically served by these proposals, it was the middle class. Participants assumed the economy worked well enough for them, and many, after all, worked and shopped elsewhere.

Investing in Everyone

Voluntary community organizations want good ideas. At the same time, they need people to contribute money, legitimacy, and work, and one way to encourage this participation is by accepting people's ideas. As a result, organizations can face a choice between good ideas and rewarding ideas (Baum 1996). Some Southeasterners felt the Coordinating Committee's desire to include something of value to so many led it to make bad choices.

The Planning Council depended on neighborhood groups' investing authority in the plan. Some believed this political need encouraged politely accepting a wide range of ideas, to avoid alienating needed supporters and to conceal disagreements among groups the leaders wanted to forge into a coalition. The cost, they argued, was not realistically appraising possible Southeast futures and framing the plan around one or a few coherent images.

An activist involved with SECO for many years says SECO's political relations with neighborhood associations kept planning leaders from taking disparate community ideas and molding them into a cohesive Southeast vision:

> A lot of efforts started to find what the areawide problems were. I think the communities now are much more concerned about their specific area, rather than the areawide problems. And, actually, if you look at the plan's recommendations, they are real specific to the specific area. They are not broad: "This is for Southeast Baltimore's needs." If you look at the industrial [economic development] plan, it picks out pockets; it doesn't talk about job creation for Southeast Baltimore in a broader sense, or it's very specific. It's site specific. And I think that is the way the communities have moved.

Reaching a broad overview and general principles for economic development would have taken more time and effort than the Coordinating Committee could call on; nevertheless,

> the strategy that was chosen for plan development lent itself to looking at smaller areas, rather than the Southeast as a whole. Because you had clusters, and the only time the clusters really got together was in the beginning and the end. And beyond that, there is this little housing group and an industrial group, and they never really related back well to the clusters. You know, the Industrial Task Force never went back to Cluster D, where most of the industrial space is, and said to the communities, "We've really identified this part of Southeast as the area where there is the most opportunity for new job creation, industrial development," and asked the communities how they feel about that. . . .
>
> I wouldn't say it was an accident. I would say that it was possibly a foreseeable outcome and that it may have been the best alternative, given the constraints the planning process had to work with . . . time, manpower, expertise, a whole range of constraints. I don't think that the plan, that the way they chose to try and do what they did is bad at all. They tried to identify major issues initially, and they had a task force that worked on that, and they had the clusters that worked on specific communities, and it's a framework for planning that in a lot of ways made a lot of sense. . . . I think there is an opportunity if more money can be found to go back and build on pieces of the plan.

Another Planning Council member felt the political norm of uncritical acceptance reinforced Southeasterners' habits of deference:

> They are intimidated by authority. . . . as direct as they are, they are intimidated by people they perceive as their superiors. . . . There is an unwillingness to explore themselves in groups. It is something that is taught . . . the Pope or the parish priest. Just respect them; don't second-guess them. Whatever your thoughts in private, don't say them in public.

As a result, early plan drafts contained uncontroversial pieces but avoided the potentially conflictual effort of working them into one compelling vision. Though impressed by the greater coherence of the final draft, he remained convinced a political desire for inclusiveness weakened the plan.

Planning leaders might not vigorously dispute these criticisms. They would emphasize how few people and how little expertise they could draw on to compose a plan in a short time. And they would argue the plan is a good first plan. It could have more comprehensive and long-term goals, but it is clear enough about directions for remaking Southeast. To a large degree, it builds on available opportunities, but many of these are far from trifling, and concrete accomplishments are necessary for consolidating investment in planning. Neighborhood groups may get to know and trust one another more, and the Planning Council could articulate more comprehensive, bolder goals.

BOUNDARIES AND COMMUNITY

Behind these disagreements about the plan lie two views of Southeast as a community. Many who argue for comprehensive recommendations believe all Southeast is a community at least of shared economic interests. Some hold, further, these interests reflect common customs and aspirations, with economic development a means to revitalizing honored traditions.

Others would counter that, despite periodic appeals to common "ethnicity," Southeast has been socially, culturally, and politically pluralistic. Economic interests have been the most consistent unifier (Fee, Shopes, and Zeidman 1991). Southeast groups have overlapping, but not identical, economic interests, and the plan reflects this pluralism. Whereas the first group wants the plan to contribute to a more socially and culturally cohesive Southeast community, the second requires simply a planning process that responds equitably to diverse interests.

These positions envision different boundaries around Southeast Baltimore. Both seek to increase the significance of lines on the map. The latter aims for economic integrity, boundaries defined by behavioral norms that would admit economic benefits from outside and retain those generated internally.

Those with the former perspective want different, more demanding cultural and social boundaries, for two reasons. Negatively, they believe that, as desirable as economic integrity would be, it is unrealistic to expect secure economic boundaries around Southeast Baltimore. Firms in Southeast, including entrepreneurs in any new industrial park, can hire workers from elsewhere. Merchants in revitalized commercial districts can live and spend profits anywhere.

Conceived as just an economic entity, Southeast Baltimore has few advantages over suburban competition in a regional market. Its labor force is accustomed to working, but many have obsolescent skills. It has inexpensive factory buildings and vacant land with built infrastructure and good transportation links. But some of the infrastructure is aging or outmoded, some buildings do not fit modern industrial technologies, some sites are on or near contaminated land, and all share the mixed image and reality of being in Baltimore City. It has cultural and locational assets, but schools are a liability, taxes a burden, crime a concern, and race an undiscussed calculation. In other words, it is hard to bound Southeast Baltimore economically so as to make it unambiguously more attractive than the suburbs.

For this practical reason, this group argues Southeasterners must make the community attractive to business firms and others by defining its boundaries as well in cultural and social terms, such as local working-class ethnic traditions. By making Southeast seem special, residents could secure the loyalty of employers and merchants who would do business in Southeast because of a basic commitment to the community.[2] More broadly, defining membership in a Southeast community in such cultural terms would give residents value, encourage those there to stay, and attract others who would commit themselves to it.

THE COMMUNITIES COMPARED

Communities need boundaries to distinguish members from outsiders, make membership valuable, and secure what the community values from the outside. Because the Jewish community and Southeast Baltimore are different kinds of communities, they approached these challenges differently but ended up facing similar questions.

The Jewish community is culturally defined: its boundaries include all Jews. The unaffiliated represent a problem because they have limited loyalty to the community. Jewish leaders faced two alternatives: to secure the commitment of the unaffiliated by affiliating them or to define them out of the community. The former approach faced long odds, and it raised uncomfortable feelings. The latter was neater and quicker. For a cultural community, this approach, consistently, was a cultural remedy, but it left the question of what besides institutional attachment made those remaining valuable.

Southeast Baltimore is a geographic area; cultural meanings and social relations can give the territory value and constitute a community. The permeability of Southeast boundaries makes it difficult to distinguish members from outsiders or to keep things of value inside. Southeast leaders weighed alternative ways of defining the territory. As an economy, the area was at a disadvantage, and economic definitions had little power to inspire loyalty. Hence leaders there, too, turned to consider other cultural definitions that would give membership value.

The chapters in part 3 next look at how the two communities defined good membership and how their assumptions shaped community planning.

PART 3

Defining Good Community Membership

CHAPTER 8

Defining the Jewish Community and Good Membership: The Orthodox and Non-Orthodox

No one who spends any time in Jewish Baltimore can avoid conflicts between the Orthodox and non-Orthodox. Explicitly religious differences flow into diverse policy conflicts. These groups disagree whether religious law or modern social and political ideas should guide decisions. They disagree whether there is any secular public realm not bound by religion. And they disagree whether to resolve disagreements through bargaining or textual exegesis.

Although the language here is Jewish, these disputes resemble other contemporary conflicts. They echo confrontations between modernists and fundamentalists. Both groups here assume they are part of one community. Indeed, that premise heats encounters and creates urgent desires for reconciliation. In these respects, relations between Orthodox and non-Orthodox Jews resemble a growing number of confrontations where groups that must live together cannot agree on common directions or ground rules for setting them or resolving differences. In Southeast Baltimore, we see related tensions between traditional working-class white ethnics and white and black newcomers.

Conflicts between Orthodox and non-Orthodox Jews concern how to define the community and what to require of members: what should hold the community together and what should give it value. Yet one of the first persons I met at The Associated asked me not to write about these divisions. Somehow they were supposed to be an undiscussed secret.

It would be impossible to write about the central dynamic of the Jewish community and Associated strategic planning without violating the request. Instead, we should honor it by taking it as a clue to understanding the community. On the one hand, it was straightforward: The Associated wanted to avoid conflict. Yet the request came accompanied by anxiety: these disagreements were so basic that even naming them could sunder the community.

However, the fact that these conflicts were public knowledge suggested the secret involved something besides their mere existence, some underlying, possibly unconscious meaning. The request thus frames a puzzle: Why would community members want to conceal from themselves the nature of relations between two dominant groups, and what does this self-deception reveal about community identity?

RELIGIOUS DIFFERENCES

To ask this question is not to deny real differences among religious groups in the Baltimore Jewish community. In the 1985 survey, 20 percent defined themselves as Orthodox, 35 percent Conservative, 29 percent Reform, and 12 percent "other" (including Reconstructionist; Tobin 1986:10).[1] Comparison with the national Jewish population helps interpret these numbers. In the United States, too, Conservatives are a large group (40%), but Reform Jews are equally numerous (41%). The Orthodox, who make up 20 percent of Baltimore Jews, comprise only 7 percent nationally (Kosmin et al. 1991:33).[2] Thus, while Conservatives form a substantial center and non-Orthodox groups constitute a large majority in Baltimore as in the United States, Baltimore is much more Orthodox and much less Reform. The fact that the proportion of Orthodox in Baltimore is triple that in the United States suggests their extraordinary influence on Baltimore Jewish life.

Religious beliefs and practices follow a rough continuum from the Orthodox on the traditional end through the Conservative to the Reconstructionist and Reform on the modern side. The Orthodox most literally interpret the Torah, observe the most extensive rituals, and consider halacha a guide to daily life. The Reform liberally interpret the Torah in modern terms, selectively observe rituals, and guide their lives more by contemporary social and political ideas than by halacha. Conservatives and Reconstructionists are in the middle (Cohen 1983; Heilman and Cohen 1989; Kosmin et al. 1991; Liebman 1973, 1988).

Denominational differences are most distinct and consistent among rabbis and other religious leaders, who have interests in articulating matters of belief and observance. Commonalities among Jewish laity blur denominational boundaries (Liebman 1973). Many Reform and Conservative Jews are indistinguishable, as are many traditional Conservatives and modern, liberal Orthodox. Many Jews, as others, choose congregations more deliberately than they enunciate religious beliefs or select a set of observances. The different denominations emerged from different national groups, and they represent not only habits of faith but also family traditions and social status.

Any simple dichotomy between "Orthodox" and "non-Orthodox" is bad sociology. It ignores differences in belief and practice between many

Conservatives and many Reform Jews. At the same time, it lumps together modern Orthodox with all traditional Orthodox, who, in turn, vary in habits of interpretation and practice. Such labeling takes away names from the Conservatives, Reform, and Reconstructionists, and it particularly deprives of voice more traditional Conservatives and modern Orthodox.

This distinction, however, fairly renders Baltimore Jewish community politics, where people dichotomize themselves into Orthodox and non-Orthodox. The Orthodox contribute to this split in two ways. First, among them, the more traditional "right wing" dominates public positions. They claim the authority of being the most legitimate Jews, they are most fervently committed to their practices, and their numbers are growing. Many question The Associated's authority because it assumes a secular realm not bound by religious law. More liberal Orthodox participate in the federation, but do so with accountability to the traditionalists. Thus relations among the Orthodox lead their spokespersons to represent more extreme positions.

In addition, the fact that Orthodox root their positions in religion increases their distance from non-Orthodox, whose rabbis articulate different religious positions and whose laity consider religion less important as a basis for public life. (At the same time, participation in The Associated, offering the opportunity to influence fiscal allocations, moderates all extremists [see Liebman 1988]).

In community affairs, the Orthodox and non-Orthodox group around political views that contrast in three related ways. First, the Orthodox base their positions in interpretation of Torah, while non-Orthodox rely on contemporary social and political thought. As a result, the Orthodox often take positions defined as more conservative (Cohen 1983).[3]

Second, the Orthodox consider halacha a guide for public as well as private life. More accurately, traditional Orthodox recognize no distinction between a private religious sphere and a public civil domain. In contrast, most non-Orthodox see religion as one institution among many in their lives and draw a line between the public world of work, politics, and society and a private religious and family life.

Third, for traditional Orthodox halacha defines not only correct positions, but also a decision method: textual interpretation, which points to right views on issues. In contrast, most non-Orthodox, as modernists and as liberals, are pluralists. They assume several positions can be legitimate, they regard different positions as derivatives of proponents' interests, and they expect to make decisions by bargaining toward consensus. Most Orthodox see disagreements not as legitimate conflicts of interest but as contests between right understanding and misinterpretation or disregard of texts. Although they may strategize politically, they do not think of themselves taking positions for political reasons.

"Orthodox" and "non-Orthodox" reasonably describe how most Associated participants think of themselves. The labels not only refer to these important differences, but they also testify to the influence of the Orthodox in defining terms of reference. At the same time, they reveal collective stakes in collapsing many overlapping differences into two. To understand what this split means for community identity and how it contributed to difficulties in strategic planning, it is necessary to examine psychological relations between Orthodox and non-Orthodox.

THE ORTHODOX AND NON-ORTHODOX AT ODDS

Orthodox Criticism of Non-Orthodox Laxity

The first American Jewish congregations followed traditional patterns now called Orthodox, but the Orthodox movement began only at the beginning of the twentieth century, in reaction to Reform and Conservatism. The "Orthodox" label made the point that new American movements had strayed from proper Judaism. When Baltimore Hebrew Congregation, for example, originally orthodox, began to reform the worship service around 1870, disgruntled members broke away to establish a more orthodox synagogue in the next block. To proclaim their judgment, they named the congregation Chizuk Amuno ("strengthening of faith").[4]

Two aspects of this story have continuing importance. One is that when Baltimore Orthodox, particularly the more traditional, look on other Jews, they see deviance and lapses.

The other is that the Orthodox have separated themselves from other Jews to practice their Judaism. Part of the reason is to avoid contaminating interaction, as traditional Orthodox keep away from both non-Orthodox Jews and Gentiles. Part of the reason is practical. Traditional Orthodox lives require a synagogue, school, kosher butcher, and *mikveh* (ritual bath), among other facilities, and geographic concentration is necessary to support these institutions. In addition, the requirement of walking to the synagogue on the Sabbath and certain holidays means living near a synagogue (Harris 1985; Heilman 1992). Traditional Baltimore Orthodox have designated boundaries to an *eruv*, a territory religiously defined as an extension of the home to allow on the Sabbath such "work" activities as carrying objects and pushing babies in strollers outside the house. An *eruv* phone directory lists only Orthodox residents and businesses.

Isolation makes it difficult for traditional Orthodox and others to know one another realistically and forces each to imagine what others are like. Where at least the Orthodox regard difference as deviance, and where a relationship to God is at issue, social relations and perceptions are likely to be acerbic.

Orthodox Jews disdain non-Orthodox religious practices. Some go so far as to question whether Conservative and Reform Jews are really Jewish. For example, one rabbi asks whether they are Jewish according to Jewish law, which specifies matrilineal descent or conversion:

> There is hardly a family in the Reform or Conservative movement where there isn't mixed marriage. [It is a matter of] self-survival. They are trying desperately to keep them within Jewish families. I have questions about their being Jewish. [If there was a conversion,] was it a religious[ly proper] conversion? The Reform consider someone Jewish if they have only a Jewish father. We don't recognize that.

Regarding religious practices, another Orthodox rabbi notes, "My congregation doesn't understand what goes on in Reform synagogues."

Breaching one of the Ten Commandments, liberal Jews do not devote the Sabbath to study, but play:

> You look at Park Heights [a main street of the Jewish community] on a Saturday afternoon in winter. The Conservative and Reform temples are closed. The Orthodox places, there isn't enough space for the youth groups. . . . I challenged the Reform and Conservative congregations to get their youth in Saturday afternoon for two hours. Off the record, they say it is their day off. I don't know what is their day on!

Traditional Orthodox identify The Associated with liberal Judaism and its lapses. Its very distinction between a civil realm and religion is unjustifiable, a rabbi asserts:

> The federation adopted the separation of civil and religious. The separation of church and state is a Christian concept. We Jews don't separate these things.

By implication, The Associated is not a Jewish institution.

Further, federation philanthropy, by following modern social welfare principles, strays from tenets of *tzedakah* [charity], as another rabbi argues:

> *Tzedakah* is usually done by volunteers. In the general [Associated] community this has ceased to exist and has been taken over by social workers. They do it on a so-called quote scientific, noninvolved basis. This is an incorrect approach so far as Jewish tradition is concerned. . . . "You should carry the load of your neighbor on your back." This has been translated into writing a check. That meets the religious obligation, but it misses the other half of *tzedakah*, which is not just to give money, but to give your personal feelings toward the needy. It is the law, practice, tradition of the social worker not to get involved.

Finally, The Associated makes decisions in a way that deviates from Jewish law: they go by consensus, rather than tradition, as a rabbi explains:

> Consensus is difficult for the Orthodox. In traditional Judaism there is no democracy. In traditional Judaism, decisions are dictated by the Torah, the written Torah and the oral Torah. And set down in the guidelines of the Shulchan Aruch [a sixteenth-century compilation of laws regarding Jewish life]. People could vote out putting on *tefillin* [phylacteries] in the morning. It could be a majority, or consensus, or unanimous vote, but it wouldn't mean anything. When the decision comes to the floor, the question is, What does the Shulchan Aruch tell us?

To make his point simply, when asked what he would call the alternative to consensus decision making, he answers,

> *Sechel,* common sense. . . . With consensus The Associated would flounder. There is a saying about the Shulchan Aruch. It consists of four sections. But there is a fifth section. What is the fifth section? *Sechel.*

Yet at the same time some say non-Orthodox are not Jewish by law or practice and The Associated follows neither Jewish law nor common sense, Orthodox complain about "Orthodox bashing."

Non-Orthodox Criticism of Orthodox Zealotry and Guilt about Laxity

As the targets of criticism, many non-Orthodox consider the Orthodox intolerant. A Reform woman declares, "I am much more tolerant of the Orthodox than they are of me." A Conservative man protests,

> I don't like the mentality of the Orthodox. . . . I find it hard to accept the Orthodox view that won't accept others' approach to Judaism, when it is others' acceptance that allows them to follow their approach. . . . All the *frums* [pious ones: traditional Orthodox] from New York, derogatorily they are called black hats [based on their dress]. . . . It is important to say it is okay for others to do different things.

Reform, Conservative, and Reconstructionist rabbis feel the Orthodox discredit their institutions. Women feel the Orthodox do not respect women. Those married to non-Jews feel ostracized.

Moreover, "The Orthodox are zealots. They are very aggressive in fighting for what they believe. . . . There are no holds barred." As if in response to the Orthodox rabbi's remark about common sense, a Conservative talks about getting consensus when community members disagree:

> This may be applicable to all but the Orthodox community: if you work with people who are intelligent, and you give them opportunities to present their point of view, and you can see something that represents your input and get something, [consensus is likely].

Instead, "The Orthodox are unbending. . . . Being intransigent pays off." Non-Orthodox are angry the Orthodox succeed in forcing The Associated and other institutions to go by their norms. A non-Orthodox leader bitterly cites the agreement to close the Jewish Community Center on Friday night and Saturday for the Sabbath:

> There is no good reason for closing it on Saturday. It doesn't make any sense, does it? It is stupid. . . . Having socialization on Saturday is not antireligious. . . . Except that the Orthodox think everyone should be praying all day. This is being oversolicitous.

Non-Orthodox frequently accuse the Orthodox of "blackmailing" them. If Associated leaders do not give them everything they demand,

> They would threaten to set up their own agencies. They would threaten to pull out of The Associated. People at The Associated are very afraid.

For example, Conservative and Reform strategic planning participants did not press their positions on education against the Orthodox "because they understood the explosion that is potential in the Orthodox community will give us a lot of trouble."

The Orthodox are stubborn, but "blackmail" is more complicated than non-Orthodox admit. First of all, the Orthodox, despite complaints and ridicule they are living a peculiar, old-fashioned European life, practice effective modern politics, getting much of what they want by threatening to walk out. Further, "blackmail" works because non-Orthodox want something from the Orthodox. Federation leaders want them to participate so The Associated can claim to be the "central address" of a single community.

More broadly, many non-Orthodox want acceptance from the Orthodox. The Orthodox seem, as they assert, "really" Jewish. They have held ground against modernity, practicing their religion with apparent faith in a time when many find it difficult to believe in much beyond their mundane lives. A liberal lay leader recognizes this motivation in explaining why The Associated gives in to the Orthodox:

> Because they [The Associated] want to keep the issue, that We are One [The Associated's fundraising slogan]. And they think they [the Orthodox] may be right. There is 52 percent intermarriage. Maybe they are right. And there is a lot of guilt involved. That is why wealthy Reform give to Bais Yaacov and Talmudical Academy [Orthodox day schools]. This will save Judaism. They have to support it for their guilt.

Associated staff and liberal laypersons recognize the federation's role in helping non-Orthodox assuage their guilt. One religious leader described the situation bluntly:

> The Associated, outrageously, gives them [the Orthodox] money. Conservative and Reform Jews writing checks to these Orthodox Jews. It is guilt. Or "You Jew for me." "You be the Jew I can't be." Or they believe they are buying a piece of heaven.

Attack on the Orthodox for Pursuing Money

The acerbic exchange between Orthodox and non-Orthodox can be understood as a disagreement about religious belief and observance and their communal implications. Mention of guilt, however, hints at something more complicated, at least among the non-Orthodox. Perhaps some contend with their own consciences as much as with the Orthodox. Another charge against the Orthodox adds to the puzzle: non-Orthodox often attack the Orthodox for pursuing money.

In a sense, this is just one of many ways the non-Orthodox put the Orthodox down by showing feet of clay beneath pious dress. A liberal rabbi finds the modern Orthodox an easy target:

> They belong to synagogues that are Orthodox but drive on Sabbath [in violation of normal Orthodox Sabbath observance]. They keep kosher at home, they eat crabs [which are not kosher] out.

Traditional Orthodox are more consistently observant, but some complain they think about money too much. They come to The Associated and individual philanthropists seeking funds for Orthodox institutions, they take what they can, and they give nothing in return. When they give to charity, they contribute only to the Orthodox community.

A Reform leader argues, "We are overly solicitous of the Orthodox, though not for financial gain. They don't give very much money." Another says, "The Orthodox don't put back into The Associated." Still another adds, "If they had their way, they would get all the money." A liberal rabbi complains they "are quick to grab off every dollar they can." Someone concludes, "For the most part, they have little interest in the non-Orthodox community. They will play ball [just to get money]." Another rabbi observes,

> The Orthodox are becoming more and more involved in the [North American] Council of Jewish Federations. . . . You know what Willie Sutton said about why he robbed banks? Because that is where the money is.

A Reform Jew cinches the case against the Orthodox, in answering a question about how to get agreement between them and the non-Orthodox:

> When you put them [the Orthodox] in the process of getting dollars, they will accept the heathen in their midst. . . . The very observant will stay because they want their money.

These people indict the Orthodox for pretending to be other-worldly while pursuing material wealth. Thus the Orthodox are the same as everyone else. Yet that is just what the Orthodox reply. They raise funds as others do. Because they have little wealth, they solicit the non-Orthodox and The Associated. Maybe others resent their success. But non-Orthodox cannot concede that point. They want the Orthodox to have nothing to do with money, as remarks about Willie Sutton and the heathen suggest.

The comments about guilt provide a clue. Those who feel, or want to feel, the Orthodox are "good" Jews who redeem the rest may scorn Orthodox fundraising because it makes it difficult to idealize the Orthodox as purely spiritual. At the same time, those who feel burdened by guilt comparing themselves with the ideal Orthodox may unconsciously want to destroy Orthodox moral authority, and so lessen the guilt. Whereas the first wish would have the Orthodox stop fundraising, the second would have them continue. Undoubtedly some non-Orthodox ambivalently hold both impulses simultaneously, fixated on Orthodox fundraising.

Yet this still does not explain why pursuing money is the offense singled out against the Orthodox. Significantly, one of the community's wealthiest men praises The Associated's fundraising in the exact terms used to attack the Orthodox:

> We know we get the major, major part of the campaign from a few people. You could say they waste so much time on all the small givers. Others say you can get money from the small people. The answer is what Willie Sutton said: "Why do you rob banks?" "Because that is where the money is."

If robbing banks is a sin for the Orthodox, it must be so for the non-Orthodox, too. Maybe some non-Orthodox unconsciously think of fundraising as robbing banks: easy but unsanctified money. Perhaps some who succeed at business feel guilty about making money while observing few rituals. Non-Orthodox could defend themselves from guilt by attributing the pursuit of money, instead, to the Orthodox, characterizing it as trafficking with the heathen, and attacking the Orthodox for what, by comparison with their own practices, is normal and only modestly successful. Such an unconscious process would allow non-Orthodox to attack the Orthodox for what they consider their own sins.

Significantly, monetary ruthlessness is a long-standing charge against Jews. Jews who attack the Orthodox over money may unconsciously be defending themselves against the charge by identifying with the anti-Semitic aggressor (Freud 1946; Gilman 1986). Instead of fearing accusers who seem so powerful, they may feel stronger by mentally putting themselves in their attackers' place, then turning and exacting the feared treatment on others who are weaker, the non-Orthodox.

Thus concerns about the Orthodox and money reflect both economic relations within the community and social and psychological relations between the community and the outside world. At the same time, the charge against the Orthodox deflects potential community conflict over economic issues. To the modest who might resent or envy those of major means, the wealthy tacitly say, Look at the Orthodox; they are the ones who pursue money without scruples.

Orthodox Doubts

Paradoxically, most criticisms of the Orthodox confirm them as orthodox: they unwaveringly adhere to traditional Judaism. What maddens others is that traditional Orthodox firmly reject modern realities and those who live with them. A Conservative Jew speculates about why the Orthodox are rigid by imagining how they think: "As soon as I allow others to have Conservatism or Reform, then I begin to question my Orthodoxy."

Perhaps, he speculates, some Orthodox question the unique correctness of the practices in which they invest so much time at the expense of modern pleasures. If doubts plague them, they may deny them, turn and associate lenient non-Orthodox observance with the doubts, and assail the mere existence of Conservatism and Reform as a way of driving out their own questions.[5]

It is difficult to know how much such doubts fuel the Orthodox attitude toward the non-Orthodox. Many who want to be Orthodox but do not accept all traditional beliefs and wish to participate in contemporary society settle in modern Orthodoxy.[6] However, they may still have difficulty reconciling traditional observance and modernity, particularly if they lack the faith to justify religious practices that are inconsistent with science and interfere with participation in modern life (Liebman 1973).

Even the most traditional ultra-Orthodox may have doubts, as Heilman, an Orthodox anthropologist, writes:

"It is a loss of orientation," Clifford Geertz argues, "that most directly gives rise to ideological activity." To the haredim [ultra-Orthodox Jews], much of contemporary life—and particularly the last half century—have been times of profound loss of orientation. These rapid and far-reaching changes made tradition more important, a matter of ideological concern (1992:100).

These Jews, Heilman argues, practice elaborate rituals with a fervor that both reflects faith and anxiously asserts it in defense against growing doubts.

Indeed, doubt seems precariously poised to unsettle faith and rituals, and rabbis counsel followers to avoid the thinking that would lead to doubt. Heilman describes a conversation with an ultra-Orthodox Hasidic Jew in Jerusalem:

> One of the Reb Arelach [a Hasidic group], whom I will call Shalom Nisan, explained to me: "Reb Arelach don't need to think; they just need to experience, and they experience very deeply, very organically. Things are and that's it. Don't ask why and how or how it would be if it were different. There's a basic lack of a need to think things over." For the Reb Arelach, Shalom Nisan explained, doubt is anathema and that is what thinking may bring. "*Safek* is 'Amalek' in gematria [a mystical system in which letters have numerical value]," he explained, noting that the letters that spell out the word "doubt" [safek] are kabbalistically [mystically] equal to the name Amalek, the Jewish incarnation of evil, the nation's greatest enemy. Reb Arelach are supposed to live without doubts, taking for granted the established truths in their world; they are expected to have no interest in reexamining these (1992:146).

Heilman describes what might be unconscious psychological dynamics both giving rise to doubt and defending against it:

> In addition to their emphasis on the spiritual and mystical is an ideology that comprehends the world beyond their own as at best irrelevant and at worst threatening and evil. Reb Arelach realize, of course, that this outside world forces itself upon them, at times even tempts them mightily. But as Shalom Nisan explained: "We know what that world is; it's goyim [Gentiles] and *pritzos* [whores]. The people who come from that world are *fremde* [foreigners]. The world is black and white. We are white." And so all kinds of efforts are made not to engage themselves with the outside world, to prevent its corrupting them (1992:147).

A world of whores could be simultaneously disgusting, tempting, and frightening. These ultra-Orthodox, Heilman explains, defend themselves against it not only by separating themselves physically, but also by persuading themselves things in the modern world are the opposite of what they seem:

> The attitude toward this outside world is not so much anger as contempt. In effect, to the Reb Arelach—as one hasid put it—the outside world is precisely the opposite of what it imagines itself to be. What it thinks is good is really bad, and what it values is worthless. Where the outsiders see light, the Reb Arelach see darkness; and what outsiders might perceive as the darkness within the world of the Reb Arelach is, as they see it, true light (1992:148).

These Israeli ultra-Orthodox suggest hypotheses about their Orthodox Baltimore counterparts. Even some traditionalists seem to feel their faith challenged by modernity. Heilman suggests those who doubt their faith or practices unconsciously defend themselves against anxiety by denying any doubt, then identifying it with less observant non-Orthodox, and, finally, heaping contempt on them for doubting.

Both sides in this conflict over orthodoxy have more at stake than religion and associated politics. They are acting out inner conflicts about the obligations and possibilities of faith in the modern world.

FAITH IN MODERNITY

The Orthodox and non-Orthodox represent positions in a dilemma about how to live as Jews in the modern world—how to have sufficient faith to justify adherence to religiously defined Judaism while also surviving, and even succeeding, in modern life. Non-Orthodox participate in modern social and economic life but may feel guilty that they don't serve a purpose higher than material gain. They admire, respect, and envy the Orthodox, who seem to have so much faith they can do without materialism. Indeed, they idealize the Orthodox, insisting on seeing them as, and trying to force them to be, people of pure faith.

Among the Orthodox, the modern Orthodox are most actively involved in modern life, but even traditionalists do not simply shun it. Some effectively influence community politics. Some make sophisticated use of modern technologies. Many are active in law, medicine, the sciences, teaching, and civic affairs.

Still, some envy the freedom with which non-Orthodox more broadly participate and succeed in the modern world. However, even if they wish to follow, they feel bound to have and keep faith for not only themselves, but all the community. In return, they expect non-Orthodox to support them materially.

The public conflict is more convoluted than it appears: each group unconsciously wants the other to be what it consciously attacks the other for being. At the same time non-Orthodox criticize the Orthodox for unwavering religiosity, they insist the Orthodox have the faith they lack and observe the rituals they ignore. In the blunt language above, they want the Orthodox to "Jew for" them. And at the same time Orthodox criticize the non-Orthodox for materialism, they insist the non-Orthodox continue to make money, but give more to them. They will have faith for all, if only they are paid for their service.

Thus the two sides reflect a tacit community division of labor, where each group takes the task it can best accomplish. However, in this splitting, each group is so forced to specialize that its members feel burdened by what they must do and impoverished by what they may not do. Each group depends on the other for the completeness of faith and modern success.

Yet community members cannot admit what they have done. They see no way to reconcile faith and modernity other than unconsciously to split them off and hope they come together. They feel discussing the bargain would force it to collapse, not only because they have no common terms to understand how they require both faith and modernity, but also because they fear analyzing faith would dissolve it.

Thus the overt community conflict is partly a social enactment of inner psychological conflicts. When someone attacks the other group (for being pious or materialistic), he also attacks an aspect of himself he feels forced to deny. Yet at the same time he unconsciously wants the other side to excel at what he cannot acknowledge.

The Orthodox–non-Orthodox conflict persists not only because it involves real differences, but also because each side needs the other. The groups do more than project unwanted aspects of themselves (unprincipled pursuit of money, doubt) onto each other. Each also projects a valued but deficient aspect of itself (the possibility of faith, material and other modern success) onto the other, asks the other to epitomize its ideal, and then reidentifies with the new, improved aspect, feeling good and whole as a result (see Klein 1946, 1955; Ogden 1979; Schafer 1968).

COMMUNITY MEMBERSHIP

The Orthodox–non-Orthodox split dominates the Jewish community for two closely related reasons. First, the groups are contesting the definition of good community membership. The Orthodox insist people follow complex cultural patterns of behavior involving religious observance and belief. Many non-Orthodox think it enough for Jews to interact with other Jews and, perhaps especially, affiliate with Jewish institutions. In their opposition, these groups frame a question for every community: whether it can persist if members simply have social and commercial relations, or whether survival depends on members' following more complex, culturally coherent patterns of behavior. Second, these groups each insist on one of the ingredients required for the very existence of a community: transcendent faith and social and economic success. People focus on their conflict—indeed, nurture it—because in maintaining this confrontation they keep the community alive. For now, paradoxically, the conflict holds the community together.

CHAPTER 9

The Orthodox, the Non-Orthodox, and Strategic Planning: The Case of Jewish Education

Planning, as politics, is the art of the possible. No matter what the private passions, when decisions are made, groups seek what they can get. The Associated, as everyone recognizes, is where the money is, and federation planning offers the opportunity to convert community values into funding priorities.

Planning for Jewish education offers an example. Orthodox and non-Orthodox disagreed about religion and community membership. They opposed each other on educational goals and spending priorities. Yet psychologically they depended on one another. Moreover, The Associated wanted agreement so it could claim to be the "central address" of a large, unified community. One aim of strategic planning was to commit the Orthodox to the predominantly non-Orthodox federation. Yet the Orthodox insisted on being different and separate as a condition for sitting at the table. The case shows how these dynamics shaped planning.

JEWISH EDUCATION

When the strategic plan was published, it stated the premise for Jewish education:

> along with an experience of Israel, Jewish education is the most powerful bonding force among American Jewry; it powerfully strengthens Jewish identity and hence the Jewish community. At a time when many of the social, economic and ideological forces affecting Jewish life tend to weaken the sense of a distinctive history and shared values, Jewish education is vital to the preservation of the legacy (Plan 1989:8).

Yet between broad agreement on this assumption and consensus on policies lay major disagreements about the aims, curriculum, and pedagogy of Jewish education. They referred ultimately to different views of the community.

115

Some, largely but not exclusively Orthodox, believe religious knowledge and practice are essential to Jewish identity. They regard full-time day schools, which include religious instruction, as proven means of teaching the knowledge and encouraging the practice. When strategic planning started, Baltimore had nine day schools: seven Orthodox, one Conservative, and one Reform. The Associated subsidized all but two new schools: the Reform program and one Orthodox. Most day school advocates are Orthodox. A few Conservative and Reform parents send children to day schools, and some send contributions to Orthodox or non-Orthodox programs.

Many non-Orthodox think of the Jewish community ethnically, constituted by institutions, including religion, and social relations, loosely bound by culture and personal identification.[1] In contrast to the Orthodox, who see the community as support for individual religious practice, many of them regard the community as an end in itself. Most non-Orthodox who value religious knowledge and practice support "supplementary" education (called "congregational" or "communal" depending on its sponsorship). These programs include Sunday school and may add one or two weekday afternoon sessions following regular school.[2] Only non-Orthodox attend these programs and consider them the most appropriate Jewish education.

Some, virtually all non-Orthodox, emphasize personal identification with the Jewish community, on whatever basis an individual chooses. They are concerned about those who do not think of themselves as Jewish. They want Jews first to feel good about being Jewish. Study and observance are secondary, matters of choice. They support educational programs that stimulate Jewish identity. These include discussion groups, recreation at the Jewish Community Center, which could create good feelings about being among Jews, and trips to Israel, which could inspire Jewish commitments. In contrast to formal day schools and supplementary programs, such "informal" education is less structured in setting, aims, curriculum, and/or pedagogy.

Different views of Jewish education lead to different institutional interests. At the end of the 1989–90 school year, just after completion of the strategic plan, 3,284 children attended the seven day schools supported by The Associated. This represented a 38 percent increase from four years earlier.

However, problems accompanied growing enrollment. Traditional Orthodox families have many children, and many have modest means. As a result, day schools provide extensive scholarships, which drain school budgets. Raising funds through higher tuition is tricky, because ensuing requests for still greater financial aid may wipe out gains. In 1990 net tuition provided for only 46 percent of day school expenses. The Associated gave day schools a subsidy amounting to about 5 percent of total expenses. Contributions paid for another 33 percent, leaving 15 percent unsupported. Schools were generating an aggregate deficit of $1.5 million to $2 million annually, and the total system debt, including capital loans, was $8 million at the end of the 1990 school year (Commission on Jewish Education, *A Strategic Plan for Jewish Education*, 1993 [hereafter, "Education Plan"]; and Jewish Day School Education Report 1991).

Day school teachers, who have good reputations, are paid approximately 20 percent to 25 percent less than teachers in Maryland independent schools. A couple of day schools have had significant delays in paying their teachers, and one faced bankruptcy before being bailed out with Associated help. Thus day schools have good reasons for coming to The Associated.

Supplementary schools enroll twice as many students, 6,614 at the beginning of the 1990–91 academic year—a 22 percent increase from four years earlier and a 28 percent increase over the decade. However, one-third of those students were in preschool, providing child care as much as Jewish education. Moreover, the actual number of days children attended (not counting preschool) declined by 6 percent during the decade, as enrollment in three-day programs (Sunday plus two afternoons) dropped significantly and two-day enrollment greatly increased (Education Plan 1993; Congregational and Communal School Report 1991). Perhaps some left three-day programs for full-time day schools, but those remaining prefer less intense Jewish education.

That condition, in turn, affects the quality of supplementary education. Because teaching in congregational or communal programs is mostly part-time, poorly paid work, few professional Jewish educators are likely to go there. Hence these programs want The Associated to help get and keep better teachers and improve the teachers they have.

Informal education, by and large, is not institutional. Most prominently, its advocates want funding for trips to Israel for adolescents. Some are interested in education for families.

EDUCATION IN STRATEGIC PLANNING

When Jewish education was put on the planning agenda, these complex, overlapping positions were often simplified into denominational terms. Debate frequently pitted formal against informal education, with largely Orthodox on one side and non-Orthodox on the other. Budgetary discussions found day school advocates, largely Orthodox, against nearly everyone else. The arguments reflected educational disagreements and competition for scarce funds but became containers for broader Ortho-dox–non-Orthodox conflicts.

The Services Subcommittee was responsible for recommending action on Jewish education, and its first draft report noted the centrality of denominational differences:

> [An argument against Associated involvement with the schools is that] such support may raise difficult and potentially divisive questions of disproportionate subsidization of Orthodox over Conservative and Reform institutions. . . .
>
> [It might be reasonable to support schools according to the amount of day school curriculum that is specifically Jewish {an approach that would aid supplementary schools}, but] Even so, such a formula would provide more support to Orthodox than to Conservative or Reform institutions. That might prove a source of contention. It would also seem to ignore one of the principal criteria for subsidy adopted by this subcommittee—namely, that priority should go to services addressed to persons at risk of not retaining their Jewish identity. Children of Orthodox homes are probably least likely to fall into this category. Should the formula then prefer children from least affiliated families? Or from poorer families? Or should we allocate support in proportion to the relative sizes of the Orthodox, Conservative and Reform communi-ties? Or to the size of their youth populations?

The final draft of the Subcommittee report did not include this dis-cussion or otherwise refer to denominational conflicts. The strategic plan did not resolve these questions, but, instead, offered three general rec-ommendations:

> *Increase funding for Jewish education.* . . . The Associated . . . should support a wide spectrum of adult education, formal and informal, and as offered by a variety of institutions. . . . it should be committed to facil-itate the access of all Jewish children. . . . The Associated must sub-stantially increase its funding of Jewish education, without assuming principal financial responsibility.
>
> *Support day and supplementary schools differently.* . . . The day schools' main need is for additional funding of core curricula. The supplementary schools' main need is to improve the effectiveness of schooling. Associ-ated support should reflect those differences. . . .
>
> *Establish a new structure.* . . . All schools must . . . retain the responsi-bility for setting their own curricula and for organizing, operating and—to the extent possible—financing themselves. They must be evaluated primarily by their own accrediting bodies. But a Baltimore entity or entities must take responsibility for three critical tasks:
>
> 1. assessing the needs . . . for Jewish education . . . ;
> 2. determining the degree to which . . . those needs are now met; and

3. making the decisions and allocating the resources necessary to help build a comprehensive, well-coordinated, efficiently administered and community-wide educational system (Plan 1989:9).

Removal of denominational references was meant to avoid conflict. Perhaps, however, reluctance to face denominational issues contributed to failure to reach agreement on educational goals. The planning process that followed offers evidence.

STRATEGIC PLANNING FOR EDUCATION

For much of the strategic plan, implementation meant detailed planning. For Jewish education, it meant making another attempt to come to agreement on basic directions. When the Strategic Planning Implementation Council was created in July 1989, its Services Task Force took up Jewish education. Soon after, in early 1990, Associated leaders set up a Commission on Jewish Education and charged it with developing a strategic plan for Jewish education.

Twenty-two at-large members were chosen to represent a range of religious, educational, and agency affiliations. Twelve more were picked as delegates from eight agencies involved in formal or informal education. Five present or former Associated leaders became ex officio members. Except for the delegates, most were men who were major contributors and senior community leaders. Concern to include day school advocates led to a membership that was one-third Orthodox.

The Commission created four subcommittees, each to analyze and make recommendations on one type of education and each comprised of advocates for that type: day school education, congregational and communal religious school education, informal education, and higher education. The first three subcommittees reported in the summer of 1991. A dispute at the Baltimore Hebrew University stopped the fourth subcommittee. After reorganization of the university, a consultant produced a report in March 1993.

The following account focuses on five meetings leading toward acceptance of a strategic plan for Jewish education in June 1993. They highlight how relations between Orthodox and non-Orthodox affected strategic planning.

Setting Priorities

Meeting One: Talking about Educational Priorities. After the first three subcommittees completed reports, staff sent commission members material for a January 1992 meeting to set priorities. A draft "Introduction to the Strategic Plan for Jewish Education" stated basic assumptions, including the equality of formal and informal education.

It was accompanied by a "Conceptual Framework/Planning Grid" for organizing the disparate subcommittee recommendations. Some were specific to one type of education. For instance, the Subcommittee on Congregational and Communal Religious School Education recommended more full-time positions in supplementary education, to attract better teachers. The day school subcommittee wanted more scholarships for day school students. Other recommendations were generic, such as the informal education subcommittee's proposal for multiyear funding. Recommendations could be placed on the grid under "Personnel," "Educational Programs/Initiatives," or "Special Populations." A column listed six target populations that might be affected by a recommendation. These were categorized by age (from "early childhood" to "adults" and including "families").

At the meeting, the chair and a staff member began by emphasizing the draft was tentative and urging members to think conceptually about commonalities between formal and informal education.

EUGENE HAMMERMAN [A LEADING TRADITIONAL ORTHODOX ADVOCATE FOR DAY SCHOOLS, COMMENTING ON THE INTRODUCTION]: There is not enough in this document about Jewish education in Baltimore. We must define Jewish education in terms of what has been successful in increasing Jewish identity. Informal Jewish education has not been successful. Successful, for example, in stopping the intermarriage rate. Outreach [largely informal education] to the unaffiliated is not the same as Jewish education.

LOUIS GREENSPAN [A SECULAR NON-ORTHODOX LEADER]: There is a policy question: Are the unaffiliated our clients?

MAX NEUSTADT [ANOTHER SECULAR NON-ORTHODOX LEADER, A STRONG ADVOCATE FOR INFORMAL EDUCATION]: I am for the unaffiliated. Formal and informal, it is all education. . . .

HAROLD WEISS [AN ORTHODOX ADVOCATE FOR DAY SCHOOLS]: The document, in being all-inclusive, is too neutral and meaningless. It doesn't identify a direction and make choices.

WILLIAM SILVER, CHAIR:[3] Staff can't make these decisions; the commission must.

RUTH CHERNOV [AGENCY REPRESENTATIVE]: Even the affiliated are not a homogeneous group. Many nominally affiliated need Jewish education to increase their affiliation. . . .

RACHEL EISENMAN [AGENCY REPRESENTATIVE]: There are dangers in focusing on the core of affiliated groups, especially when many of their children become less affiliated. I have informal education programs in my agency, and they work in pulling in the unaffiliated.

WEISS: Okay, but informal education is only bait for the real thing: intensive Jewish education.

ROGER KOBRIN [NON-ORTHODOX DAY SCHOOL ADVOCATE]: More important than interested and connected people, as the informal education people emphasize, are educated and knowledgeable people. Not civil Jews, but Jewish Jews. . . .

ESTHER DAVIDOFF [AGENCY REPRESENTATIVE]: The key is to focus on Torah-based Jewish education, whether formal or informal. I would propose to eliminate the words "formal" and "informal," and to focus on what is learned. . . .

SAUL AARONSON, STAFF:[4] This is a draft. Read the observation that Jewish education is a lifelong enterprise. Keep in mind that The Associated funds only part of Jewish education, and that is what we are talking about. Please give me any written comments you have on the draft. For now, I would like a formal sign-off on the grid as a framework.

WEISS: I move that Saul complete the grid. [Second. Some hands raised.] Now that we have gotten past that, I would like to argue again for preparing the introduction at the end, rather than now.

SILVER: We won't ask you to sign off on it now.

WEISS: Okay. Though it is too all-inclusive now.

SILVER: We can amend it later.

WEISS: Okay. . . .

DAVIDOFF: I would like to ask that by the next meeting we have the grid filled in also with current budget figures for programs in each box [so we can see who now gets how much].

AARONSON: Maybe at a later meeting. We can't do it by next time.

BETTY STEIN [AGENCY REPRESENTATIVE]: I feel that, after the talk about the relative importance of outreach and inreach [mainly formal education for the affiliated], there is no consensus on it.

AARONSON: Right. I don't hear consensus either on affiliated and unaffiliated.

SILVER: Our aim is to include all—for example, outreach and inreach.

NEUSTADT: I want to reinforce Esther's request for budget figures. I'd like to see at least round numbers.

AARONSON: Okay. We can do it. I was just waiting to hear you say "great job."

SILVER: I want to thank the staff for a good job, as always.

Analysis. This meeting's rhythm is typical. The chair invited an Orthodox leader to open discussion, and he articulated disagreements with non-Orthodox positions. Some subsequent speakers elaborated differences, while others sought common ground. The Orthodox were most likely to emphasize disagreements and to push for debate and decision on differences, while non-Orthodox, aided by Associated leaders and staff, sought consensus.

Periodically, the chair and others talked about whether there was consensus on issues, whether, in effect, staff were authorized to draft language. This was the context in which staff hoped for "formal sign-off" on the conceptual introduction and grid. Weiss criticized the language as unacceptably inclusive. The chair threw the decision back to the Commission. Later, Stein and staff agreed they did not hear consensus on basic issues.

Typical, also, is how people presented their positions. Most argued from personal experience, often as parents or as students, sometimes just as observers. No one appealed to expert knowledge. Even with disagreements over desired outcomes, educational research might shed light on how effectively different programs contributed to their goals. No one considered the possibility that research might focus deliberation.

One reason is that members, except agency representatives, were chosen for their political representation or influence, not educational expertise. More generally, the Commission was a lay policy-making group; staff were supposed to provide specialized knowledge. The Board of Jewish Education had such expertise but in the Commission was regarded as only one of several agencies competing for funding.

Discussion moved among general statements about the value of programs, arguments about target populations, and allusions to characteristics of a good community. Members confused program components with student outcomes, but staff did not push for or offer clarification. Perhaps people were sensitive to limitations in their knowledge and refrained from raising questions they could not discuss.

Maybe people avoided talking more systematically about what education should do because differences seemed irreconcilable, and talking specifically might be not only futile, but dangerous. The non-Orthodox were most concerned about jeopardizing apparent community harmony, while Orthodox worried conflict would limit disbursements to their programs. These might be the reasons, as well, why members did not consider that scientific knowledge could organize their debate: if research served as a basis for measuring different positions, groups would be forced to confront each other directly, with risky results. Perhaps people believed eventual decisions would involve compromises conceding language and funds to everyone, and conceptual clarity did not matter.

The ninety-minute meeting was too brief for detailed deliberation. The generalities in which people talked, if anything, exaggerated disagreements. Yet neither wishes for clarity nor interests in consensus led anyone to ask for further discussion. Staff interpreted ambiguous observations about consensus as authorization to proceed, and no one objected or gave more specific directions.

Meeting Two: Voting on Priorities. Staff next mailed members a ballot listing every recommendation mentioned in any subcommittee report. Recommendations were grouped under "Personnel," "Programs," and

"Special Populations." People were asked to check (but not rank) their top five priorities of nine listings for personnel and twelve of twenty-six for programs, and to note the three for special populations. Only twenty members voted.

The removal of recommendations from the contexts of advocative reports to a conceptual grid, as well as mail balloting, were efforts to avoid conflict and facilitate agreement. The chair introduced the following meeting as "pivotal" and hoped the Commission would pivot toward consensus.

SILVER: We'll discuss each category of proposals in turn. Let's spend twenty minutes on personnel.

HAMMERMAN: [He read a long letter he had sent the chair and staff after the last meeting. He continued:] We can't talk about formal and informal education in the same breath. Personnel, for example: they have different personnel needs. We must talk about each of them separately. Formal education is institutional, regularized. Informal education is ad hoc, both in what people ask for and how people respond to the requests. These are two different constituencies. . . .

SILVER: I'm not surprised you are saying that. I think we would have great difficulty getting consensus from the committee by separating the two, because one would come out higher than the other. If we consider differences of opinion, we will never get consensus.

WEISS: Why are we doing this prioritizing? What does voting on priorities mean? Does it mean how dollars will be spent? Or does it just mean how things are valued? For example, trips to Israel, which everyone valued high, versus day schools. Trips to Israel might be valued high, but that doesn't mean that a great deal of money should be spent on them.

YITZCHAK WEINSTEIN [AN EDUCATOR]: Note the emphasis on the word "schooling." This is formal education. Then there is also communal education. And informal education. . . . Isn't Israel a school in itself? All three—schooling, communal, and informal—should be integrated. Let's deal with these issues by going through specific recommendations. . . .

JEROME ORNSTEIN [A TRADITIONALLY RELIGIOUS NON-ORTHODOX LEADER]: I think there is a continuum, formal and informal. One is not more important than the other. The valuation here is that all are equal.

SILVER: Don't worry about money yet.

WEISS [TO THOSE AROUND HIM]: But that's what it is all about.

SILVER: [The recommendation to] "Increase salaries and benefits": day schools will come in with a proposal that fits in. But there could be someone defined as a teacher at the Jewish Community Center.

HAMMERMAN: Formal and informal education are not the ends of a continuum. They are different.

SILVER: Let's avoid dividing up into formal and informal. Doing that would lead to conflict, no decision, no consensus. . . .

[A staff member distributed tallies from the voting, and the chair read the results. They reflected commission representation. Nineteen or twenty votes went to personnel recommendations put forth by all three subcommittees—to increase salaries and benefits, promote professional development, and improve recruitment and placement. Fifteen to eighteen votes went to recommendations from the supplementary school and/or informal education groups—to promote Israel experiences, reach out to the "marginally affiliated" and college youth, and commit funds on a multi-year basis. Day school recommendations for operating subsidies and capitation grants got fourteen and ten votes, respectively.]

JACOB LITWAK [AN EDUCATOR]: The priorities are inconsistent. Why did greater teacher recognition get only eight votes?

WEISS: People were given a fixed number of unweighted votes, and this is how it ended up.

SILVER: Let's turn to programs. [He listed the priorities, which included a "system manager."]

ALEXANDRA NORMAN [NON-ORTHODOX LEADER]: Regarding the system manager: this would lead to money going to a big bureaucracy.

SILVER: This was a high, high priority for the Informal Education Subcommittee.

WEISS: What is the meaning of eighteen votes for experience in Israel?

SILVER: It is not yet the top priority. It is only one of the priority items. There will be a further vote. . . .

HAMMERMAN: We should limit the "system manager" to informal education. Or call it a "coordinator for Jewish education" for informal education.

[In a long discussion of the "system manager," questions concerned to whom the manager would be accountable and whether it would just collect and disseminate information or have power over programs.]

FRED GINSBURG [AGENCY REPRESENTATIVE]: For example, the system manager would be responsible for "encouraging interagency collaboration on programming and reducing possible redundancies." What power would it have?

ABEL CHECHIN [AGENCY REPRESENTATIVE WITH DAY SCHOOL ALLEGIANCES]: I would suggest substituting "identifying opportunities for interagency collaboration." . . .

SILVER. What about "information resource person"?

GINSBURG. Take out "empower" from "Empower a 'system manager.'"

SILVER. Would you accept "Establish an informational resource"?

AARONSON. It is informing the community.

SILVER. We are getting close to consensus on this entity. . . . I am trying to move to [recommendations on] specific populations. [Discussion continued to focus on programs, and ending time arrived.] We will convene the steering committee of the subcommittee chairs to draft this into the text of the plan. . . . Well, we got through it!

Analysis. Staff designed the survey to get consensus among views by finding agreements on specific recommendations. Weiss criticized it methodologically, noting votes could not express preference rankings or weights. But his strongest objection was that breaking down committee reports into discrete recommendations avoided direct confrontation between overall positions.

Again, as Orthodox speakers emphasized disagreements, the chair tried to avoid confrontation and find consensus. Hammerman began by reading his long letter, arguing formal and informal education be considered separately. The chair rejected the idea, insisting the two types of education constituted ends of a continuum. Separating them would force people to value one over the other, creating winners and losers. Such an outcome would not be consensus and was unacceptable. After the meeting, several people complained to staff that Hammerman had taken too much time. They felt people should refer briefly to their positions but not advocate them at length. A longer presentation not only could offend those who disagreed but might be considered to require a response, which could lead to public conflict.

Most ignored anyone who said they should proceed to setting priorities. The only proposal specifically discussed was a "system manager," put forth by the Informal Education Subcommittee to coordinate informal education resources, but favored by Associated administration as a way of centrally managing all programs. Opposition came primarily from day school advocates who did not want outside control. Both invoking their minority interests and evoking others' anxiety about federation intrusion into agencies, they turned a "system manager" into an "informational resource." Seizing on that agreement, the chair finally assumed sufficient consensus to guide subcommittee chairs (though, in fact, they never met to draft language).

Although the survey and discussion indicated broad agreement about giving more money to education, recruiting more students, and facilitating Israel trips, there was no specific decision about planning or funding. Nevertheless, no one objected discussion had been incomplete (for example, in not getting to special populations) or had not led toward consensus on text. Probably members assumed important decisions would be made in private negotiations and, therefore, were willing to turn initiative over to staff.

Meeting Three: Approving an Educational Budget. The absence of specific plan priorities did not keep The Associated from taking educational initiatives, as the president solicited individual gifts and foundation grants for special programs. However, the Commission's failure to agree on priorities created an awkward situation when it was forced to switch from its planning role to a budgetary role in the federation's fiscal cycle. The Commission had to decide on how to allocate a new supplementary $300,000 Fund for Jewish Education, intended to support innovation.

The Commission held three hearings on agency requests before a May 1992 meeting, where it would have to make decisions implying priorities. Five agencies, all involved in formal education, requested a total of $488,403, with the Council on Jewish Day School Education asking the most—$199,372, two-thirds of the available fund and 41 percent of total requests.[5] Prior to the meeting, staff negotiated with agencies to lower requests, to make them look realistic and magnanimous while avoiding a fight.

The chair, who had been party to the negotiations, called the meeting to order with a grin. He began by saying the Board of Jewish Education "showed great fiscal management and great planning for 1993," summarized the agency's new position, and announced what "The Associated leadership" would give in return. He then asked each agency to report.

The Board formally announced its scaled-back request, followed similarly by all other agencies except the Day School Council. After the first four had compromised, the day school spokesman subtracted their total from $300,000 and lowered his request to equal the remainder, to accompanying laughter.[6] He now asked for only $142,599, but this was 48 percent of requests. Requests equaled available funds, and conflict could be avoided.

At the end of presentations, an agency representative proposed to "give *koved* [respect] to the chair," and everyone applauded. The chair said he "would like to give a tribute to the staff. They make me look good." Everyone applauded. He called for a vote, and the budget passed without objection.

After the meeting, an agency representative congratulated himself for contributing to a harmonious decision by lowering his request. An Orthodox day school advocate told staff the Baltimore federation was exceptional in America for such a conciliatory way of working. Staff members congratulated one another on the amicable outcome.

Analysis. Unlike plan language, dollars are not abstract. Allocating the Fund for Jewish Education was a tangible way the Commission paid off. However, the problem, as many saw it, was that the Commission had neither a plan nor a consensus about the relative priority of formal and informal education. Nevertheless, the committee had to make a specific decision on money.

When original budget requests exceeded available funds, the meeting could have ended in conflict. To prevent this, staff privately negotiated with agencies. The chairman's grin seemed to reflect appreciation of the intensity of potential conflict, knowledge that deals had been made, and recognition that others knew of them. The meeting would end happily. When speakers presented revised budget requests, no one discussed the merit of any, no one spoke of educational priorities, and no one openly criticized the day schools for inflexibility. Applause and congratulatory comments expressed relief at avoiding conflict. Staff (by negotiating) made the chair look good (in running a harmonious meeting).

Thus the meeting had two outcomes. One was a budgetary decision that gave nearly half the available money to day schools, most of the rest to supplementary education, and none specifically to informal education. These allocations bore no obvious relationship to Commission members' policy preferences. The second outcome was apparent consensus. Final celebratory remarks suggested most Commission members wanted to avoid conflict more than they cared about spending priorities.

The episode illustrates the power of an intransigent minority in a group that wants consensus. Yet the Orthodox are a special minority. For many non-Orthodox, including those who disagree on policy, they have special authority as traditional Jews. Perhaps the non-Orthodox adopted this budget not only because they cherish unity, but also because, unconsciously, they want to support the Orthodox.

Adopting a Strategic Plan

Staff aimed to conclude the Commission's third year with adoption of a plan. While an outside consultant prepared the higher education report in the fall and winter of 1992, the commission did not meet. Meanwhile, Associated leaders designed a new structure for Jewish education, where the Commission would become part of a Center for the Advancement of Jewish Education. When federation leaders announced the new structure would begin on July 1, 1993, they declared the intention to raise $10 million for a Jewish education fund. In June, the last month of the fiscal year and of Silver's chairmanship, the Commission met twice to approve a plan.

Meeting Four: Considering Guiding Principles. Prior to the first meeting, staff sent out a conceptual outline for a plan, including a timetable for the next several years and enunciation of ten "understandings and guiding/overriding principles" and three "core issues" based on earlier Commission discussions and talks with interested parties.

Silver opened the meeting by talking about how work would proceed through the new structure in the fall and then directed, "What we have to do is adopt what you have received today and then move into determining and implementing more specific goals next year and later on."

NEUSTADT: I am puzzled about what is the relationship between this next study group and the last study groups that were the four committees that made rather specific recommendations.

SILVER: As a result of the four study groups, there were fifty-three recommendations, but we don't know which to attack first. I don't think we will say day schools first, but across the board. But under these categories, what in each segment is most important.

NEUSTADT: Didn't we do that already? . . .

SILVER: There is not yet consensus. . . . We have not had a concrete description here about what we are trying to do to enhance Jewish education. For example, improve synagogue membership, or improve synagogue attendance. For example, increase the number of people who go to Israel. Or get more members for The Associated.

NEUSTADT: All of the above.

SILVER: In what order?

NEUSTADT: It is concurrent. The prioritization of these I have trouble with.

SILVER: We are not going to say day school education is more important than informal education. . . .

HAMMERMAN: One priority that you have not mentioned at all is paramount: each child in this community who wants a Jewish education should be helped by this commission to get a Jewish education. We are not getting anywhere. And we should leave this up to the individual denominations, be it Reform, Conservative, or Orthodox. . . . We are not going to prioritize anything.

SILVER: I am glad you said that. The ten items [in the outline] are the truths we have found. Taking our youth and giving them a good Jewish education will be our paramount goal. . . . But everyone may not see it that way.

HAMMERMAN: Shouldn't we discuss this?

SILVER: Not today. . . .

NEUSTADT: I think we will end up with a new mission statement that will be the old mission statement. . . . I sat for a year on a committee that addressed the issue of informal Jewish education. . . . Is [our proposed coordinator for informal education] going to occur because we are going to have another committee for a year? I think we are ready to implement now. . . .

AARONSON: We could have sent everyone a twenty-page document today [to remind you of the four subcommittee reports]. A year ago there was a conceptual grid, a chart. We said, what is missing is context. There was so much to absorb in one setting. So we need to focus on priorities. . . .

HAMMERMAN [after several people argue the new committees should devote the next year to setting deliberate priorities]: I have the answer: First, we have an infrastructure in this community: day schools, community schools, higher education. We don't have to reinvent the wheel. And we have a market-place, where people can choose what they want. . . .

JEROME FITTERMAN [ONE OF THE COMMITTEE CHAIRS FOR THE NEW STRUCTURE]: I don't want you to take offense, but I am saying that we need to decide [on priorities].

HAMMERMAN: We have been doing that for three years.

SILVER: Maybe we will do it for another year.

[Hammerman and Neustadt start to argue about goals, constituencies, and educational priorities.]

SILVER: Each of you has an opinion. . . . We have to ask these questions. It will take time. Meanwhile, nobody has been cut off from funding. . . .

[Members discuss some of the points in the conceptual outline.]

WEISS: Everyone here does agree that everyone who wants a Jewish education should have it. And everyone agrees that there are those who don't know they should have it, and it is our duty to persuade them. Jews have been arguing for millennia. We are going to have to face the divisive matter of where we are going to put our money in the next five years. Not everyone can have their own first priority. Not everything can be first. Let's get on with it! First you have got to decide which of the groups is first and then get on with it. . . .

[Members begin to talk about how to conceptualize Jews in terms of their identity and which institutions should take responsibility for working with each group.]

AARONSON [trying to focus discussion on the outline's questions "What elements define an active, literate Jew?" and "What elements comprise an active, vital Jewish community?"]: Would you agree to put these questions in the document?

WEISS: No. It assumes the ultimate is the literate Jew. It may be something else.

AARONSON: Change the word. . . .

SILVER: "Committed."

WEISS: Too broad. . . . You could have a failure of a Jewish community that is literate and knowledgeable but doesn't practice or believe.

NEUSTADT: You are defining who is a good Jew and who is a bad Jew. I don't think we want to do this.

WEISS: We could have a highly educated intermarried Jewish community, but . . .

AARONSON: We are trying to draft the introduction to the document. Maybe what we ought to do is take a shot at the whole document. . . .

SILVER: There have been some good and interesting questions. I don't think we have a consensus [laughter]. We have got to ask ourselves the critical right questions before . . . action recommendations. We don't agree on which questions to ask ourselves. . . . Do we have a consensus that we have to try to figure out what to do here? . . . The strategic plan—we've got it sitting there; it's on the shelf.

AARONSON: What do you want to do? Send out the document? . . .

HAMMERMAN: Prioritize. That should be the real purpose of the next meeting. . . .

LEO PRINZ [AGENCY REPRESENTATIVE]: I have a request: send out the forty or fifty priorities.

SILVER: Okay, but don't lock them into your mind. We will give you the plan. Then we will give you the introduction.

Analysis. This was the first meeting on a plan for Jewish education in fifteen months. Many had expected the Commission to take up where it had left off, wrestling with disagreements and trying to set priorities. Instead, they found leaders and staff had agreed on the essence of a plan; it was general, and prioritization and implementation would be further postponed.

Some expressed impatience at a repetitive process. A number insisted on addressing differences at once. Orthodox day school advocates argued for making explicit choices. Neustadt said he wanted money for a coordinator for informal education but believed various purposes should be funded. Hammerman, while maintaining his position that Jewish education must be religious education, even went so far as to say each denomination should choose its own approach.

Yet repeatedly Silver thwarted calls for decision or efforts to discuss substantive issues. He insisted members would not choose between day schooling and informal education. He tried to focus attention on questions to ask, on which people might agree, rather than answers, about which people disagreed. But he discovered that even the word "literate," in what he thought a general question, threatened to set Orthodox against non-Orthodox in defining who is a Jew. He concluded, to laughter of agreement, there was no consensus.

When people wondered how they should proceed, Silver explained that staff had already drafted a plan. This meeting was arranged to endorse the conceptual outline, which could be the basis for a plan. Now he took the absence of any vehement dissent as authorization to release the plan. The introduction would be revised to reflect the discussion and fit the plan.

No one expressed surprise that staff had already written a plan, nor did anyone object to this way of proceeding. Perhaps, as before, some were relieved to avoid public conflict and to place responsibility on staff. Perhaps some believed staff knew better what to say in an educational plan. Some, as well, might assume they would have more influence in private conversations with staff than in Commission meetings. Finally, some cared more about budget allocations than plan wording.

Meeting Five: Adopting a Plan. In preparation for the intended final meeting, staff sent out two documents. One was a draft of the plan's body, including a summary of the study process and findings and recommendations from the four subcommittee reports. Recommendations were grouped under "Personnel," "Programs/Initiatives," and "Special Populations" in order of votes received in earlier balloting. Higher education recommendations, which came in later, were listed after the others in each section. A second document was a revised introduction. The meeting notice announced the agenda to be discussion of the introduction.

Silver opened the meeting with his hope, since his term ended with the month, this would be the last meeting. He reported that a "think group" of staff and a few Commission members had drafted the revised introduction.

Aaronson called attention to changes. A sentence declaring "Jewish education . . . critical in ensuring and enhancing Jewish continuity" was put at the front of "Definitions." The new draft dropped the divisive question "What elements define an active, literate Jew?" and focused more inclusively on "What qualities define an active, committed Jewish community?" Consistently, the first newly framed "Goal" was pluralistic:

> Promote the broadest range of educational opportunities to all members of our Jewish community that will enhance the personal meaning they derive from being Jewish.

The final "Goal" referred to "monitoring and evaluation," "benchmarks," "accountability," and "formal measurement of stated desired outcomes."

A "think group" member, not Orthodox but committed to day schooling, moved adoption. Several people briefly discussed wording in a "Guiding Principle" that said "Jewish survival is . . . dependent upon a strong sense of individual/personal Jewish identity," among other things, with the question whether "sense of . . . identity" was enough to demand of individuals. An Orthodox member objected to general language about "an active, committed" community but acknowledged amendments would only be compromises affecting little.

The "principles, definitions, questions, and goals enunciated in the document" were unanimously adopted, subject to revisions suggested at the meeting, as "the introduction to the plan." After the meeting, staff compiled "Building a Stronger Community: Toward the Year 2000—A Strategic Plan for Jewish Education" from the introduction and the draft plan body.

Analysis. After more than three years, the Commission on Jewish Education produced a strategic plan. Credit could go to staff who drafted the document. New language was conciliatorily inclusive. Words implying a single correct definition of a good community member were deleted.

However, because traditional Orthodox insisted on defining member-ship religiously, pluralism was a defeat for them. For example, the switch to emphasis on a good community, rather than good members, recognized various possible definitions. Leaving definitions of community member-ship to individuals' "personal meanings" went still further. It was not sim-ply pluralistic, but also general enough, to declare independence for the non-Orthodox from Orthodox norms. Finally, references to "account-ability" and "monitoring," in the context of Orthodox resistance to fun-ders' evaluating their use of money, signaled a likely concrete defeat for the Orthodox.

Another explanation for the plan's acceptance is the chair's leader-ship. By temperament a reconciler, he would listen to anyone. Though not Orthodox, his support for Jewish education included contributions to Orthodox schools. He believed his success in stewarding a plan reflected trust in his neutrality and integrity. The fact that his term was ending encouraged members to pay him a tribute by accepting a plan.

Yet the Commission never formally adopted the plan, nor did it come to consensus on points about which members raised questions. The plan, including summaries of subcommittees' work, was a compilation, rather than a statement of agreed on principles and priorities.

RECAPITULATION

The Center for the Advancement of Jewish Education started in the fall of 1993. It was an elaborate structure, where, for example, a Committee on Financial Resource Development raised funds while a Committee on Educational Planning and Service Delivery planned.

After more than thirty meetings at many levels, in March 1994 the Commission approved a ranking of eight educational programs. Debate focused on the top three. First was a proposal for an endowed educator benefits program estimated to need $1 million to $2 million per year, requiring, in turn, a $25 million fund. Second was financial aid for Israel experiences, priced at $120,000 annually. Third were family education programs, at $602,000 over the first four years.

The top program would benefit mainly Orthodox day schools, since they had most of the educators and could use the money to shore up their budgets. Israel experiences and family education were informal pro-grams favored by non-Orthodox. Members debated without deciding whether the ranking meant raising $25 million for educator benefits before putting money into other programs.

This decision resembled earlier ones. A non-Orthodox majority dis-agreed with an Orthodox minority on policy but made a decision that could give them money far out of proportion to their representation among decision makers or the general population. This was another time where the Orthodox benefited from non-Orthodox fear of public conflict. At the same time, the disparity in funds for the first and other programs seemed to express feelings the Orthodox ideally represented the community.

Soon after, Associated leaders concluded the vote was ambiguous, perhaps misinformed, and potentially divisive, and they planned to start over the next year.

CHAPTER 10

Consensus Decision Making

No two words are spoken more often, or more often together, at The Associated than "community" and "consensus." They were the watchwords of strategic planning. Yet, just as we have seen how ambiguous the meanings of "community" are, we have also seen how elusive "consensus" is. Both words express clear emotional aims of unity, but they cover over contradictory feelings that can have the practical consequence of impeding planning.

The Associated's predicament highlights differences between communities and organizations. A community is amorphous. Boundaries and membership definitions may be unclear, and contradictory criteria may coexist. Within the boundaries, members engage in wide-ranging, fluid interactions. Organizations, including community organizations, require structure, with delineated boundaries, membership, roles, authority, and responsibilities. Organizations are often ambiguous, but some definition is necessary for work (Baum 1987).

Both communities and organizations are dynamic, and "structure" is a moment in an ongoing process. The greater the differences among community members, the more dynamic, fluid, and amorphous that process will be. Nevertheless, an organizational decision is a relatively "static" moment when participants must agree to be in a specific place and follow certain procedures to take a position they will accept. While a community may be highly diverse, in the act of making a decision, a community organization must be unified.

Organizations lack the complexity to recognize and respond to all the identities and interests community members bring with them. Hence organizations must choose the best of imperfect decision procedures to represent those interests. Doing so depends on realistically assessing similarities and differences.

Jewish education was perhaps the most difficult issue in strategic planning. It involved efforts to articulate organizational goals and strategies and fit spending priorities to them where community differences were great and not evidently reconcilable. This chapter looks at the uses of "consensus" decision making as a means of representing and creating community.

135

PLANNING AND COMMUNITY DECISION MAKING

Planning is a response to three types of differences human beings encounter. One is a difference between people and their environment. The world does not spontaneously satisfy desires; strategic effort is necessary. Second, future conditions differ from the present. Because both desires and resources change, alternatives must be explored. Third, people differ from one another. Consequently, introspection is not the same as a social survey, interests must be studied, and conflicts must be resolved. This last set of differences affect which desires will be the focus of strategic efforts to arrange future resources. Realistic planning must consider differences a subject for analysis and make decisions in a way that acknowledges competing claims for priority. Neutrality is impossible.

Research for planning is a formal, specialized activity in many organizations. In addition, decision rules are themselves research procedures, prescribing who may present information about perceptions and interests, as well as how the proffered information will be evaluated. Majority voting, for example, declares the correct perception to be that held by the most persons. Consensus decision making, in contrast, requires that all parties agree on one description of reality.

Where differences are relatively small and conflicts mild or infrequent, consensus decision making is reasonable. The assumption that members will reach unanimity expresses a belief that people share common interests and encourages members to talk about how they see their interests. Uncoerced unanimity may occur under several conditions. Some problems have good solutions, and parties with overlapping interests may find a mutually satisfactory course of action. People may so empathize with others' concerns that they go along with what others want, especially when others feel their desires deeply. Or people may feel unanimity is inherently good and decide to go along with the majority to affirm and create emotional unity (Mansbridge 1983).

However, when differences are greater, when parties are more self-interested or more intransigent, and when conflicts are frequent, consensus culture may discourage minorities from pressing their views and encourage them to acquiesce when they do not really agree. Majority rule may be a better path to decisions. Its effectiveness requires that all participate voluntarily, have relatively equal power, and agree on the legitimacy of every interest. Each party can expect to be in the majority sufficiently as not to be aggrieved by any majority that overrules it.

Several conditions make majority rule difficult. First, if power is so concentrated that some interests have little or no chance to be part of a majority, the excluded may regard majority decisions as illegitimate. Second, expertise or doctrine may persuade some parties that only certain positions are acceptable and lead them to oppose majority decision making that could include other positions. Third, actors may be so firmly invested in one view of their interests that they cannot compromise.

Nevertheless, majority rule can work in communities with considerable diversity if managed by a central institution everyone considers legitimate. However, when the community is large and issues are complex, managers may be tempted to narrow the definitions of issues and the range of participants to reach agreements, and excluded interests may rebel or leave. Or else managers frame issues so abstractly that agreements lead to little action, and parties withdraw from an ineffective system.

If conflicts are too great to allow majority rule to produce broadly legitimate decisions, but if all parties still share an interest in acting together, they may create new procedures. Their success depends on willingness to examine what they believe separates them.

Organizations choose decision rules, however, not only for their realistic fit with social conditions, but also for the fantasies they encourage regarding the community.

For example, majority rule can enable groups with moderate conflicts to make decisions if the parties are willing both to compete and to negotiate. On the one hand, some people may enjoy the caring relationships that form alliances to press shared causes, and they may appreciate the decrease of tension that follows negotiated agreements. However, they may feel anxious about acting aggressively to promote their interests against others. Some people fear doing battle. Some are afraid of losing: not just being injured, but also being shamed after exposing their wants and then not being strong enough to prevail. Some feel anxious about winning, guilty about successfully influencing or harming others or afraid of reprisal. Some also feel anxious about the burdens of winning: being responsible for a policy, which will be judged, and being responsible for other persons. Thus, even though majority rule may fit social conditions, it may arouse troubling feelings.

Majority rule presents leaders with specific dangers. It assumes differences and directs groups to see differences. It reinforces individualism and group autonomy. By formally identifying winners and losers, majority rule not only shames consistent losers but brands them deviants and makes them potential dissidents. It becomes easy for them to move from criticizing policy to challenging the ground rules and leaving.

In contrast, consensus norms reassuringly assume a harmony of interests. They imply a world where caring far outweighs aggression. People are similar, they easily join together, and their collective power strengthens all. No one will feel weak or ashamed about inadequacies. There will be no dangerous conflict, and no one need fear battle. Consensus defines dissidents as eventual allies. Consensus rules empower minorities: by holding their ground, they can force the majority to move toward them or prevent a decision. Deliberation may be aggressive, but it will be guided by reason. The end is a caring agreement, where no one loses and no one is shamed. These premises suggest comforting fantasies to people anxious about aggression and conflict. They offer political reassurance to leaders who want control.

Organizations may reasonably make decisions by consensus to affirm common interests. But they act unrealistically if they adopt consensus rules with the aim of giving competing interests self-protective vetoes. Because the conflicts that necessitate such vetoes are inconsistent with a reality of common interests, a group that requires vetoes will rarely discover widely shared positions (Mansbridge 1983). However, it may never recognize that consensus rules do not fit social conditions if it wants to be reassured by the fantasies that go with the rules. People imagine that difference, conflict, and aggression dissolve under consensus norms. Wishful thinking may substitute for realistic planning and decision making.

The challenge to any organization is to analyze differences among community members and choose procedures that fit reality and lead to legitimate decisions.

THE ASSOCIATED AND THE COMMUNITY

So far, we have examined two differences within the Jewish community. One sets the unaffiliated off from the affiliated. Indeed, some of the affiliated are not even sure the unaffiliated are part of the community. Differences between the Orthodox and non-Orthodox divide them fundamentally: not only conceptions of the community and policy preferences, but also assumptions about bases for policy preferences and ground rules for resolving differences.

Associated staff and lay leaders resist publicly recognizing differences. They describe the Baltimore Jewish community as uniquely homogeneous among American Jewish communities. It has long traditions and is both physically concentrated and socially cohesive. The generations in Baltimore Jewish families have grown up and done business together, they feel a strong attachment to the area, and children stay in the community. In this view, the centrality of The Associated reflects the community. The annual campaign is highly successful not simply because of local wealth, but because of exceptional generosity. Representatives of prominent families make up a cohesive leadership. Unlike in other cities, there are no divisive feuds, and all leaders come together to address common problems.

This account is condensed in an Associated fundraising slogan: "We are one." All Baltimore Jews are one community. Some Orthodox give a simple rejoinder: "We are not one." A non-Orthodox rabbi, speaking with Associated staff and leadership, amended the phrase: "We are one, but we are many." A top staff member answered, "We are different, and we are the same." Differences, he suggested, are superficial.

Although the portrait of a unified community seems to contradict a reality of splits, the idea of Jewish peoplehood has a long history (Kaplan 1981 [1934]). For traditional Orthodox it invokes the belief all Jews were present with Moses at Mount Sinai. It fits other Jews' sentiments, by redefining Jewry from a religious community, within which there are disagreements and from which there are defections, to an ethnic community, which includes everything those who think of themselves as Jews do.

Moreover, the assertion of unity serves important psychological purposes. Not only does it reflect shared history, but it expresses a wish that all Jews could make up one community, all would care for one another, and the community would be strong. Seeing the community this way responds to the memory of the Holocaust, a history of persecution, and contemporary anti-Semitism. It offers security in a world that does not always accept Jews. Strategically, in religious and ethnic politics, a cohesive community matters. Psychologically, a single community represents security, and any split seems to endanger all.

Associated leaders and staff share these psychological interests and have congruent political interests. The Associated can be, as it claims, the "central address" of the community only if there is a unified community. The federation's wealth and power depend on representing as many as possible. Acknowledging differences would offer a legitimate basis for competing organizing and fundraising.

Hence, even though the Orthodox–non-Orthodox conflict divides many people, The Associated publicly declares Baltimore has a single Jewish community. Following from and reinforcing this view, The Associated elects to make decisions by consensus. In doing so, it follows the pattern of other North American federations (Elazar 1976). This choice of decision procedures affected strategic planning.

CONSENSUS

"Consensus" at The Associated has two aspects: decision outcomes, the proportion of participants who support a choice; and the process of reaching a decision.

The Outcome

The Associated has no specific definition of "consensus" as an outcome. It connotes unanimity, though, as a staff member concedes, "We don't have unanimity. There is majority rules. . . . But it is not a majority of one." A lay leader emphasizes, "We never want to come out of a meeting with a vote of 51–49." Although it could produce a decision, it would create the problem that half the parties, and their constituencies, would be angry. They might insist on continuing the debate. They might criticize The Associated. They might reduce or withdraw contributions to the federation. Their actions would challenge The Associated's claim to be the "central address." As another staff member puts it, "If we are 6–5, we offend five people. If we are 10–1, we only offend one."

Would two-thirds represent an acceptable majority for "consensus"? There can be no explicit answer, or else it would be impossible to claim consensus. One staff members says 60–40 would be unstable; another says two-thirds would be acceptable. The first argues that 80–20 or even 90–10 would be desirable, and the second does not disagree. The answer depends on the situation. The criterion is negative: Would a defeated minority do anything outweighing the benefit of a decision?

Associated staff and lay leaders try to get agreement from all participants. A lay leader central to strategic planning observes, "You don't want to come out with a majority opinion. You want total consensus [unanimity]." Yet people tie modifiers to "consensus" that recognize the ambiguity of even this rule. For example, a staff member says strategic planning participants were told decisions would not be made on the basis of "false consensus," apparent unanimity covering over disagreements— as might be the case at other times.

The Process

A Quaker meeting offers one image of creating consensus: individuals speak together until they agree. Occasionally someone at The Associated likens its decision process to a Quaker meeting, but few would insist on the comparison. A lay leader describes the strategic planning process whereby the organization's name was changed from Associated Jewish Charities and Welfare Fund to The Associated: Jewish Community Federation of Baltimore:

> That was a very good process. And that was voted on. For years and years there had been criticism and concern with the name. . . . Part of the criticism—which was absolutely correct—is that "Charities" was no longer the effective word, nor was "Welfare." We are a community. We serve more people than charity. People in need transcend poor people. . . . We were thinking this may be causing a lot of young people not to participate. There was no vehicle to change it. No context. As we started doing the strategic plan, [the opportunity arose]. There was a lot of heated debate. This is something that we did well. Something the community did buy into. There was a lot of debate in the [Relationships]

Subcommittee. And then a lot of debate in the full Strategic Planning Committee.

It did not pass the first time. We recommended from the Subcommittee that the full Strategic Planning Committee address the issue. There was no consensus [even in the Committee]. The only consensus we could arrive at was to address the issue. In this case the process really was good. It worked. It was the first item on the agenda of the [Communications, Image-Building, and Community Relations Task Force, set up by the Strategic Planning Implementation Council]. It really got battled around. We looked for words that were important. Many of us in power wanted the word "federation." It was used elsewhere around the country. And we felt you could not lose the name "Associated," because that is what people related to. Also, "Associated" was a significant word in Baltimore. You have Associated Catholic Charities, Associated Black Charities.

This was processed. I don't think it was overprocessed. It was voted on. You don't vote when you will not win or when you will have a split vote. We were close to unanimous or unanimous. Then we carefully outlined the project in presenting it to *The Jewish Times*. We didn't want to leak it before we had announced it to the [Associated] Board. This was a superb example of committee process. I have heard really good things about the name change. . . . It is one of the best examples. The idea was not completed in the strategic plan, because we could not get consensus. At one time I thought we might get [a facilitator to help us make a decision]. It was not railroaded. We thought it would be easier than it was. I really feel we did it right.

This is not a linear process moving smoothly to agreement. After heated disagreement within the Subcommittee about whether to change the name at all, members came to agree the name should be changed but could not agree on a new name. They simply recommended to "Change the name" (Relationships Subcommittee Report 1989:8) and postponed specific action to the Strategic Planning Committee. When they could not agree on a name, they recommended "Seek a more appropriate name" (Plan 1989:11) and pushed action off to implementation. The Task Force considered names and chose one.

Along the way, committee chairs made head counts or took straw votes but avoided formal voting if near-unanimity was unlikely. As in all committees, voting was infrequent or ritualistic. Sometimes the chair called for votes from "those opposed," sometimes not. Informal votes were never recorded, and minutes never suggested any vote was other than unanimous. Meanwhile, those who wanted specific name changes lobbied Subcommittee, Committee, and Task Force members. This is conventional politics, with a rule of avoiding decision until near-unanimity is possible.

A staff member fills in details about how consensus is often reached, at the same time modifying the requirements for consensus as an outcome:

> If you look at Webster's definition of consensus, everyone's interests are somehow being met by the decision that is made, serving all the interested parties. Ninety-five to 99 to 100 percent of the time we don't have "true consensus." We have "modified consensus." The modification is related to politics. The politics is, He who has the gold rules. Where there is consensus in the purest sense is among those who have the gold. The consensus is built around the leadership of the organization.
>
> The staff's job is taking this consensus and selling it to everyone else. The consensus is most important at the very top. It is less important lower down on the rungs. Most of the time the people who are most important are the people with responsibility for resource development [giving money]. In the end, people will acquiesce because they know the big boys have signed off. They know the likelihood of fighting it is minimal. They will buy in in order to get a piece of the pie for themselves. People are intimidated by the leadership of the organization.

In other words, "consensus" depends on near-unanimity among wealthy donors. Other committee members, recognizing they have less power, are likely to go along, unless they have strong objections. Arguably, debate leads to what another staff member calls "informed consensus," but the consensus may be informed as much about the dominant interests as about the substantive issue.

Dealing with Conflict

Yet the Orthodox actively dissented and, despite their lack of wealth, carried weight. They succeeded by exploiting two desires of largely non-Orthodox federation leadership. One is to be accepted by the Orthodox, who represent ideal Jews to many non-Orthodox. The other is to have unanimous "consensus."

For example, the $488,000 in requests for the $300,000 Fund for Jewish Education presented the challenge of reconciling requests with available funds in a way that satisfied Orthodox and non-Orthodox. Commission members might have debated and agreed on priorities. Alternatively, agencies and their Commission advocates could have bargained privately with one another. Instead, top staff negotiated individually with agency representatives, encouraging or offering incentives for each to reduce its request.

These "behind-the-scenes" negotiations are so much a part of normal politics at The Associated, they are hardly private or hidden. Everybody expects them, and nearly everyone regards them as the real work and locus of decision. Sometimes they involve direct negotiation between parties. Often Associated staff negotiate with individual parties. In either case, top management are central, because of their links to community leaders and philanthropists.

A staff member often involved in brokering agreements talks of working out "managed consensus" by using

> persuasion, influence, coalition building. I wouldn't say "threats"; I would say "persuasion." . . . I say they should think in terms of what is good for the overall community. I say that if they want something later on, they should go along on this issue.

Another speaks of occasionally "buying someone off" with a position or contribution to a program. Participation and power in negotiations, he says, follow "the Golden Rule," described above. Still, an agency board member reports, on issues where the Orthodox hold strong views at variance with others, Associated staff may bargain first with the Orthodox and then urge non-Orthodox moderates to go along with the results.

Some outside the leadership criticize the process. One complains that, because decision making is "behind the scenes," public meetings, particularly of large groups like the Commission, are "a joke." And "everybody knows they are a joke." There is no public debate on issues; decisions have already been worked out "behind the scenes," and everyone comes simply to "rubber stamp" them. Some believe they are making decisions, but many do not, he says, and become cynical.

Why doesn't he speak up when he disagrees, at least to go on record? At small meetings, he says, he does, but he would be seen as disruptive in larger gatherings. Staff would get angry. He wants to be considered a "team player" who supports the party line in public and, consequently, will get something later. Moreover, he goes on, he knows how to play the game behind the scenes, even though he is not wealthy, and he does what he can.

At the same time he is angry about elite private decision making, he colludes with it, never to disrupt public harmony. This approach can be considered prudent politics. But it represents more.

Many agree public meetings "rubber stamp" decisions made elsewhere. The less powerful complain more openly. Top leaders may acknowledge decision making is not democratic. But no one moves to change the arrangements. More is involved than just efforts by the powerful to keep procedures that benefit them. For example, at the end of the first meeting, Neustadt, an elder statesman, added his weight to the request for budget figures, sure to explicate and thus heighten conflict. A staff member agreed to comply but first wanted a compliment for good work. His good work, as he saw it, was to try to transcend conflict with a conceptual framework and a grid. The chair, also a powerful man, gave the compliment, and the meeting ended.

After some disagreements at meeting 2, the chair concluded the meeting with a sense of relief: "Well, we got through it!" without a blowup. His initial grin at meeting 3 expressed similar satisfaction at avoiding conflict. Applause and self-congratulation later echoed this relief.

"Behind-the-scenes" politics makes this possible. Even powerful leaders fear public conflict, and they displace conflicts onto the staff, expecting them to resolve differences. Publicly, community members can act as if there are no divisions, as if they have no community-rending disagreements. Politically, this arrangement benefits a powerful elite.

Psychologically, it protects everyone from anxiety about splitting the community. In the politics of consensus, Associated managers try to get as near unanimity as possible. Agreement normally starts with lay leaders, but anyone who is not a "team player" harms others as well as himself. He makes himself a loser and can make the majority feel guilty. Further, he makes it impossible for participants to think of themselves as members (or leaders) of a cohesive community. Instead, assurance of eventual consensus helps avoid guilt about acting aggressively and shame about failing. All can bask in the warmth of caring among members of a unified community. On the other hand, the managers who negotiate backstage agreements are exhausted, not just by the effort called for, but also by taking on community members' anxiety, guilt, and shame.

Participants are likely to explain unanimity by saying that constituencies have sufficiently overlapping interests and enough good sense to discover reasonable solutions to problems. As often, many begin with the emotional assumption that unanimity is intrinsically good and will go along with either the leaders or a strong minority in order to affirm and create a feeling of unity.

CONSENSUS AND COMMUNITY: REALITY AND FANTASY

Strategic planning was an effort to subsume the politics of budgetary interests under agreed-on principles and priorities. This challenge was complicated by another aim, seen in the case of Jewish education. Equating the federation with the community, Associated leaders sought to reconcile community social and cultural differences with organizational decision procedures.

Confrontations between Orthodox and non-Orthodox were most problematic because they concerned not only policy, but also definitions of community membership, and the groups lacked common language to discuss their differences. Consensus decision making offers a fantasy solution to these problems. Staff take in differences and produce virtually unanimous decisions. From real differences they offer the possibility of imagining unity. Yet these procedures carry costs. People complain staff and leaders control so much to get unanimity, they avoid dealing with "real issues." Under consensus norms, an intransigent minority can get its way or block the majority, especially when the minority has special moral standing. Agreements may be highly abstract or fragmentary. Or else, as in four years of planning for Jewish education, the majority may go on for a long time neither defeating the minority nor coming to terms with it.

When psychological and political wishes for unity make groups anxious about differences, they have trouble realistically recognizing not only how they differ, but also what they have in common. Fantasy may displace planning.

CHAPTER 11

Defining Good Membership in Southeast Baltimore: Good-Heartedness, Homeownership, and the Problem of Race

Southeast Baltimore, unlike the Jewish community, is a geographic area, but there, too, people define themselves culturally in a way that gives the community virtue and distinguishes some residents as ideal members.

Southeasterners' vocabulary for membership contrasts strikingly with that of the Jewish community, but both define membership so as to make the community good by linking everyday affairs to something transcendent. Jewish traditions favor an explicitly religious language. Because Southeast Baltimore is religiously and ethnically diverse, no single religious norm would be acceptable there. Yet a culture of goodness emerged in Southeast that has the attributes of a civil religion. It is the culture of good-hearted homeownership.

THE SOUTHEAST CHARACTER: GOOD-HEARTEDNESS

One of the most common words Southeasterners use to describe themselves is "average." Unlike at The Associated, they rarely speak of their community as "unique." Yet many Southeast residents feel it is extraordinary to be as "average" as they are. What they mean emerges with the discovery that not everyone is "average": some are not that good. Averageness is a way of living. A long-time resident calls it "good-heartedness."

In The Associated, an ethnic view of community membership competes with the religious position, though religion has greater authority. In Southeast Baltimore no ideal stands against good-hearted homeownership, though this view of membership seems to follow class and racial lines. We first listen to how the good-hearted describe themselves, then look at class and race.

Exceptional Averageness

A woman living at the eastern, suburban edge of Southeast Baltimore describes her community as "average":

> I would say that it's an average community, a middle-class community. So the prices of homes in that area are . . . modest. They are priced modestly, so that just about anybody could afford a home in that area. . . . You can still buy a home that's not too high-priced, which means people can put more money into fixing up the house, and that way it's comfortable.

This description is remarkably humble: the community is "average," the prices of houses are "modest," "just about anybody" could and does live there, and it's "comfortable."

In sketching the area's history, she delineates the strengths of these "average" people:

> We have a lot of people who have grown up in this neighborhood to begin with. It's a working-class neighborhood, blue-collar. We have General Motors right around us, Lever Brothers. We are not far from Sparrows Point, and, at one time, Holabird . . . that was an Army base; it's the Holabird Industrial Park now. And right immediately behind us, we have O'Donnell Heights city [public] housing projects. . . . From what I understand, they were built for the people from the Army base. . . . Plus we have people from Sparrows Point, and, I guess, during World War II, those homes were built in 1942, so they were built for all those people that were going to Sparrows Point to work and General Motors.

Interestingly, she uses three different terms to describe community members' class position. When talking about what people have in common, she calls them "middle-class," but, when reviewing history, she calls them "working-class" and "blue-collar." One way to interpret the shift in terms is as an account of social mobility. In the past, people were "working-class," and they have become "middle-class." Yet one might also read the series of labels in order as successive revisions in what she wants to call her community's people.

First, she labels them "middle-class" as one more way of saying they are average, as when she says, "We fit in there in a very average way. We are there in the middle." "Middle-class" connotes settledness and respectability. Then, perhaps, she draws a more precise meaning to "middle-class." The term accurately describes people's manners and aspirations, but it exaggerates their means. They do not have what many others have, nor do they have as much as they want. "Working-class" might be more accurate. And yet, with the briefest of pauses, she makes one more revision. In many ways, "blue-collar" is equivalent to "working-class." It describes people who work with their hands, who generally have lower incomes and lower status than many "middle-class" people who work with their heads.

But there is an important difference. "Class" labels refer to a continuum from the wealthiest "upper class" to the most destitute "lower class," or even "underclass." These labels compare people, denoting those who are better, because better off, and those who are worse off, and worse. "Collar" labels, in contrast, refer not to the outcomes of working, but to the content of work. "Blue-collar" and "white-collar" are just different types of work, each with its own merits. Thus "blue-collar" families can claim all the virtues that once unambiguously adhered to the "working class," while avoiding class comparisons made still more invidious by the postindustrial economy and recession. "Blue-collar" communities have the dignity and respectability of the "middle class" without worry about what they do not have. And they can take pride, as in this woman's account, from having built the nation.

That is what a neighbor suggests in her own encomium to the Southeast community:

> The community is very patriotic. . . . They are very conservative. They do care about their homes and the areas in which they live . . . and they're pretty much just regular, down-to-earth, average people. It's largely blue-collar, I believe . . . because . . . the Point, GM, Esskay, Western Electric are large employers in this particular area in the Southeast area. So a lot of the people in this area are blue-collar and have worked or are working in these type places.

Continuing, and repeating others, she says,

> Southeast Baltimore is a pretty good area. . . . Everybody pretty much is down-to-earth, good people. For the most part they get along, and they are just average, everyday living, working people.

And—the key point—they are extraordinary for being average:

> So they are all just average people. A lot of them have exceptional qualities. . . . And actually the entire area, if you get right down to it, is pretty exceptional, just because of the ability of the people to come together when they need to do it. Whether it's a problem or something that they need to do that's not a problem, something good like the community fair.

The virtue of the exceptional average people of Southeast Baltimore is that they value community and take care of one another:

> There are a lot of people active in one form of community service or another. They are either active in senior centers and senior activities, or they're active with the Rec Council and the school, like the PTA . . . or they're active in the community association. . . .

> I think people are realizing that with the types of things that are going on nowadays with government and the budget and things like that, that people have to do things on their own in order to get them done, in order to help government get things done. And people are realizing that they can't just sit back and let somebody else do it, that they have to become active and help it along. So this area tries to promote community involvement and awareness and community service. . . .
>
> They can all get together for a good time, they can all get together for a good cause, and they can all get together and try to problem solve when it is necessary. They all pretty much have the same basic family-moral-work ethic, that type of thing.

This proud community self-reliance has another side, hinted at in comments about the lapses of government:

> Politics is very iffy. A lot of people don't trust politicians. We've had good experience working with some, not so good experience working with some, and no one particular politician necessarily. . . . From the political end they don't feel they get a lot of straight answers. They feel they get . . . statistics and things that are geared to say what the government wants them to say in order for the community to approve such a project. So there needs to be a lot more trust created between the community and government. . . . The community has always been straight with the government. The government . . . needs to be just as straight with the community.

Southeasterners take care of themselves because they feel they cannot depend on government or others to help them.[1]

Good-Hearted Virtues

These values reflect the immigrant experience. Poor people came to America in search of equality and the opportunity to make something of themselves. This history is evident in a community worker's articulation of basic Southeast cultural assumptions:

> Equality of access might be one. It always boggled my mind that people got so upset when they couldn't have access to the water [as a result of Gold Coast development]. It is cultural outrage. . . .
>
> Opportunity for kids. People identify with them. They think it is an absolute crime, that in this community at large [once] everyone could leave high school and get a job, and this is not a reality today. . . .
>
> Respect might be another. I see this as a common, basic principle shared across the board in all Southeast. It probably came out of the church and immigrant experience. I hear that . . . youth have no more respect for older people, and they can talk back to them. . . .
>
> You work for what you get. . . . Not ever being able to understand welfare. So there is a little bit, no, a lot, of resentment about people who don't work for what they get.

This is the Protestant Ethic, and those who live by it feel the virtue of the righteous. A third-generation Southeast native begins to describe the Southeast character by emphasizing self-reliance: "One of the East Baltimore[2] ethics is this: I can do it myself, without ever stopping to think about it, asking people's help." In the portrayal that follows, he recognizes flaws in the Southeast character but claims a special moral position for its "good-heartedness":

> There is a place called East Baltimore. There is an East Baltimore ethic. . . . Good-heartedness. . . . If you try and do good, the world will be okay, the world will treat you well. . . . People shouldn't have to do something for nothing. They should do something for something. There is honesty in that. . . . [The community] is full of a bunch of good-hearted people. That is the authentic character of East Baltimore. . . . People are honest.

"Honesty" is a multifaceted virtue. It is a matter of reciprocity, where reward repays effort. It is also pure candor: people "wear their hearts on their sleeves." Moreover, they are unpretentious; they know what people and things are worth:

> I think they are different from other places. When I talk with them, they don't tell me about their new car, acquisition things. That is like the suburbs. Here the conversation is about real things: bad neighbors, trash, and rats. . . .
>
> I was in Florida, talking with someone, and the minute they opened their mouth, you knew they were from East Baltimore. It was not the accent, but what they said, the lack of pretension and subtlety. My best friend from high school, he says exactly what is on his mind. [Sometimes he says stupid things, but he says what is on his mind.] I think, the more education we get, the more we hide behind words.

Southeasterners are not perfect, but one should view their shortcomings sympathetically. Many suffer from "a lack of education. They are people who have been beaten down. They don't know how to deal with anything."

> I don't want to portray them as innocent. . . . Certainly they are prejudiced. Most grew up thinking if they behaved okay, the world will be okay, and they found out this isn't true. Their world is under assault. Crime. Problems in the schools are real. They are under assault by the government. . . . Or some agglomeration of other citizens, who run a Section 8 [renter subsidy] Program that is not monitored and does not work. And they confine poverty to the city. Schools don't teach anything, and nobody takes a stand. It has all gotten away from us. That is what the people who live here have seen, and that is what makes them cynical.

Still, at its core, good-hearted honesty expresses the essence of blue-collar morality:

> If you walk up and down the streets of East Baltimore and talk with people . . . they are working-class, though some of them don't like work at all. They believe in doing an honest day's work, doing the right thing, keeping their house clean, raising their children right, believing in God, whatever. . . . They are working-class. They work for a living. . . . I just think of them as just people. They are not professional people.

Finally, at least for him, the good-hearted can come from any race or ethnic group:

> There are subsets . . . whites, blacks, Hispanics now. . . . From the blacks I know—who are not that many—they have the same hopeful, good-hearted outlook about how things ought to be.

HOMEOWNERSHIP

These people emphasize an association between average, down-to-earth, good-hearted culture and homeownership, the tangible symbol of virtue. Owning a home is the American Dream to which immigrants aspired. It is a sign of settling in America. A young man reflects on this heritage:

> Homeownership was the big thing. The mother lived with them, the father lived with them, grandparents. The house was gold. A child would say to his parents, "I get the house when you die." When someone died, the house wasn't advertised, but people made phone calls. I never saw a house for sale. I don't remember seeing for sale signs when growing up.

Homes are measures of forebears' honor and the physical manifestation of extended families that support their members.

When Southeast residents talk about what would improve their community, they regularly say "promote homeownership." The president of a neighborhood association declares, "Most people that own their homes are a different kind of people." A community leader summarizes the view that homeowners are good neighbors: "People who are homeowners tend to take better care of their property and tend to have more stake in the neighborhood." Renters, in contrast, have "not quite the stake in the community," a minister comments. They "pretty much wouldn't be ones to get involved in things," a second-generation resident observes. Homeowners good-heartedly care for others in their community.

THE CULTURE IN DANGER

Yet many see this culture in danger. They note renters replacing owners and blacks replacing whites. New neighbors are less likely to be homeowners and seem unlikely to be good-hearted. A resident of a neighbor-hood in economic and racial transition describes the Southeast ethos as fragile:

> If and when the area turns black, it will be different. It will be a different culture beyond color. I think there is something about "You try to treat each other well" from East Baltimore. The ethic resides more in the place, and as people leave here, they will lose it. There is a kind of crit-ical mass. If too many people don't have it, then the place will lose it as well.

Renters, particularly black renters, symbolize threats to a way of life. For example, when rumors of rental housing construction began circu-lating in a community on the suburban edge of Southeast Baltimore, the association president called a meeting, and he reports what neighbors said:

> Some of them said . . . the prices were too low, and . . . they were afraid blacks were going to move into the area. . . . Well, our neighborhood, I would say, is maybe 95 to 98 percent white, and it does affect the home-owners, because they are afraid the property values will go down . . . and that's the biggest thing. . . . I would say the biggest thing is the property values, the crime, and they just don't want that their lifestyle would be drastically changed.

Homeownership, property values, and a virtuous lifestyle are linked. Renting challenges homeownership and property values financially, and it threatens the lifestyle socially and morally.

HOW OWNERS SEE RENTERS

Who Lives Where

Southeast Baltimore households are almost evenly split between owners and renters: 44 percent rented in 1990. Renters and owners tend to live in different areas, with renters concentrated on the western side of Southeast, in lower-income neighborhoods closer to downtown. Sixty percent of renters lived in eleven of twenty-six Southeast Census tracts. In the ten Census tracts with the highest proportions of renters, where 36 percent of Southeasterners (including most public housing tenants) lived, 67 per-cent of occupied units had renters. In contrast, in the nine tracts with the lowest proportions of renters, where 37 percent of the population lived, only 27 percent of units had renters.

The proportion of renting households in Southeast rose from 42 percent during the 1980s. However, renting increased more in some areas than others and even declined in places. For example, two waterfront tracts had by far the sharpest increase in renting. Almost all renters (93%) were white. In the tract including the Gold Coast, renting grew 141 percent, but median household income was $32,857, much greater than the City median of $24,045. In the tract including Fell's Point, where renting grew 78 percent, median income was only $23,194. Both contrasted with the O'Donnell Heights public housing project tract, where 66 percent of renters were white but the median was only $9,243 and renting fell 4 percent.

Black renters generally were poor. For example, the five tracts with the largest concentrations of black renters had median household incomes between $10,809 and $18,764. By and large, the percentages of renting households in these tracts stayed the same between 1980 and 1990, increasing between 2 percent and 4 percent in three tracts, declining by 3 percent in another, and declining by 13 percent in another.

Homeownership dropped 2 percent, but trends varied. The greatest percentage decline was in a tract along the east end of the waterfront, where homeownership decreased 20 percent and renting increased 29 percent. Some of this change reflected Gold Coast development, and median income was $25,560. Seven other tracts had ownership drops of between 10 percent and 14 percent, but three also had rental declines as part of overall population loss.

Three of these tracts had significant conversions from owning to renting, most notably one north of Patterson Park where owner-occupied units declined by 14 percent while renter-occupied units increased by 23 percent (though still only to 29%). Median income was $23,304. This tract was one of six straddling the racial boundary at the northern edge of Southeast Baltimore, and the area had the marks of a neighborhood in transition. In each tract, more than 6.5 percent of housing units were sold in 1990, almost twice the Baltimore City rate of 3.5 percent. Five tracts had net increases in renters. Five had median household incomes below the City median. In every tract, more than 10 percent of units had housing code violations (compared to 9% for Baltimore), and in one 25.5 percent had violations. Three tracts had vacancy rates higher than the City average of 9 percent; in one, one unit in seven was vacant. One tract had an abandonment rate more than twice the City average of 2 percent; the rate in another was more than three times as high.

Racially, Southeast Baltimore, like much of the rest of the City, is segregated. Southeast was 72 percent white in 1990, while Baltimore City was 59 percent black. Ninety percent of Southeast whites lived in nineteen Census tracts where they comprised 90 percent of the population, while 80 percent of blacks lived in seven tracts where they made up 71 percent of the population.

The relationship between race and renting is complex. Blacks were more than twice as likely as whites to rent (77% versus 35%), but, because of the overall Southeast racial makeup, 64 percent of renters were white. Thus there is good reason to think of blacks as renters but little to equate renters and blacks. Renters, as all residents, live racially separated. In six of the eleven tracts where renters were concentrated, the renters were predominantly white, and in five they were predominantly black. In four of the eleven tracts more than 75 percent of renting households were white, and in three more than 85 percent were black.

Hence Southeast owners are likely to have owners for neighbors, and when their neighbors are renters, they are likely to be white. Thus in the nine tracts with the lowest proportions of renters, the population was 95 percent white, and only one percent of occupied units had black renters; in the ten tracts with the highest proportions of renters, the population was 51 percent white, and 36 percent of occupied units had black renters.

Concerns about Renters

Still, Patterson Park neighborhoods are changing conspicuously, and even owners whose neighbors are almost all white homeowners worry about the future. Anxiety focuses on renters, with black renters often symbolizing the worst possibilities. One concern stems from the belief renters are not community-minded. Renters are seen as having little financial or emotional stake in their housing or neighborhood. They do not control their unit, and, if they have low incomes, they have little money to put into maintenance. Moreover, few low-income residents have the time and ability to take part in community affairs. These views have some factual basis, but they are typical homeowner stereotypes of renters (Goetz and Sidney 1994; Perin 1977).

In addition, some renters are annoyingly or dangerously antisocial. Not only do they seem less likely to care about their housing, but some are careless, some destroy property, and some are involved in drugs or crime. A long-time resident says vandalism drove him from his old neighborhood, and he explains the problem in terms of renters' lacking stakes in the community:

> Homeownership is the key. I don't care what color people are. There were bottles and trash. People had the decency not to break the bottles, but they didn't have the decency not to leave them. You could sweep today, but it will be there tomorrow. . . . You could hear more sirens. But you often couldn't hear them because of all the noise from people getting out of bars at two in the morning.

A third concern about renters focuses on how they will destroy "property values," a phrase that ambiguously joins economic investment in housing and emotional investment in the good-hearted culture. For example, the community leader near the County line proudly describes his community. It is old. His family used to own a lot of land there. It has many long-time residents. It has single-family detached homes. The homes are close to work. He uses typical terms to characterize its virtues: it is a "hands-on kind of neighborhood," with "down-to-earth people," "average citizens."

But he has begun to worry about renters and "property values":

> We have an open plot of woods back here that a developer's been trying to build some homes on for about the last four, five years. Well, at some of the meetings we had people, some of them said they didn't want Section 8 housing in there because they didn't want low-income housing. It's going to affect their property values. . . .
>
> I'd say, basically, the community, they don't want any change that's going to really disrupt their lives, or what they perceive as something going to disrupt their lives. We fought to try to keep a tax-exempt group from setting up a mental health clinic down here . . . and we went to Zoning to fight them. Well, that was an outgrowth of the fear in the neighborhood that they were going to bring in mentally retarded patients right out of Spring Grove, Crownsville, Springfield [state hospitals], whatever, and try to mainstream into the society through our neighborhoods. And, having worked with the Southeast Police Community Relations Council and some of the officers there, I know they don't have the manpower to take and provide guards and everything down there, adequately provide the security that would have been needed. . . .
>
> We have three schools within half a mile of there . . . and neighbors are all around that area, and . . . our neighborhood was concerned this would affect our property values. They would have these people wandering the streets at all hours, which the organization did not adequately safeguard, that we perceived that would be a problem.

In lumping renters with the mentally ill, he draws on the original Greek view of "idiots": they are outside civil society and a threat to it.

QUESTIONS OF RACE

Earlier he equated renters with blacks before talking about cascading dangers to community values. Another activist, reacting to such blanket racial statements, describes many Southeasterners as distinctly un-good-hearted:

> This part of East Baltimore is a fairly typical white, blue-collar neighborhood. Fairly overt, blatant racism is part of the culture, reinforced through the family and other relationships.

There is a long history of racial animosity in Southeast Baltimore. Some of its earliest expressions grew out of job competition between European immigrants and blacks, often encouraged by employers who wanted to promote labor disarray, defeat unions, and keep wages down (Olson 1980).

When whites talk about a neighborhood "turning black," whatever else they mean, they are making claims about historical and moral priority. Whites, they say, came first and established a community with certain values; blacks challenge its boundaries and norms of behavior. A house, they go on, is not an isolated physical structure, but a door into a community, and a community's integrity depends on managing entry. In this framework, blacks' arrival is like the earlier movement of Italians into a German area. In both cases, the outcome depends on how the first group interprets the newcomers' differences and evaluates the possibilities of assimilation.

Racial Boundaries

A few whites assert race is irrelevant to Southeast community life. An association president says,

> Southeast has become one big melting pot, and we just more or less work together and live together as if it's happening, and we aren't even consciously aware of the racial thing. I mean, on an individual basis some people may feel this or that, but as a whole community, we don't really see a racial effect.

Most Southeasterners, however, acknowledge widespread racial tensions.

Many residents and neighbors of Butcher's Hill, an area of gentrification, believe middle-class whites there are exceptionally tolerant. "Those people up there," a man living nearby states, "they have a different way of thinking than the regular people around here." A Butcher's Hill resident proudly reports,

> In our neighborhood, we handle racial tensions pretty well. I like the thing that our neighborhood is more open and not so judgmental as other neighborhoods, who have a lot of problems with racial issues.

"But then," she acknowledges,

> we don't have a big junior high school in our neighborhood either, which is the main problem in Baltimore-Linwood, because most of the students are black, and they come from another neighborhood, or they come from all over. The people who live there don't want to send their kids to that school because there have been a lot of problems there.

Putting black students in a Southeast middle school, whatever else it does, violates residential segregation. A former New Yorker contrasts Baltimore with that city:

This is a very Southern town. It still has a lot of Southern roots; it is still very segregated. Not that New York isn't in the same sense that . . . South Bronx was mostly Puerto Rican, and Harlem mostly black. But . . . it's not as linear as it is here. Except for the area of Washington Hill, you can actually draw lines on streets and say, white people live on this side of the street, and black people live on that side of the street.

A white woman born in Southeast begins to draw the map by explaining, "Baltimore Street is the color line, with white south and black north." A man conducts a mental tour of the area:

You go up to a certain area, going north, and it's just like the whites almost stopped. You might find a stray white or a stray black between, I think, Baltimore Street is. . . . On the west side of the park it's, I think, pretty much Baltimore Street, and going west it's Fayette or something like . . . There is generally a street like Fayette, I think Fairmount in some areas, and it's . . . you just don't go in those neighborhoods. Very rarely you walk through those neighborhoods if you are of the wrong persuasion.

Blacks describe the maps similarly, including such details as where they have lived and where it is risky to live. A community worker notes many whites see Southeast ending at the racial boundaries:

They differentiate [Southeast] from East Baltimore, which is predominantly black, so there is a real clear definition. You know Southeast Baltimore stops, stops and starts, primarily where the racial lines happen to be drawn, you know, on the streets that separate the black communities from the whites.

Many people do not readily leave the familiarity, security, and presumed safety of their turf, defined partly by race. Community associations that want both black and white members consider this when choosing meeting sites. A member of a predominantly white organization explains:

We meet at the White House up there in the park once a month. . . . There is a black church on the corner between Fayette and Montford, and they offered their church as a meeting place, and we alternate the two, because the community meetings are not very well integrated, and the black people do not feel comfortable going out to the park. And so we decided that way we can integrate things better by alternating the meeting sites. It's a much more integrated crowd when you go a little further, really. And people don't mind working together, and they are very sort of antsy about coming to meetings in each others' neighborhoods. That church is at the very edge of what a lot of people consider the black and white line, fence. So that worked out really well.

In the Old South, whites could live near blacks because caste distinctions reassured whites they were separate from and better than blacks.

In the North where there were norms of relative equality, many whites wanted residential segregation to maintain a status boundary. In contemporary Baltimore, a Southern city in the post-civil rights era, geographic boundaries have especial importance for some whites in establishing their physical and social separateness from blacks. Hence territorial boundaries can be embedded in tension.

A liberal white explains:

> If I was a black man, I wouldn't want to walk down here after the dark . . . like I wouldn't want to walk up there, north of Baltimore Street, for the most part, in the black neighborhoods after dark.

He cites a well-known incident that dramatizes the stresses. It involves a violation of geographic and social boundaries:

> A couple of years ago, a guy got run down because he was walking down the street with a . . . He was a black man walking down the street with a white woman, and they got mad at him. They started chasing him, and he ran out to the middle of Eastern Avenue [in white territory], and the car accidentally hit him.

"He worked at Haussner's [a famous restaurant in a white neighborhood]," someone else explains;

> this black man was walking with a white woman and was harassed and chased into the street. A truck ran over his head. Skinhead literature began appearing on cars in Baltimore-Linwood. A bar had a sign in the window which said, "Death to all niggers." There was a Nazi bookstore on Eastern Avenue that was firebombed.

She notes the incident led SECO to organize Rejoicing In Community Harmony (RICH), a coalition to improve race relations, but she immediately goes on. She mentions a minister who gave a Halloween party for a group of children that included blacks: "People put excrement on the window. Someone drove by and threw a rock that hit a girl."

Making Sense of Racial Differences

The meanings of race in daily life are social constructions. Skin color may be used to group people not only by appearance, but also by ways of acting and presumed virtue. It symbolizes explanations for apparent differences in behavior. Differences may be seen as great or small, unbridgeable or changeable. People considered different can be judged as a group or individually. Perceived differences may be interpreted as intrinsic characteristics, reactions to conditions, or choices.

Blacks and whites talk about race and housing differently. Blacks see race as a central, but unfair, influence on housing decisions and emphasize the freedom to choose where to live. Whites are more likely to talk about people's behavior, either as part of or apart from their race, and whether it makes them desirable neighbors.

Blacks recount stories of realtors' steering them to traditionally black neighborhoods when they wanted to buy homes. For example, a man complains,

> When I bought my house, they never told me about Butcher's Hill; they never told me about Baltimore-Linwood. They were steering blacks this side [north] of Monument Street.

They describe their parents' or their own pioneering as the first blacks on white blocks. Some describe blockbusting or landlords' exploiting prejudice and fear. Another man says bad landlords

> were deliberately putting bad people in the blocks. Then elderly white homeowners next door moved. The white investors put in negative black tenants scaring out elderly whites and some blacks. They try to drain as much money out of the property as they can get. Then they let it sit.[3]

Some whites acknowledge prejudice, most often in others. A service worker who has practiced in Southeast for years reports,

> Except in a few neighborhoods which are being regentrified, there is not much interest in integration. Some of the older people in this community, they grew up prejudiced. It's part of their life experience, and they have absolutely no interest in changing.

A few recognize how prejudice affects them, as does this relative newcomer to Southeast Baltimore:

> One of the black marks on this community is the prejudice. I don't know if it is a Baltimore thing. It exists. It is like the first line of defense or blame. There is prejudice. There is even some hatred. It is contagious. I've caught myself. When my brother's car was broken into, I assumed it was a black kid from the projects. And I didn't know that.

Yet few whites speak of blanket prejudice against blacks. For example, an activist rebuts a complaint of racism against her neighbors by focusing on individual blacks' behavior:

> In our [community association] meeting a few years ago, someone called the police because they said they were not admitted to our meeting, and they said that was because of race. But this woman at the same time had a problem child in the school over here at the middle school. So we don't know what the reason was for this, because at the same time we had Dr. Smith from the Department of Recreation, and he was our guest speaker, and he was a black person, very nice. It's a shame that he

died of a heart attack about two years later. Very nice person, and we had a crowd; we had a full house that night. So I think it depends on how people behave as how they are perceived.

It is unclear how the black woman was treated at the meeting, but the speaker justifies maybe having excluded her by distinguishing good and bad black behavior. The acceptable black had a Ph.D., whereas the unacceptable one "had a problem child."

The Problem of Black Renters

Those who admit worrying about blacks justify their fears by focusing on black renters, who differ in not only race, but class and tenure. A community leader, mixing fact and fantasy, conjures a dire image of black neighbors:

> They had the same thing when some of the blacks started moving into O'Donnell Heights, and people were afraid of crime and stuff like that, and to a certain degree it has happened, with all the drugs and things, and the Jamaicans moving in, they had, I think it was last year, a couple of murders up there, where they killed a couple of women and children in the middle of the night. . . . That's what I think the most . . . we would fear down in our neighborhood if it changes.

Others complain, more specifically, about black renters who fail to maintain their housing or damage it, are noisy, or commit other antisocial acts.

Charges against black renters are not unfounded, but no one has carefully studied renter problems. As a result, people are left to speculate from familiar incidents. While some are afraid of black renters, others are concerned for them, and still others carefully distinguish blacks and renters. Analyses fall into three categories. Two are structural, emphasizing external influences on behavior. One of these equates renters with blacks and dwells on race. The other groups all low-income renters and emphasizes their class. A third considers individual influences on homeowners' or renters' behavior foremost, instead of or on top of race and class.

Racial Explanations. Some whites, many of them working-class with limited formal education, interpret housing issues racially and see virtually all problematic renters as black. They believe something about the conditions of being black, no matter how sympathetically one might view blacks, makes blacks most likely in the foreseeable future to be poor, to have to rent, and to engage in behavior inconsistent with good-hearted culture. Many assume differences between white homeowners and black renters reflect immutable differences in conditions and character.

Although these whites explain their views in terms of their experiences, they often also draw a moral split between good whites and bad blacks that simplifies their world and assures them of status (see Jordan 1968). Even if a middle-class black family satisfied all stated expectations of neighbors, these whites would feel diminished being part of a community that included blacks. Buffeted by changes that erode their importance, they can find satisfaction in Manichaean explanations that simply blame black renters.

Other whites, more likely middle-class and professional, see the influence of race differently. Discrimination in employment, education, and lending, not biology, they say, has limited blacks' opportunities to learn, earn, and purchase housing. If some black renters are undesirable neighbors, they argue, it is only because they have been forced into circumstances where they have few models of or rewards for civility (see Wilson 1987).

Class Explanations.   Other whites, also mostly middle-class and professional, recognize some black renters create problems but prefer class to racial explanations. They emphasize social opportunities and constraints over biology, culture, or personal character. The middle class can buy and maintain homes, whereas the poor must rent and depend on landlords for upkeep.

These whites point to the poverty of many black and white renters alike, portray them as victims of the economy and landlords, and characterize their actions as reflections of limiting economic circumstances. For example, a long-time community leader states,

> In neighborhoods where there is transition, there is some tension. My hope is, when it is happening, it is because of the income level, the fact that you have low-income renters.

A community worker agrees, indicting absentee landlords:

> I think . . . I could be real wrong . . . most of the prejudice that we classify as racism comes from housing and crime. I don't think it is really innate because your skin is different from mine. Landlords rent horrible buildings to renters. They don't demand they be kept clean. And sanitary conditions are not kept up.

Another activist explains that homeowners' anger at black tenants who behave differently reflects class differences unrelated to race:

> I don't think race is a factor. It's the nobody-listens thing. When you are a working person, and you get up at 6 A.M., and somebody keeps you up till 3 A.M., that is a real problem. That isn't racism. Although there are components that are. And people are willing to move more quickly. And you see a lot of middle-class blacks leaving these neighborhoods. That makes it a class thing, classism.

These whites shy away from analyses that highlight race, perhaps to avoid discomfort at comparisons, possibly to avoid discouragement about change. Still, they sometimes take the economic point of view in tacit argument against racial interpretation. For example, the first activist quoted above expresses the "hope" that differences are a matter of class. The second hesitates, acknowledges she "could be real wrong," but finally asserts that antipathy toward black renters responds to how they are forced to live because they are poor, not their race. The third, after citing the exodus of middle-class blacks, seems to conclude with relief the problem is "a class thing, classism," not race.

Individual Explanations. The story contrasting the black Ph.D. and the black woman with "a problem child" attests that not all blacks are the same, that individuals have control over their lives. Here is another explanation for renter behavior.

For example, a community worker poses a conundrum and offers an hypothesis. Thousands of white wage-earners, he observes, worked side by side in the factories, but only some bought homes. Why? Perhaps the families that scrimped, saved, and purchased were better organized than those that continued to rent. And some of the latter, less competent families may, indeed, take poor care of their residences and engage in antisocial activity. Moreover, what is true of whites must also be true of blacks. Many who take this view do not deny the harm of racism or the limits of class but offer an explanation for variations among residents of seemingly similar circumstances.

Implications for Intervention. These perspectives all value homeownership but take different attitudes toward low-income and black renters. Quasi-biological racial and individual interpretations are conservative, assuming social programs can do little to improve conditions for those whose genetics or habits limit their ability to take advantage of opportunities. Thus improving neighborhoods by increasing homeownership would mean putting better persons in current residents' places. Those who take the racial view would replace black renters (and maybe also owners) with white owners.

Those who emphasize individual character might find it easiest to recruit households with the ability to buy homes. Alternatively, they might try to teach dysfunctional renters the habits they need to become homeowners and good-hearted community members.

People who take a class view are most optimistic. As a framework, economics has an advantage over race: though class structures are rigid, they seem to offer greater possibility for movement than castelike racial relations. Creating new economic opportunities, these people assume, will lead individuals to change to exploit them. As a guide to intervention, the economic view has tactical strengths: advocating universalistic policies to benefit all low-income renters would avoid problems of focusing on blacks (Wilson 1980, 1987).

Many who think of housing this way hold the ideal of a multiracial community of middle-class homeowners. This project involves expanding opportunities simultaneously for low-income renters, so they can purchase homes, and for working-class whites, so they can develop middle-class security and tolerance and accept neighbors different from themselves.

In this view, racially prejudiced working-class whites are also victims. Economic stresses and parochialism lead them to scapegoat blacks, as a community leader suggests:

> Because of the pressures that are happening on this blue-collar neighborhood and low socioeconomic groups, people are seeing a lot of these racial conflicts, because the pie is just not big enough, and everybody is trying to get their piece of pie. I think a lot of white people see and feel that they are not getting some of the things the minorities are, because of the law they can get, in the sense of equal opportunity and things like that. . . . But they have the same problems as the minority. . . .
>
> I think also because this area is still very blue-collar, and many of the people don't have good educational backgrounds, that they haven't been exposed or taught what racial issues are and how to behave with each other, we are still relying on the things that our parents did and the attitudes of our parents, because you never left your neighborhood. I think when people leave their neighborhoods and go to college or work someplace else, if they move back into the neighborhood, they bring back those influences. But . . . if you ask a lot of people who were born here [in Southeast], they've never been to West Baltimore. There are people who live in Highlandtown who have never been to the Inner Harbor [about a mile away].

These activists envision improving the lot of blue-collar families, not just enabling renters to buy, but giving families economic security and getting their children the education that brings sophistication, so that middle-class white and black homeowners can live in harmony. A woman describes the ideal:

> I think people who live in racially mixed neighborhoods know it's no big deal. . . . Successful racial mixing of neighborhoods depends on whether the people are homeowners or renters. People who are homeowners tend to take better care of their property and tend to have more at stake in the neighborhood. . . . If we get black and white homeowners working together, then that will help to eliminate racial problems. It's the homeowners idea, not the racial idea, that makes so much difference.

HOMEOWNERSHIP AND COMMUNITY MEMBERSHIP

Southeasterners value homeownership for its tangible benefits, such as controlling property, and, if necessary, making money on an investment. At the same time, they value its symbolic returns: status, legitimacy, and community membership. We look more closely at how concerns about community membership shape thinking about homeownership.

Faith and Modernity

Good-hearted homeownership has dual meaning as a community investment. Homeownership is a financial commitment to a collectivity, analogous to affiliation with the organized Jewish community. Good-heartedness is a moral commitment, not simply an agreement to abide by a shared code of decency, but an act of faith in transcendent principles of community life. It is analogous to Jewish religious belief.

Good-hearted homeownership combines the faith of good-heartedness, justifying community, with the economic success represented by homeownership, providing the means for community life. For immigrants, good-heartedness asserted traditional values, while buying a home established a stake in the new world. Yet these two elements have not held together. Good-heartedness presumes communal responsibility, but homeownership is the realm of autonomy.

Contrary to the assumption that homeowners are inherently good-hearted, anyone can buy a house, including the house next door. Some consider a house just an investment, another means to making money. They—or their tenants—are not necessarily good neighbors, it is harder to be good-hearted, and the family home turns out to provide an unreliable stake in the modern world.

Many defend shaken faith in good-heartedness by insisting more fervently on the virtue of homeownership, as does the activist who contemns renters as idiots.

Renters, the Unaffiliated, and Community Membership

That analogy evokes characterizations of the unaffiliated in the Jewish community. Renters and the unaffiliated are both diverse, but in each community one group, homeowners or the affiliated, differentiate the population into two homogeneous groups and designate the other part disloyal and undesirable.

The division, turning on a tangible sign of investment in the community, imperfectly follows class lines, implying ability to invest financially is related to ability or willingness to invest emotionally. There is something to this view, but there are many exceptions: unaffiliated Jews who identify with the community, and Jews whose affiliation means no more than writing a check; renters who care for the Southeast community, and owners, including absentee landlords, who do not.

Moreover, the unaffiliated and renters face obstacles to community participation, and some feel excluded. Jews with limited incomes may be unable to afford synagogue membership and may be ashamed to ask for lower fees. Most can afford some contribution to The Associated, but few can make gifts that bring influence. Some feel put off by the federation's emphasis on money (Cohen 1993; Relationships Report 1988:6–7).

Southeast renters, especially the poor, face various difficulties participating in community associations. Single parents have trouble attending meetings. Adults with little formal education often feel uneasy at public gatherings. They may be embarrassed about their language or lack of sophistication. Parliamentary procedures may confuse them. Those who talk glibly may intimidate them. Further, some Southeast neighborhood organizations are homeowner associations that do not let renters join or attend.

Homeowners have psychological incentives to ignore such facts. While geographic Southeast is a troubled territory, drawing moral lines between owners and renters helps bound a cultural community of those who are loyal. Recognizing renters who care about the community would locate the virtue of good-heartedness among more residents, potentially increasing the community's total value. But homeownership would no longer be a sure sign of grace, and owners could not automatically claim goodness. It is safer to assert a link between good-heartedness and homeownership and to paint renters as vicious. Tying tenure to race helps literally to draw black-and-white lines between renters and owners. Racial anxiety adds to concerns about renter disloyalty, and black renters come to epitomize those dangers.

Thus a moral distinction between owners and renters offers an unambiguous definition of good community membership. Thinking this way makes it possible to idealize homeowners as good-hearted, see Southeast Baltimore as virtuous, and find justifications and directions for continuing the community. These cultural and psychological meanings of homeownership reinforced economic and social interests in homeownership in shaping Southeast planning, as we see in the following chapter.

CHAPTER 12

Homeownership and Community Preservation

Homeownership is the American Dream. It is a sign of success and offers the best possibility for shelter control available in America.[1] Hence many renters want to own. Southeasterners who promote homeownership both desire good neighbors and wish success on renters around them. Yet a preference for homeownership leads to practical dilemmas.

HOUSING DILEMMAS

Nearly half of Southeast households do not own homes. Even among whites, one-third are renters. Moreover, renters vary considerably, from well-to-do whites on the Gold Coast through moderate-income whites and blacks to the very poor of all groups, many of them public housing tenants. Although renting has increased slightly overall, the meaning of the increase varies, even where homeownership has also declined. In some places this conversion means black renters are moving into homes whites once owned and occupied, whereas elsewhere well-off whites are renting apartments that replaced homes owned by modest white families. In a few areas decline in homeownership reflects both changes in tenure and population loss.

The low cost of Southeast housing facilitates homeownership. The average 1990 sale price for a single-family structure was below $50,000 in nineteen tracts, below $40,000 in eleven tracts, and below $30,000 in three tracts. Many Southeast renters could afford mortgage payments, but they would need extraordinary assistance to make a downpayment and pay closing costs, overcome an unattractive credit history, and get a lender's attention. Moreover, 57 percent of renter households had annual incomes below $20,000.[2] Many Southeasterners are unlikely to own homes in the near future.

Those planning for housing faced a choice. They could treat Southeast as a social community and try to improve the quality of current residents' housing, with quality defined by residents' preferences. Alternatively, they could take Southeast as a territory and aim to improve the quality of occu-

167

pants for existing housing, with quality defined extraneously.

The first approach would maximize residents' opportunities to move up. Renters in run-down housing could get units fixed up or move to better places. Those who rented expensively could find cheaper, at least comparable, alternatives. Renters who wanted to own could buy. Owners interested in improving their homes could do so. Owners who wanted better or larger housing could find something suitable.

Whereas that approach emphasizes individual choice, the other would begin with a norm for collective life and consider whose choices were compatible. Although the specific nature of this approach would depend on the definition of "quality" residents, for those planning it meant getting better neighbors. They might be more likely to bolster property values, maintain public space, provide a sense of security, or offer sociability. These ends could be achieved by "upgrading" present residents. If their preferences matched planners' values, the two approaches merged. However, if residents' wishes or means did not fit planners' norms, the alternative would be to recruit outsiders to displace undesirable current residents.

Cultural norms encouraged a homeownership policy, which would discount and try to replace poor renters. Moreover, such a policy would discriminate racially. Southeast is like the rest of the United States: blacks earn less than whites, at any income are less likely to own homes, are less likely to move from renting to owning, and are more likely to move from owning to renting (Amin and Mariam 1987; Morrow-Jones 1993).

For planning participants the policy choice was not abstract. Some, including those who spoke sympathetically about renters, insisted on serving low-income families. Yet housing policies would concretely affect who would be their neighbors. Renters might be less likely good neighbors than owners. It did not matter that one's social analysis exonerated renters from responsibility for rat infestation, if the renters and rats lived next door. Viewing antisocial behavior as an unfortunate product of poverty did not make drugs, crime, or noise more tolerable.

Furthermore, even if some activists could accept the mixed lot of renters as potential neighbors, much of the Southeast population was more conservative and anxious about renters, particularly blacks. Politically, a planning council that encouraged renting as a low-income housing policy risked alienating working-class constituents.

PLANNING FOR HOUSING

At the first cluster workshop, a Coordinating Committee member announced themes of Southeast community planning: "Preserve what we love in our home. Build on it. Get rid of what we don't like." The community was a home, and people would be evaluated as family members.

During the eighteen months of planning that followed, discussion of housing traced two paths. Tacitly, and quickly, it moved away from housing for low-income residents. Overtly, it moved steadily toward promoting homeownership.

Avoiding Housing for the Poor

A few at the first workshop argued for low-income or rental housing. As would be typical of the planning process, this minority included middle-class people who had moved to Southeast, most prominently members of the Coordinating Committee, and former public housing tenants. However, others had little interest in the poor, and even most of the advocates, themselves homeowners, preferred owning to renting.

For example, a former public housing resident, asserting the importance of subsidized housing, called for more "public housing, low rise." Another said, instead, they should "aim at owner-occupied or owner-rented" housing. She explained: "No absentee landlord rental housing. . . . Owner-occupied rental housing." Later, a woman suggested "in-law development in some rowhouses in neighborhoods." Another woman encouraged developers to build "senior citizen housing."

The latter rentals were acceptable because tenants were tied to the community. In-laws were family members. Tenants of owner-occupied buildings might be relatives; at the least, they lived under the landlord's eye. Senior citizens would likely be long-term residents who could no longer manage homes; at any rate, they would be quiet.

Still, most of what people said about housing introduced themes often repeated. A Coordinating Committee member argued for "increas[ing] homeownership for all incomes." A long-time black resident elaborated, "Housing and jobs." A neighborhood association officer articulated common assumptions in advocating "ownership of property, which leads to pride, which spills over in communities." A staff member affirmed the discussion by reiterating "Homeownership."

At the second cluster workshop, participants similarly endorsed homeownership while articulating concerns about renters. A Coordinating Committee member presented data showing a high proportion of units bought by investors. But he spoke in defense of renters. Renters are not bad people, he said; he had been a renter. Many renters go on to buy.

All the same, a long-time resident commented, "There are bad people coming in. Investors don't screen their tenants. They bring in crime and drugs." A black homeowner allowed that "Section 8 housing is okay, but" too much on a block is a problem. People come from public housing, their kids fight our kids, they have bad sanitation habits. There are slum landlords. Landlords move bad families to other properties they own, and then people move from those other neighborhoods.

Landlords who like Section 8 income and live elsewhere may not know or care about tenants' antisocial behavior.

The man who just spoke said an important neighborhood issue was to "encourage [Johns] Hopkins [Medical Institutions] people to become homeowners in the area." Another now mentioned "problems with the behavior of HUD [U.S. Department of Housing and Urban Development] housing tenants—irresponsibleness to the neighborhood," and the first rejoined, "Limit the number of properties Neighborhood Rental Services can have in a neighborhood." The second came back: "Change HUD regulations regarding acceptable tenant behavior and behavior leading to eviction." And the first returned, "Weed and feed-type program: homeownership."

A minister interrupted: "Include renters." But a man followed immediately with complaints about "a problem with uncooperative absentee landlords who are nasty to talk to." A neighborhood leader insisted on finding a way to "make landlords responsible for tenant behavior." Several others went on to argue for homeownership.

Race and Renting. When people discussed renting, they distinguished "good," usually old, renters from "bad," usually new, ones. Older renters had reasonable, if modest, incomes and shared good-hearted commitments to the community, whereas newer renters earned little and sporadically and regarded the area as just a niche in the housing market. Absentee landlords, outside investors, and public housing administrators who admitted these new residents might be the real culprits, but renting seemed too problematic to warrant serious effort.

The difficulties of influencing a community's rental housing market were daunting enough. Keeping and getting renters, probably low-income families, who would be good neighbors, while pushing and keeping out those who would cause trouble called for exceptional agreement, wisdom, and power. What deterred planning participants from considering even incremental interventions was rental housing's ties to race.

The preparatory meeting for the first cluster workshop highlighted the dangers. Cluster A is socially, economically, and racially diverse. Almost at the meeting's start, Angelo Buono, a white businessman, sitting next to the only black in the room, launched into the first of several diatribes. Focusing on public housing abutting his neighborhood, he sounded a tocsin:

There is a problem here, in the neighborhood, in the city, in the whole country. We are getting away from community involvement. We are moving toward doomsday. But one neighborhood can't protect itself. We need the whole city. But first we have to stop—and I mean *stop*—all crime. And we have to force our officials to get off their butts and do something. . . . The bad situation, the bad economy is like a blessing in disguise. It might unite all communities.

Getting to the point:

We must have no more public housing in Southeast Baltimore. No people on public assistance. We are burdened with our own problems, without having these people thrown in. And these people are irresponsible.

The meeting's purpose was to set the workshop agenda, not debate issues, and the chair ruled Buono out of order. But he resumed:

There will be developers who will want to come in here and develop certain blocks. It is important that they not come in here and build refugee camps.

A man reproached him, saying the poor deserved good housing:

You might be able to sleep in your house and feel safer. I am not a rich person. But if we don't have affordable housing like that gentleman wants, they have to be somewhere. There has to be a place for poor people.

Buono answered, "I am for affordable housing." But that was not all. He outlined his vision for a planning process to include people he spoke for:

If we are going to attract responsible people, we should have a discussion. And we should have a constitution up front. So that if you have a master plan, you say, Number One, Crime.

Again someone interrupted to say the meeting's purpose was not to debate issues, but he continued:

I don't want to isolate myself from poor people, people on public assistance. But I do believe in the right to separate myself. Zoning. And then they put public housing right in my own back yard. These are things I am interested in. If the workshop will consider them, I am interested in it.

Soon after, the meeting adjourned.

Buono attended the cluster workshop. Perhaps chastened by his earlier experience, he did not say much, but he made his position clear. During a slide presentation on demographics, he asked, "How many residents are property owners? Public housing has destroyed neighborhoods of thirty years ago." During an exercise to advise hypothetical future developers, Buono enunciated, "No public housing, no subsidized housing, no low-rent housing."

It is unclear whether many at either meeting knew Buono. In some circles he had a reputation as a man who, among other things, wrote angry letters to newspapers and businesses about whatever bothered him. He came to these meetings because the Coordinating Committee had asked neighborhood leaders to invite community members, and someone had brought him. He had an incendiary way of talking, insistent on being heard, not obviously interested in listening. He seemed exasperated his world was out of control.

When he called public housing projects "refugee camps," a staff member scribbled "racist" on a yellow pad and passed it to another staff member. Whether the characterization was accurate or not, he spoke for many in Southeast. If planning were to be inclusive, it would have to make room for these positions. Yet at the cluster workshop, where a third of participants were black, people tacitly agreed to ignore what he said. Later, word went out he was unwelcome, and he did not return.

Regardless of his manner, he raised central policy issues: What would the plan say about housing the poor? What would it say about balancing homeownership and renting? In the end, neither issue was addressed. One explanation is the cultural primacy of homeownership. More than that, however, the fear and anger Buono's tone represented showed how difficult it would be to discuss these issues. Rentals and low-income housing meant housing for blacks. They were racial issues, and they could not be addressed in isolation from Southeast racial tensions.

No one believed the inchoate planning process could contain and resolve racial conflicts. Participants shared the premise they would reach common understandings by avoiding divisive issues. Hence, perhaps blacks more than whites, they put aside intense feelings that could set people against one another.

As with Jewish education at The Associated, a policy issue about which people reasonably disagreed was entangled in strong emotions about who could be considered a good community member, and participants preferred apparent agreement to dangerous discussion. Emphasis on unity not only excluded certain substantive issues, but it also excluded people who could not be trusted to avoid raising them divisively.

Promoting Homeownership

Patterson Park Neighborhoods Initiative. In February 1993 a coalition of community associations and nonprofits sent the Department of Housing and Community Development a proposal for Community Development Block Grant funds for the Patterson Park Neighborhoods Initiative (PPNI), a project to stabilize the transitional area in the north. PPNI focused on neighborhoods forming an inverted U over the top of Patterson Park. With about 32,000 people and 13,000 housing units, it included just over 40 percent of both in Southeast. Funding began in July.

The Initiative is part of the story of Southeast planning. Its sponsoring coalition included associations representing a large part of Southeast. Leaders of these groups and involved nonprofits were active in Southeast planning. SECO and SDI were cosponsors and instrumental in winning funding. Because of the project's timing, magnitude, and sophistication, as well as its director's Planning Council involvement, it influenced Southeast planning for housing.

The PPNI proposal declared the virtues of homeownership:

> [H]omeowners take better care of their property than renters, and for that reason alone it is preferable to have a high percentage of homeowners. In addition, homeowners also lend stability to an area because the house is an investment and deciding to sell is not an easily made decision, nor can the house necessarily be sold readily for the desired price. In contrast, a renter can move relatively easily as soon as the lease, if there is one, expires (Patterson Park Neighborhoods Intervention Initiative 1993:19; hereafter PPNII[3]).

The largest part of the PPNI proposal was a "Comprehensive Home Ownership Plan." It declared goals of keeping current residents, owners and renters, attracting new homeowners, and preventing houses from going to absentee owners. It presented detailed strategies for promoting homeownership: marketing the area to potential buyers, offering financial incentives and programs for buyers and existing owners, and engaging in property acquisition, control, development, and management. The budget included capital and revolving funds to support these efforts.

This plan was followed by a brief "Plan to Upgrade Rental Unit and Tenant Quality." It began by affirming there "always will be a place for rentals in our neighborhoods" but then distinguished good and bad renters:

> Traditionally, rental units had been owned by area residents and many were rented on a long term basis to people who had a commitment to the area. Recently, that image has been replaced by rental units owned by absentee landlords, and rented to people who have no allegiance to the area (PPNII 1993:25).

The plan is worth quoting at length because it presents a clear position in analyzing renter problems and identifying points of community leverage in response:

- A major concern of neighborhoods has been a rapid increase of Section 8 tenants who simply have not been educated in community living and the extent of their personal responsibility for the good of the community. Just as this is true of only a percentage of section 8 tenants, it is also true to some extent of tenants (vs. homeowners) in general. Two avenues are available:

- Tenant counseling, education and training.

- Insistence on compliance with Section 8 regulations on the part of government agencies responsible for implementing them.

Finally, some of our areas contain among the highest number of section 8 tenants in the city. Efforts will be made to restrict any increases in the number of such tenants where effective education, training and control is not possible.

- Institute a program to get landlords committed to the area. After all, they have an investment here. . . . We can help landlords by advertising for renters on behalf of our neighborhoods, that is, we can build a pipeline of quality renters as well as a pipeline of potential homeowners; we may also be able to offer property management for a fee. On the other hand, we can see that housing and sanitation codes are enforced; we can use the nuisance and padlock laws with respect to bad tenants; we can use the receivership law on vacant houses. . . .

- Another major concern is conversion, legal or illegal of single family units to multiple-unit dwellings. Such conversions often increase the population density beyond that which the area can support. It can also make a home unfit for single family homeownership because of the cost of reconversion. . . .

  Legislation has recently been introduced in the Baltimore City Council which prevents conversion to multi-family units for two story residential houses without sufficient lot area. . . .

- Try to increase the population of renters generally regarded as desirable, such as:
  - people who work downtown
  - Hopkins and Bayview transient professionals
  - college students
  - immigrants
  - children of area residents. . . .

- A final rental upgrade strategy is encouraging private neighborhood ownership and management of rental property, i.e. try to return to the basic conditions when rental worked, when properties were in the hands of those who lived here. Private ownership might be individual or cooperative and may take the form of simple encouragement, or referral to appropriate training programs, or actual assistance. Assistance might include referrals for financing, direction in formation of cooperatives, publicity, etc. (PPNII 1993: 25–26).

The PPNI proposal emphasized homeownership for those who could, with a little help, afford to buy. The rental plan focused on controlling the behavior of problematic renters, recruiting more desirable, middle-class tenants, and limiting rental units. It was not a housing plan for those who chose or had to rent, but strategies for getting owners better neighbors.

Housing Task Force. About the time the PPNI proposal came out, following the four cluster workshops, the Planning Council formed a Housing Task Force to develop the plan's recommendations. Some who signed up strongly supported housing for the poor and saw renters as deserving. However, as people began to consider specific proposals, these abstract commitments encountered concrete obstacles. In general, the Council lacked a firm constituency for low-income or rental housing. In particular, the realities of dealing with problematic tenants and absentee public and private landlords were daunting.

In March, the Task Force chair reported to the Council. The group had identified housing problems from comments at cluster workshops and was drawing on the PPNI proposal, which the chair called "a good model for any area in stress." The Task Force would attend to both ownership and renting.

The Coordinating Committee and other core participants met in May to consider how to structure the overall plan. The Housing Task Force chair presented a draft report. The mission statement declared,

> A housing plan should build on existing resources, and promote safe, attractive, well maintained housing for existing residents and newcomers. Therefore there should be housing for both homeowners and renters of varied income levels.

The report supported homeownership most prominently with efforts to "Keep Senior Citizens in their housing as long as possible," "Employer linked housing programs," a campaign to "Market area to new residents and develop programs to make area more marketable," and "Work with banks to provide more sensitive loan program for first time homeowners and rehab loans" (Housing Task Force 1993:1, 2; hereafter Housing).

Although the report was sympathetic to renters and low-income families, proposals were cautious and qualified. It recommended "Programs for *Good* Rentals" (Housing 1993:2; emphasis added), such as neighborhood-based management, efforts to hold managers accountable to the local community, and encouraging neighborhood associations to admit renters as members.

A lengthy recommendation concerned "Low Income Housing." A section on public housing supported tenant involvement in decisions on proposed replacement of high-rise buildings with low-rise and scattered site housing, with the scattered site housing to be controlled by organizations with neighborhood accountability. It encouraged management accountability to residents. Regarding Section 8, it proposed to "Study effects of program and educate to prevent stereotyping" (Housing 1993:2).

The only proposal that might add to the supply of rental housing was a broader recommendation to "Require all new housing developments over 50 units to have 20% for low income" (Housing 1993:1). Otherwise, in terms of expanding housing opportunities for the poor, the recommendation concentrated on making low-income persons, including public housing residents, homeowners, for example, through credit counseling and financial assistance.

Extraordinary financing mechanisms would be needed for many low-income renters to buy homes. The proposals would make rental housing and tenants more acceptable to their neighbors but not increase their number. The report aimed to get homeowners better neighbors, but not increase Southeast housing opportunities for those whose incomes forced them to rent.

Southeast Community Plan. The Southeast Community Plan, released in December, combined general language inclusive of renters, specific proposals for promoting homeownership, and caution regarding rental housing. The mission statement advocated "promot[ing] safe and well maintained housing for all residents." It announced six principles for housing initiatives and projects: "provide housing for both homeowners and renters of varied income levels," "strengthen neighborhoods," "be sensitive to the area's history," "be compatible in terms of scale and density," "prevent real estate speculation," and "create a marketing plan targeted to and coordinated with business and industrial growth" (Plan 1993:25).

The first principle declared an interest in low-income housing and rental housing. However, sensitivity to the area's history and concern to strengthen neighborhoods could mean deferring to working-class white communities that did not want black renters. Preventing real estate speculation is not opposed to providing decent rental housing, but a more positive statement would encourage local nonprofit organizations to purchase and/or manage rental housing. Finally, a marketing plan's emphasis is homebuying. These tensions are evident in specific proposals.

The first priority housing recommendation referred to homeownership: "Develop Employer-Assisted Housing/Live Near Work Initiative."

Targeting large employers such as Johns Hopkins and General Motors, the proposal aimed to publicize the area as an attractive place for workers to live and "to assist employees in purchasing in adjacent neighborhoods" (Plan 1993:26).

The next priority recommendation mentioned both ownership and renting but gave only qualified support to renting. "Start[ing] a Canton/Highlandtown Housing Initiative" aimed to "Stabilize the neighborhoods south and east of Patterson Park by promoting home ownership and quality rental housing." "Three key objectives for such an initiative are: retain current homeowners; attract new homeowners; and promote quality rental housing" (Plan 1993:27). Although no one could quarrel with an insistence on "quality" rental housing, no text required that owner-occupied housing or homeowners have "quality." Implicitly, any homeowner was better than a renter.

A recommendation to "Advocate for Legislation Requiring Affordable Housing Set-aside" was concerned with people of limited means. The recommendation focused on ownership, but an appendix calculated subsidies needed to lower housing costs for families earning $20,000 to $25,000 to rent (Plan 1993:30, 55).

The strongest support for renting came in a recommendation to "Assess and Expand Resources and Capacity of Existing Housing Non-Profits." The discussion noted nonprofits "provide good rental units and management," in addition to "promot[ing] first time home buying and increas[ing] home ownership in Southeast" (Plan 1993:29).

In addition, the plan included recommendations to support other programs. One was to "Support Decreasing the Number of Public Housing High Rises at Lafayette Courts and Flag House" (Plan 1993:47). On the one hand, this supported a class of low-income renters. However, depending on where the Housing Authority relocated tenants, Southeast might end up with fewer public housing residents.

Another recommendation was to "Support Patterson Park Neighborhoods Initiative" (Plan 1993:49).

SOUTHEAST RESIDENTS AND THEIR COMMUNITY

Housing is not just a building, but a door into a community, and Southeast planning participants made housing policy to fit community norms. Although core activists recognized low-income residents' needs, they acknowledged the cultural dominance of good-hearted homeownership. The plan gave rhetorical support to needs of the poor and renters, but specific recommendations would increase homeownership.

Realistically, homeownership offered a chance to stabilize the housing market and community. Moreover, homeowners who took part in planning had social and economic interests in neighbors like themselves. At the same time, the dangers of addressing any issue so deeply implicated in race discouraged people from considering housing for the poor and renters.

The culture of good-hearted homeownership rationalized these interests and fears. Promoting homeownership was a way to strengthen the community by binding it to the past and invoking a heroic image to lead it through unsettling changes.[4] "Community," "property values," and "stability" were not just racial code words. They expressed anxiety and hope about maintaining meaning, value, and connection in a turbulent world people poorly grasped and desperately wished to control. Homeownership was a means to recovering the good community.

COMMUNITY MEMBERSHIP AND COMMUNITY PLANNING

White Southeast liberals, mostly college-educated, largely middle-class, contrast their tolerance for blacks with the anxiety or hostility of many working-class whites. The liberals accept the modern world and, for better or worse, have made terms with it. White ethnics, as admirable as they are, want a world that is fading. These perceptions resemble non-Orthodox Jews' portrayal of the Orthodox, and psychological relations between the two Southeast groups parallel those in the Jewish community.

Many white liberals simultaneously demonize and idealize white ethnics. Some working-class whites speak anxiously or hostilely about blacks, and middle-class observers accurately see them as prejudiced. Yet most Americans are victims of racial fear and prejudice. Liberals are troubled by conflicts between what they believe and say and what they sometimes find themselves feeling or doing. They can rescue a sense of purity by unconsciously denying their own prejudices, splitting them from their tolerant views, and projecting them onto white ethnics. The fact that some white ethnics talk and act against blacks makes the liberals' prejudice unconsciously added onto them seem part of one whole, realistic picture. Thus white ethnics not only appear prejudiced, but seem the only prejudiced white group.

At the same time, even while recognizing white ethnics' shortcomings, many middle-class whites idealize them. Earlier immigrant generations, while trying to survive, lived with intimacy, tradition, ritual, and faith uncommon in modern life. Many middle-class whites, living in a world where work is abstract, institutions are bureaucratic, and organizations are outside local control, want deeper meaning, goodness, and caring. They project these desires onto the few remaining traces of vital ethnicity and magnify them into idealized ethnic communities. Seen this way, white ethnics give the community transcendent value by linking it to Europe, the struggles of immigration, and the American Dream.[5]

For their part, white ethnics join in idealizing their communities (Stein and Hill 1977). They consider their traditions the best way to live, even as they recognize how far everyday conditions have strayed. Reacting anxiously to change, some see middle-class white newcomers as both agents of destruction and saviors of a sort. Often they have vilified them as gentrifiers, outsiders who came in and, by renovating old houses, pushed up assessments and taxes. Long-time residents recite dollar figures to tell how gentrification hurt the little people. These newcomers are not good-hearted. They see Southeast as a housing market, not a community, and they epitomize a world where everything is for sale.

And yet they are homeowners. And, by and large, they are white. Another side of gentrification is that it keeps black renters out. Moreover, as it turns out, some are tireless advocates for the Southeast community. Even if they sometimes talk too glibly and presume to know more than others who have lived in Southeast for generations, they are a link to the modern world. They know how to get public funds and foundation grants. They can deal with the complicated corporate world. They are good people who can bring some money and power to Southeast.

Relations in Southeast Baltimore lack the intensity of those in the Jewish community, largely because Southeast has no single tradition with the authority and vitality of Orthodoxy, but desires and anxieties are similar. Relations between middle-class white liberals and working-class white ethnics shape a bargain. Liberals who are uncomfortable with their prejudice can put it on white ethnics. Working-class whites can see middle-class gentrifiers as agents of destructive societal change. At the same time, middle-class whites accept white ethnics as a community ideal, and white ethnics value middle-class residents for the good they can bring from outside.

Practically, this alliance leads to seeking resources for promoting good-hearted homeownership and avoiding divisive issues. In a parallel, though more convoluted way, non-Orthodox Jews idealize the Orthodox and give money to day schools.

We see in both communities signs of a general phenomenon, where groups divide themselves for purposes of allocating good and bad desires and impulses (see Volkan 1988). What these cases show further, strikingly, is how groups that use one another as symbols of what they fear or hate depend on each other. Psychologically, one group needs another to represent the feelings it does not want to acknowledge in itself. Psychologically or materially, one group wants the rewards of another's engaging in activities the first is unable, afraid, or ashamed to. Politically, particularly in communities that feel under siege, there are good reasons to join forces, but these cases show that the terms of alliance reflect deep-seated wishes and anxieties as much as overt interests.

Communities express these concerns in discussing what a good member should do or be. When planning touches on these matters, community members are likely to consider unity more important than specific substantive outcomes.

PART 4

Managing Resources

CHAPTER 13

Resources in the Jewish Community: The Wealthy and the Nonwealthy

Community organizations need resources to support activities. They may assess dues, solicit funds, or ask for donations of goods or services. Community organizations generally inhabit the world of low finance. Most have few members and are unincorporated. If incorporated, they have officers but maybe no paid staff. In any case, with whatever funds they collect, more likely than not, they live a hand-to-mouth existence.[1]

The Associated and SECO/SDI are incorporated and have boards. They run programs, for which they actively raise funds, and they have significant budgets. They have staffs to maintain the organization, plan and manage programs, and bring in resources. The Southeast Planning Council was formed to create a plan and oversee implementation. It is unincorporated, and SECO has been its fiduciary agent. During planning, SECO contributed staff time, and the Goldseker Foundation paid for additional SECO work and a consultant. The Planning Council lost staff shortly after the plan was finished.

The Associated and the Southeast organizations present contrasting pictures. The Associated raises virtually all funds from a relatively wealthy community. It manages an annual budget of about $30 million and supports many organizations and programs. SECO and SDI can raise little money from community members and rely heavily on outside grants. Their combined annual budget is about $1 million. The Planning Council got $76,000 in grants for planning. It seeks implementation funds without staff help.

The Planning Council and The Associated both engage in community organizing and programmatic activities, but the different available resources affect the balance and character of these activities. The Associated concentrates organizing on those whose participation is likely to be accompanied by significant gifts, and funds support staff to manage programs. In contrast, the Planning Council had to begin by organizing constituencies for its work and continues involving community members not only to maintain authority, but to help get recommendations implemented.

COMMUNITY ORGANIZATION AND FUNDRAISING

Ambiguous usages of "community" point to tensions between community organization and fundraising at The Associated. When leaders use "community" to mean all Baltimore Jews, they designate the federation a community organization and suggest an interest in organizing the 92,000. However, those who restrict "community" to Associated givers emphasize fundraising. Fundraising is community organizing, but when time, money, and effort are abundant but limited, fundraising and broader community organization compete.

The Associated concentrates on fundraising because that has been its historic purpose and because it can do so successfully. However, focusing on a wealthy minority creates two community problems. First, it reinforces the boundary between affiliated and unaffiliated and draws another between wealthy and non-wealthy. At the same time, giving status to the wealthy challenges religious and ethnic definitions of community membership without offering a compelling alternative.

THE GOLDEN RULE

When people refer to "the Golden Rule" in Associated decision making, they are saying several things about the federation. One is that "He who has the gold rules"—the wealthy make decisions. Another is that, in fact, people differentiate community members by wealth.

A third, more subtle message prescribes social norms. An anonymous wit formulated the modern joke on the biblical Golden Rule, which was an exhortation to kindly social relations: do unto others as you would have them do unto you. In the Jewish tradition, Hillel phrased the advice differently: what is hateful to you, do not do to your fellow man. In either version, the original Golden Rule encouraged mutuality and equality. The comic twist turns these premises on their head: people are not equal, and mutuality is unlikely.

Yet the Golden Rule represents fundraising success. The Associated is a voluntary organization. Membership is a matter of choice, as is giving. The federation's most efficient fundraising strategy is to concentrate on the wealthiest families and offer them something for their money. At the same time, it must collect and spend funds in a way that satisfies, or does not offend, others—in terms of where money goes or what money flow implies regarding community membership.

Fundraising distinguishes the wealthy, who provide most resources and use some services, from the nonwealthy, who provide few resources and use many services.[2] Wealth brings power and status, and fundraising calls attention to hierarchies in the latter. Moreover, a hierarchy based on wealth implicitly competes with the Orthodox–non-Orthodox dimension as a principle of community status. Orthodoxy is more democratic, in that it is easier for anyone to observe rituals than to acquire wealth. It is also more legitimate, because being Orthodox (or Conservative, Reconstructionist, or Reform) is a way of being Jewish; indeed, for many it is at the core of being Jewish. Earning or sharing wealth has no such connection.

At the same time, wealth affects the Orthodox and non-Orthodox differently. For the Orthodox and others who consider themselves part of a religiously defined community, wealth and class differences are irrelevant to Jewish identity. Faith, study, and observance matter. In contrast, for the non-Orthodox who think of the community ethnically, there is no set standard for defining the community. A Jewish community is however Jews live. Social divisions, such as class differences, threaten the ethnically defined community by breaking it into smaller groups.

Practically also, Orthodox and non-Orthodox are differently affected by the distribution of wealth. Almost all the most wealthy are not Orthodox, while few Orthodox have great wealth. The Associated offers services to all Jews, regardless of income, and sliding fees ensure the poor can get help. The average income of agency clients varies with the services offered. Jewish Family Services, for example, is particularly likely to serve the poor.[3] Moreover, the Orthodox strongly prefer Jewish services (Tobin 1986:140–43). Hence the Orthodox are especially likely to go to Jewish Family Services, where, for example, they use half the hours of the children's unit, and Baltimore Hebrew University, where they comprise one-third of students (Tobin 1986:53).

Even exclusively Orthodox institutions, such as day schools, depend on aid from The Associated and non-Orthodox donors. Thus while many non-Orthodox have no deep religious identity to hold them together in the face of economic divisions, the Orthodox, who are joined by religious faith, still recognize their dependence on others who do not share the faith.

Hence, while The Associated values the wealthy, if it calls too much attention to their wealth, it risks splitting the community and losing claims to represent a large, unified population. For this reason, few openly speak of the wealthy, much less the nonwealthy.[4] The Associated uses euphemisms, such as "the leadership," which emphasizes the political role of the wealthy, rather than economic assets that put them in the role. An economic euphemism describes the wealthy as people with "resources." Other economic labels, such as "big givers" or, in the words of the plan, "substantial contributors" and "major donors" (Plan 1989:15), emphasize the ways the wealthy turn over their money to others. Less formally, and less respectfully, some refer to the wealthy as "heavy hitters."

Philanthropy is the delicate effort to join the incompatible principles of wealth and community. The domain of wealth is that of aggression, where people strive against one another in the hope of standing out over them. Yet the competition and the resultant inequality contradict both the reality and the idea of a community of equals who care for one another. While financial success brings pride, the less successful, even when they look on admiringly, often also feel shame at their lesser accomplishments and resentment at the power of the more successful. In turn, the successful may feel guilty, as well as proud. Thus philanthropy must reconcile the wealthy with the community in two ways. It must avoid or remove the nonwealthy's shame and resentment. And it must allow the wealthy to put their money into community purposes without guilt.

This operation encourages all to adopt a double consciousness, recognizing but forgetting differences. Those who solicit the wealthy must evoke just enough guilt to encourage a contribution for the less fortunate, but not so much as to turn the wealthy away. The intermediaries must persuade everyone the wealthy are acting on good intentions: they are not motivated by guilt, and they are not really that much richer than anyone else.

This latter transaction is subtle, for, on the one hand, it is someone's wealth that makes the philanthropic effort appropriate, but, on the other, if the wealth seems too great, it arouses the shame, resentment, and guilt that doom giving. Most people show gratitude at getting a gift and so allow donors to feel appreciated, but a mediator must be vigilant against slips. It is the touchiness of this role that makes Associated staff uneasy speaking of "the Golden Rule."

RELATIONS BETWEEN THE WEALTHY AND NONWEALTHY

Converting Wealth into Righteousness

The Hebrew word for charity is *tzedakah*. It means "righteousness," with the connotation that it is a holy act to give to others. The Associated commonly describes its work as *tzedakah*. A staff member emphasized this theme to the Relationships Subcommittee:

> By the time the Bible was written, Jewish ethical principles were well-established as guidelines for action. The Bible is replete with injunctions to care for the widow, the orphan, the needy and the stranger. The concept of a 'community chest' existed more than 2000 years ago, when it was a requirement that community leaders have responsibilities for collections and disbursement of charity funds. By the Middle Ages, Jewish and self-governing communities had reenforced these trends. By this time, the concept of Tzedakah had become inseparable from that of

Mitzvah, the performance of good deeds. To be a good Jew, meant doing good deeds as a member of the community. . . .

This historical record indicates that throughout these periods, fundraising was a crucial and continuous activity. While the chief communal functions were religious, educational, judicial and charitable, fiscal activity was the bloodstream of the entire organism.

Referring to the present, a fundraiser describes the federation's role in relation to wealthy families:

> We represent an important part of their lives. Most inherited wealth. Few made it on their own, though there are some exceptions. They are very concerned about how they are perceived. I am amazed. These people have a lot of money, but they are interested in recognition.

He goes on:

> I was talking with someone the other day, and he was commenting on a eulogy that he heard at a funeral. He said that they never mention how much wealth someone had or how many deals he made. They talk about what he did in the community, their deeds. They don't talk about how many mergers or leveraged buyouts he had.

A member of a wealthy family talks about why he serves as a political and financial leader of the Jewish community: "I believe you need to make a meaningful contribution to your community. I don't want to be just a taker." He continues, in what might seem a new direction: "I have a laissez-faire view as leader. I am not a very observant Reform Jew." He often disagrees with the Orthodox but accepts them because they are observant Jews. In this way, as with his contributing to the community, he balances having a lot and observing a little.

Another fundraiser thus describes his role as "a Jewish Robin Hood," taking from the rich to give to the poor. He mentions three hundred elderly whom The Associated helps bathe daily and the needy who get bags of food each Friday for the Sabbath. "Robin Hood" connotes unfair inequalities, but the end result should please everyone.

Idealization of the Wealthy

Indeed, many who are not wealthy, especially those close to the federation, idealize the wealthy. The Associated annual report lists donors by size of contribution, and the *Baltimore Jewish Times* reports on gifts to Jewish institutions.

Many community members invoke the same names to show the inseparability of certain Jewish families and good works in Baltimore. A community activist notes,

> The Jews are giving the money—the Symphony, the Walters [Art Gallery]. Whenever people go to raise money, they go to these people: the Blausteins, Hirschhorns, Meyerhoffs, Rosenbergs.

Public admiration for these families reflects, in turn, on all the Jewish community, as another leader argues:

> We have a strong Jewish community. A lot of influential members of the [Baltimore] community are Jewish. Their names appear all the time. For example, Meyerhoff, Hackerman. Those outside the Jewish community admire the organization of the Jewish community. . . . I am involved in the local chapter of a national charitable organization. They admire the Jewish community and the amount of money it can raise, its ability to plan, to fundraise.

Agency administrators feel elevated by the wealthy, as a director explains regarding what distinguishes his organization: "We have the resources: money and people, influential people. Shoshana Cardin, the Hoffberger family, the Meyerhoffs, Weinberg."

This wealth makes Baltimore Jews proud of their community. Two agency directors echo one another:

> Baltimore is strong, a unique Jewish community. . . . It is insular in strength. It has a great deal of wealth.

> Baltimore has a unique Jewish community. . . . It has incredible community leadership. About 100 or 150 people. They are very wealthy. They are committed to The Associated. In their hearts and souls, they are Baltimoreans. Some are old money, some not.

Another activist emphasizes a similar theme:

> In the secular community, they are impressed by our fundraising. We have less than ninety thousand people, and we raised $22 million in our general campaign, not counting the other drives. They feel awe. They see the relatively orderly fashion in which we disperse our funds and the relatively orderly fashion in which funds get to people. We are admired.

The examples of the symphony and museum indicate the wealthy give money to non-Jewish institutions, as well as Jewish causes. Thus Associated staff have incentives to cultivate good relations with the wealthy. And they like them. One solicitor comments, "We get a lot of money here. Three hundred fifty people give $10,000 or more each year. That is a lot of money for me; I don't know about you."

Resentment of the Wealthy

As individuals, Jews can develop their own work and social relationships. In religious observance, they have many choices. However, as members of the organized Jewish community—The Associated—they take places in a delineated hierarchy of wealth, status, and power. Some in limited financial circumstances resent having little influence in the community organization.

A man of modest means who occasionally works in federation committees talks about the dominance of a wealthy elite:

> It has now all come down to thirty-nine families who run [the Jewish community in] Baltimore. Not all of them are publicly visible. Not all are committee chairs. Only a couple are on the [Associated Board] Executive Committee. But they are consulted: "Hey, Joe, what do you think about this?" These thirty-nine families give 80 percent of The Associated's money.[5] There is a lot of activity around collecting money from other people, but it is all show.

A member of one of these families offers a similar assessment:

> The federation does not conduct any community elections. It does not have election day and elect officers of the federation.[6] The nominating committee is fairly inbred. Some of these people earned the right to be where they are. They give the money to turn the wheels. The rich run the federation. [No poor person will become head of the federation.]

A staff member concurs:

> When push comes to shove, the key decisions are made by a power elite. People who have given the most money. People who have stuck around. We are fortunate to have a large core of these people in Baltimore. They constitute the decision-making process of The Associated.

As a fundraising tactic, the federation sets norms of giving for various offices, thus codifying an association between wealth and power. For example, the chair of the Board is expected to make an annual gift of at least $100,000. Chairs of major committees may be expected to give $10,000, perhaps as much as $25,000 if the chair sits on the Executive Committee. Persons of modest means with strong interest or expertise in an area can get on committees, but they typically describe themselves as exceptions—committed, but not wealthy and not likely to move into influential positions.[7]

Tensions can arise when what is a lot of money to a donor is still relatively small in this context, as a staff member explains in the hypothetical example of

> a lawyer who gives $5,000 to the annual campaign. He is successful, making $100,000 or $120,000 a year. Five thousand dollars is a significant amount of money. So he wants in on the action. He wants to be on the Board. So we can put him on the Board. But what does it get him? A meal [at meetings] and the packet of Board briefing materials. He won't have influence. Every vote is not equal.

Even a substantial gift may not bring immediate power, as another staff member explains:

> Say a new contributor gives $150,000. That is a significant amount of money. He wants to be put on the Executive Committee and be put in line to be chair. But we have people waiting in line ten years to be chair. This is a dilemma. Either we displace others, and they are angry, or we risk not getting the money. I will give you a specific example. A forty-year old young man from Nashville had a successful business there. But he felt the place was too small for him. He looked around to see where he might move, and he decided to move to Baltimore. He purchased a site to build a home here. He could give $100,000 to the campaign. In Nashville he had been campaign chair and president. He wanted to be campaign chair in two or three years here. We said, No, it couldn't be done. And he didn't move here.

Several people talk about a man who tried to overcome these odds. Describing himself, he says,

> I am a little bit of an antithesis. I didn't come from a family of money. I am not wealthy, though I make a decent living. For most positions in The Associated, most people can hold those positions. Though I know for some positions at The Associated, you have to give certain amounts for these positions. In 1982 I [held a particular office]. I felt a certain level of giving went with that.

Someone else says of this man's getting his position that he "early on decided to move up the ladder and made a pledge for a $25,000 gift. Somehow he got or borrowed the money, and he made the gift." The man concludes his description of his entry into the Associated hierarchy saying, "I am a person who is evidence that it is not just dough or the family you are from." And yet another observes that

> he is not on the slate coming up this Thursday at the annual meeting. I think it was because he was not from the right families. . . . Someone around here told me he would never make it to chairman for that reason.

Perhaps inaccurate, still, this explanation reflects the view that not only does money matter, but old money matters more.

People who cannot give a lot of money but want to contribute time in leadership positions run into barriers, as a disheartened former volunteer relates:

> I am at a certain level of giving that prevents me from moving up the line. . . . There are two positions I am interested in, but I have been told point-blank that I can't have them because of my level of giving. . . . It was a surprise. I always expected there would be something else for me to do. [A staff member told me,] "This is not a democracy, you don't

have a gift, you need to try something else." I invested fifteen years of my life. If you don't have the gift, there is no place for you in the system. What I have experienced is what a lot of people had told me about. . . . I felt abandoned.

The closer you get to the top, the clearer you see it. [For the average person, it looks like everyone is equal, but] this is not a democratic society. It is absolutely monetary. The gift determines your position. You can get to be president of an agency with a fairly minimal gift. You can't get above a [board] subcommittee chair [with a small gift]. You can't get to be a chair without giving. . . . [The community members don't know what size gifts are expected, but staff do].

I thought there was a place in the system for a lay leader who was committed to the system and had some professional expertise in the area. That should supersede money.

Nonwealthy feel stigmatized by status calibrated in wealth. A rabbi complains that at

The Associated your position is based on what you give, your wealth. That will not provide for a sense of how we deal with mortality and eternity. Those are people's main concerns.

A religious layman of moderate income who engages in Jewish study says The Associated has "gone from its wealth of knowledge to the knowledge of wealth." It deprecates religiosity and knowledge.

Moreover, the wealthy are not always deeply religious or scholarly, as an Associated staff member notes in comparing federation leaders to synagogue leaders:

There is an intellectual substance that one needs to become a synagogue leader. You have to give money, but you also have to be committed philosophically to what the synagogue believes in. Here, all we are asking for is money. But we don't ask for a religious commitment. You can be an atheist and be the head of The Associated.

People can get into leadership positions without special expertise. A major donor mentions a current crisis in

an agency headed [on its board] by campaign heavy hitters. And it will be difficult to disagree with them. Like most organizations, you try to listen to people who are smarter.

But, he says, these leaders do not understand the problems and resist good advice. Another big giver notes, "It's not that rich people can't be smart, but there is a lot of dead wood." Nonwealthy cite examples of federation leaders whose money compensated for their ability. For them, these instances degrade the Golden Rule.

Associated staff work hard to support lay leaders. Staff write scripts for running meetings. They brief leaders so they can speak knowledgeably and authoritatively. Repeatedly, leaders acknowledge staff by saying, "They make me look good."

The Associated has three interests in supporting lay leaders these ways. The first is to promote effective meetings. After all, many leaders are busy and lack time, even when they have the ability, to master complex issues.

Moreover, a growing number of matters are too complicated for many laypersons, and staff gain influence from their ability to formulate proposals and evaluate alternatives. Although the chair of strategic planning endorsed the norm "that lay leaders set policy with the informed advice of the professional" (Cardin 1989:133), subtle changes in meanings of "lay leaders" and "professional staff" reflect shifting influence. Whereas traditionally people talked of "lay *leaders*" served by "professional *staff*," increasingly they contrast the limitations of "*lay* leaders" vis-à-vis "*professional* staff."

However, federation norms dictate that community members make decisions. Hence staff have a second interest in equipping lay leaders to handle their responsibilities. Assisting them in making decisions reassures community members of all incomes who prefer some democracy to technocracy.

Third, making wealthy leaders look good to the nonwealthy gives legitimacy to the Golden Rule. It does not defuse anger that power is tied to wealth, but it suggests that wealthy persons who have power have intellectual authority to go with it.

But what of the Golden Rule itself? Interestingly, a staff member makes this comment "off the record": "Not everyone comes to the table as equals. Wealth does count here. People have different speaking privileges." Why is this admission off the record? Who does not believe this is true? It is off the record because Associated decision makers would like it to be a secret. They would like to believe the nonwealthy do not see the wealthy run things. And this wish comes from recognition that nonwealthy resent the Golden Rule and the golden rulers.

Consistently, when another staff member is asked why The Associated is not more candid about decision making, he responds,

> Perception matters. When I was in school, I read . . . *The Power Elite.* . . . It is about the perception of Americans. We call ourselves a democracy, but we know who controls things. Why doesn't every paper tell people that the power elite controls America? We [at The Associated] are in the process of selling in addition to decision making. We have to continue to raise money, in the fairest, most objective manner possible. There *is* a power elite here.

He acknowledges that a "power elite" runs the federation and recognizes that nonwealthy community members know. Still, he believes federation actions will be legitimate in the larger community only if they seem democratic.

On the one hand, the wealthy are essential to supporting programs, and The Associated follows common custom in giving them formal influence. These practices arouse bad feelings, however, because The Associated is a community organization as well as a fundraising organization, and community members expect democratic participation. Hence the wealthy have two interests: one is to direct allocations according to their priorities, and the other is to persuade nonwealthy that differences in power are fair, trivial, or illusory. We look next at how strategic planning responded to these interests.

CHAPTER 14

Setting Community Priorities

One purpose of strategic planning was to set spending priorities. Another was to raise necessary funds. The federation had done these things before, but strategic planning was an effort to do both more systematically. In addition, it was promoted as a way of setting priorities in a community perspective. Practically, one challenge was to set priorities that reinforced, or did not contradict, normative concepts of community membership. Another was to reconcile the power of wealthy contributors with those membership norms and general notions of equality.

DECIDING ON SERVICE PRIORITIES

How much of which services should The Associated provide to whom? In answering this question, the Services Subcommittee would direct spending. Decisions on organizational priorities would also define the community by recognizing certain needs and setting forth how people, perhaps with help, should live.

When the committee convened in April 1988, staff raised three issues. One was geographic: Should agencies offer services in customary Park Heights locations, Owings Mills, or both? The question involved constituencies: many Park Heights Jews were relatively poor and traditionally Orthodox, whereas most suburban Jews were financially comfortable and not Orthodox.

Second, should services still be offered as charity, or should the federation deliver more money-making services to paying clients? This question also touched on constituencies—how to balance traditional assistance to the poor with services for donors and others with good incomes.

Third, staff introduced a budgeting proposal. At the time, each agency made funding requests to a separate committee, which evaluated proposals in light of the agency's past record. Instead, budget committees would be organized by target populations, or constituencies. Agencies would ask for funds to serve specific populations before committees evaluating all requests related to those populations. Central to this arrangement was setting priorities among constituencies.

The budgeting proposal became a focus of strategic planning for services, and outcomes can be viewed in two perspectives. The first looks at budgeting and power relations between the federation and agencies. Moving from agency-based to constituency-based planning and budgeting had an unassailable rational appeal (better serving more deserving groups) but also potentially significant political and fiscal consequences. Requiring agencies to justify requests in terms of federation priorities and evaluating requests in terms of client needs rather than past agency performance would increase Associated control. However, an agency director could frame programs in terms of priorities to even out negotiations.

Restructuring committees to focus on target populations would force agencies to face several committees, rather than one. The arrangement would increase directors' work and could give the federation more opportunities to say no. However, a director might turn separate reviews into new chances for support.

Perhaps as important in shaping the balance of power was a latent feature of the proposal, possibly clearer to Associated staff than lay leaders. The new arrangement required sophistication beyond many budget committee members. Budgets could become largely the province of agency and federation professionals, with agency directors' abilities a key variable.

A second perspective on deliberations focuses on constituencies' priorities as service recipients and their tacit evaluation as community members. In prioritizing constituencies, the committee would identify groups most deserving of communal support. In ranking services, it would judge which activities community members should most be able to do.

Establishing Funding Criteria

The Services Subcommittee would first set criteria for funding, then prioritize services by rating them against the criteria. With relatively little discussion, the committee agreed on criteria. After affirming services should be offered on the basis of need, not means, members supported the following statement:

> The Associated Jewish Charities and Welfare Fund should support services that
>
> 1. Provide basic services that are not available through public sources at an adequate level for the Jewish poor.
> 2. Promote Jewish identity by strengthening ties to the Jewish family/community for:
>   a. Jews at risk of not feeling Jewish
>   b. Jews who want inherently Jewish services.

The statement defined an Associated role: providing basic services for the Jewish poor when the public sector does not adequately do so and providing inherently Jewish services for those who want them. In addition, it defined community membership. Socially, members should be close to and take care of family members and other Jews, including the poor. Psychologically, members should identify with other Jews. The statement also designated certain groups particularly deserving: the poor, those inclined not to feel Jewish, those who want Jewish services, and those with family difficulties.

Although such an abstract policy was easy to agree on, different interpretations would favor different agencies. It might benefit those serving the poor, but any agency could claim to provide "inherently Jewish services." These criteria were the bare beginning of allocation decisions.

The criteria also took a position on community boundaries. The unaffiliated might be considered at risk of not feeling Jewish and thus a prime constituency. However, some on the committee felt that, because the unaffiliated had not made a basic institutional commitment to the community, they were outside it, not deserving of federation funds. A member of the staff team acknowledged this ambivalence and offered a way out. Outreach to the unaffiliated, he said, was "the 'highest priority' challenge for The Associated in its long-range strategic plan," but "we should be aware that there may likely be a minimal return (in terms of attracting involvement/affiliation from the presently unaffiliated) from a potentially large outlay of community resources for such outreach programs."

At the same time, the criteria touched, but skirted, questions of what community membership required. On the one hand, references to "Jewish" poor and "feeling Jewish" could be interpreted liberally as meaning anyone was a good member who thought of him- or herself as a Jew and was so thought of by others. On the other hand, "Jewish identity" and "inherently Jewish services" seemed to demand more. Was feeling Jewish sufficient for Jewish identity, or did it require specific knowledge and observance? Was any federation agency program a Jewish service, or must it follow specific halachic principles?

Such questions lay at the heart of disagreements about community membership. Yet Associated leaders wanted to keep all denominations and avoid taking sides. Planning participants agreed on ambiguous language that allowed various interpretations and left agencies to their own positions.

The committee was also circumspect about community members' economic status. The first principle apparently designated the poor the most deserving group, consistent with The Associated's charity tradition. However, a growing number of economically successful members wanted the federation to serve them too. Moreover, just referring to the poor called attention to income inequalities and risked arousing bad feelings.

Ensuing discussion softened references to the poor. For example, in listing the federation's "customers," someone started with the "economically needy," but another immediately added the "socially needy," comprising anyone requiring assistance, and someone else suggested "those otherwise unserved by existing services," including anyone wanting services. Another person argued "all Jews" were customers, thus eliminating the notion of need altogether. Someone else suggested customers should include not just service clients, but also donors.

Later, a staff person offered that serving the poor might mean doing nothing more than at present. He estimated between one-fourth and one-third of the Associated budget went to the poor and said that could be enough. As well, he noted, priority for deserving populations could be measured in several ways, including the number of persons served, the number of dollars spent, and the percentage of persons in the category. Different definitions would support different policies and budgets.

The committee revised the statement for the plan. The most significant change was in the first criterion, which now read,

> Provide the Jewish poor *and disadvantaged* with essential services not available through public sources at an adequate level of quality or quantity (Plan 1989:3; emphasis added).

The recommendation broadened the first target population beyond an economic category and suggested Jews of all stations could similarly be disadvantaged.

Ranking Services

After the committee agreed on criteria, staff distributed a list of Associated agency services, along with groupings of "subpopulations" making up "constituencies" corresponding to the criteria. "The poor" included the elderly, families, single parents, immigrants, the unemployed, and the handicapped and disabled. Those "at risk of not feeling Jewish" included youth and the college aged, singles, families, and immigrants. "People who want inherently Jewish services" included the elderly, youth and college aged, families, and singles. Although the second and third constituencies were defined in Jewish terms, the subpopulations did not refer to anything Jewish or religious. Only one of the subpopulations of the poor, the unemployed, was defined economically.

Committee members rated services against the criteria as Level I ("fundamental"), Level II ("important"), Level III ("legitimate"), or Level IV ("optional"). However, ratings were not unanimous, and the committee left further efforts to later. In the fall of 1989 the Strategic Planning Implementation Council passed the task to the Services Task Force. The effort to set priorities continued for over a year.

Reformulating constituencies helped get agreement. Instead of the poor, those at risk of not feeling Jewish, and people wanting inherently Jewish services, subpopulations were grouped into nine new constituencies: children and adolescents, young adults, adults, families, disabled at risk, elderly, immigrants, the general community, and Jewish education. These groups represented mainly life cycle stages, through which most people passed. This change avoided conflict over requirements for being Jewish and removed a potentially divisive focus on the poor.

Work went through several rankings, debates, and votes until it reached the Strategic Planning Implementation Council, the Associated Board, and the Executive Committee. This process allowed many people to make a case, examine the results of cumulative rankings, consider the fairness and consistency of the rankings, and try again until everyone was satisfied.

Some observers, mostly lay leaders, say many people simply watched the interests of agencies they supported and rated services accordingly. Others, mostly staff, report they saw people putting aside their sympathies and voting for community interests. Many, they say, got caught up in the abstractions of ranking services and did not recognize budgetary implications. They note that some who served on agency boards acted against their agencies' interests.

With the newly formulated constituencies, the Jewish Family Services (JFS) did well. It represented the federation's traditional charity orientation. It also delivered a wide, growing range of individual and family services to middle-income clients. In contrast, the Jewish Big Brother/Big Sister League was a small agency with few programs. One was the Jewish Alcohol and Drug Abuse Service, and planning participants questioned the need for a Jewish alcohol and drug program. Its advocates likened it to Alcoholics Anonymous and cited AA's religious orientation. Consistently, they held, there should be a Jewish alcohol and drug abuse service. This argument led raters to give the service a high ranking, though some may just have reasoned that every agency should have some highly ranked programs.

The case of the Jewish Community Center (JCC) supports the view that abstract ranking prevailed over agency interests. If JFS was a big winner in priority setting, the JCC was generally seen as a big loser. Even though the JCC was part of a century-old tradition, it did not deliver services to the poor or disadvantaged, nor did it provide social services. It ran social and recreational activities. Its advocates argued these programs were important because they drew into the organized Jewish community people who did not affiliate with the federation or synagogues. The JCC called its programs informal Jewish education, teaching Jews to enjoy being in the community. They pointed out JCC services earned money. Perhaps this argument undercut claims for higher rankings, but none carried much weight. In the end, most services were at Levels II and III.

The JCC case was a significant exception to an informal norm that eased agreement: reciprocity in raising rankings when advocates insisted a service was essential. As priority setting went through successive stages, fewer and fewer services were at either Level III or IV. Most ended up at Level I or II. In the end, forty-five services were at Level I, seventy-one at Level II, twenty at Level III, and three at Level IV.

In the growing economy of the late 1980s, most believed federation income would increase, and, whatever the final rankings, all agencies would do better than in the past. In this mood, The Associated originally proposed to fund Level I services at 105 percent of their base allocation, Level II at 100 percent, and only Levels III and IV below 100 percent.

SERVICE PRIORITIES AND BUDGETARY OUTCOMES

The outcomes of this process can be measured in several ways. The first strategic plan recommendation states,

> The community's service priorities . . . should be established in terms of the needs of clients. They should focus not on the programs particular agencies operate, but on the services the various client groups need, regardless of which entity is to provide them. Priorities . . . in effect at any given time should guide both the service agencies and the Associated's planning and budgeting decisions (Plan 1989:4).

For advocates of budgeting reform, this outcome alone, apart from any rankings, was the measure of success. In FY93, budget committees were reorganized by constituency groups.

Constituencies and agencies might measure the results in terms of rankings, but they were open to interpretation, and a smart agency director would put programs in Level I terms.

Moreover, rankings said nothing about budgeting. Should all Level I services, for example, receive identical allocations? The reason why not was that programs were not the same size in terms of clients served, staff, cost per unit of service, or any other meaningful measure. For example, adoption services, coalition-building activities, day school teacher retention, and adult employment services were all Level I. They served different numbers of clients and required different investments per client. They entailed significantly different allocations. Further, although the priority levels differentiated the importance of services, the rankings alone did not specify proportions of the budget for different levels.

Finally, though priorities referred to groups' needs, they were not based on systematic need assessment. Committee members rated services from personal impressions. A staff member noted, "There are no objective criteria of community need. It is based on perceptions, after talking with people." Thus the federation and agencies would negotiate in a loosely defined field.

In this context, how did budget restructuring and prioritizing affect allocations? A comparison of spending for FY91, before restructuring, and recommended funding for FY96, three years after, shows considerable consistency.

The totals for local services in the 2 years are similar, declining by 0.1 percent from $13,710,390 in FY91 to $13,698,504 in FY95.[1] Of 18 agencies funded in both years, 6 increased their share of the budget, 3 stayed the same, and 9 lost in share. Six of the changes were less than 10 percent of the 1991 share,[2] 7 were between 10 percent and 20 percent, and 5 ranged between 30 percent and 73 percent, though some of the large percentage changes involved small budgets. In dollars, 10 agencies changed by less than $34,129, 4.5 percent of the average 1991 agency allocation. Still, even these figures exaggerate fluctuations, since some agencies get outside income and The Associated adjusts allocations in response.

Five agencies had both large percentage and dollar changes, but most reflected extraneous financial conditions rather than service rankings. Levindale (providing medical and residential services for the elderly and disabled) increased in share by 43 percent and $110,770, and Sinai Hospital's share dropped by 14 percent and $362,780. Levindale's increase largely went to new facilities. Still, half of Levindale's federation funds (in a $31 million budget) and nearly all of Sinai's federation funds (in a $300 million budget) came from endowment, with fluctuations in return the main influence on allocation.

The JCC's share dropped by 12 percent and $300,025. Though the decline was consistent with rankings, decisions were based largely on the JCC's ability to raise money from fees.

Two changes reflected service rankings. The Jewish Big Brother/Big Sister League's share grew by 38 percent and $103,601, largely for expanding Jewish Alcohol and Drug Abuse Services. Needs were growing for Level I services. The Council on Jewish Day School Education grew in share by 31 percent and $249,016, as the overall federation spending share on Jewish education rose 10 percent and $191,740,[3] with most growth from the Fund for Jewish Education. This change represented both service rankings and relations between Orthodox and non-Orthodox.

The general constancy of agency allocations expresses political and intellectual conservatism. More sophisticated need assessment and program evaluation might suggest systematic shifts, but such a development is unlikely. The Associated budgeting process is deliberately political. Federation staff want discretion in negotiating with agencies. Defining the terms of need assessments and setting standards for measuring services could give the federation considerable control, but an explicit empirical analysis would give everyone something to appeal to.

Moreover, such formal analysis would vitiate a main reason for including major contributors on committees and boards. They want to see their ideas adopted in programs in which they can invest. They support particular agencies as vehicles for turning personal wealth into good works. A systematic need assessment might help better match spending to needs, but it would also take away donors' prerogatives, influence, and interest.

PRIORITIZING SERVICES AND VALUING COMMUNITY MEMBERS

Service priorities are loosely coupled to allocations because federation staff, agency directors, and program advocates often prefer to make decisions based on interests, where rankings justify rather than drive choices. Still, the priorities shed light on how planning participants valued community groups.

Services Subcommittee members and staff redefined constituencies while planning. They started with three, consistent with the service criteria: the poor, those who might not feel Jewish, and those who wanted Jewish services. They ended up with nine "constituent groups."

The final list differed from the original in two significant ways. First, no groups were described in terms of Jewish identity, religious or otherwise. As a matter of service delivery, this is noteworthy, because religious groups differ in preferences for Jewish services and use of specific federation services. Moreover, Jewish identity was a prominent, worrisome topic during planning. People argued for religious and ethnic viewpoints. Yet all these variations were subsumed within constituencies that marked stages in a life cycle. Differences over Jewish identity, including religious conflicts, were apparently too divisive, and those who framed the final list tried to avoid disagreement, even if doing so meant removing references to community members' Jewishness.

In addition, the groups did not include the poor, the unemployed, or even the disadvantaged. The poor were Jewish federations' traditional concern. However, they were lumped with everyone else in the life cycle groups. One explanation is Associated leaders' desire to serve the middle-class majority as well as the poor. Related is the wish to avoid drawing attention to economic status and disparities in wealth.

The final priorities fill in a picture of the community by showing the activities decision makers valued. Although a precise measure of the rankings is impossible because services differ in size, a rough analysis is suggestive.

The most Level I rankings (12) were concerned with raising children. These services help parents begin families, bring up children, and address problems their children create or encounter while growing up. Examples are adoption, day care, Big Brother/Big Sister services, foster care, and services for juvenile offenders.

The next most Level I rankings (8) involved Jewish education, including college programs. These encourage and enable people to think of themselves as and be Jewish.

Another group of Level I rankings (8) concerned "foreign relations." Most called services for the "general community," they involve managing relations with the outside world. Examples include advocacy for Israel, education on anti-Semitism, legislative advocacy, stabilization of black-Jewish neighborhoods, and securing Jewish meals and chaplaincy for Jewish patients in non-Jewish hospitals.

Straddling Level I (6 services) and Level II (5; one in Level III) were services for the poor. Many services are offered on sliding scales tied to income; these are services specifically for persons with financial problems. They include acute health care for indigent Jews, financial aid and personal budget management, adult employment services, and advocacy for benefits and services from non-Associated sources.

One of the lowest-ranked constituencies was immigrants. Only one of eleven immigrant services (employment) was Level I, and eight were Level II. Because few services were Level III or IV, this position is significant.

In the community these rankings portray, people move through the life cycle, growing up, starting families, raising children, and aging. Orthodox, Conservative, Reform, Reconstructionist, secular, and unaffiliated Jews have similar desires and occasional needs for aid. If religion matters, it is a private matter. It is an issue of personal taste, perhaps discussed with service workers, but not an object of public policy. This pluralistic view of Jewish community membership is politic for The Associated; it is the dominant view of the non-Orthodox.

In this picture, wealth has nothing to do with the life course. It does not affect how children grow or how adults raise families. Employment is a concern, but an individual problem rather than a disadvantage of class. Economic difficulties, as religious orientations, are private, perhaps discussed with service workers, but more general economic problems are not matters for public policy. So, too, with economic success. It is an individual matter, one The Associated appreciates, but not an object for public review.

Thus strategic planning for services not only set budgetary priorities, but also evaluated community members. Strikingly, the final ranking conceptualized people as more or less autonomous individuals moving through the life cycle, rather than as members of cultural or economic groups. This might be a reasonable service policy, leaving agencies to respond to relevant group differences. However, as a tacit statement about the community, atomism argued against not only the significance of accumulated wealth, but also the shared Jewishness that made the community distinctive.

RAISING FUNDS

The Finance Subcommittee would strategize to raise funds for services. Members took a lot of time to analyze financial trends and projections, but they did not seriously disagree about much. They were uncertain how much money would be needed over the next decade, but they had little doubt about where to look for most of it: among a small group of wealthy families.

The committee weighed a proposal to seek more public funds. That would increase revenues but would require offering nonsectarian services. The Associated traditionally served only Jewish clients, and its wealth allowed it to avoid government programs. In contrast with federations that pursued public money, the plan recommended caution:

> Government and foundation funding should be sought by the service agencies only for services consistent with agency missions and capacities. Funding for nonsectarian services should be sought only as authorized by the Associated . . . (Plan 1989:25).[4]

The committee emphasized new approaches to traditional givers and initiatives toward Jews who had not given as much as Associated leaders estimated they could. Recommendation 23 was specific:

a. implement a program to reach some 675 non-givers and under-givers with six-figure incomes.

b. invest more resources in developing the $1,000 to $10,000 segment of the annual campaign.

c. create a $100,000-and-over program to give greater recognition to donors as incentive to increase their gifts and to bring others up to that level.

d. create a similar program at the $50,000–$99,000 level.

e. more aggressively seek one-time gifts from donors who have experienced windfalls or unusually high incomes.

f. create mechanisms to endow major campaign gifts in perpetuity.

g. develop testamentary endowment gifts for unrestricted or designated use by agencies.

h. seek more grants from philanthropic funds, support foundations and other sources outside the Jewish community for selected special needs, locally and overseas.

i. seek the conversion of family and corporate foundations to philanthropic funds and supporting foundations (Plan 1989:24).

The aging of wealthy family leaders, often coupled with their children's lesser interest in Jewish affairs, encouraged a growing focus on endowments. They would reduce pressure on the annual campaign and, if unrestricted, give decision makers greater discretion.

Although service priorities submerged the wealthy in the general population, fundraising highlighted them, risking bad feelings about economic differences.

MANAGING RELATIONS BETWEEN THE WEALTHY AND THE NONWEALTHY

The Relationships Subcommittee was charged with improving relations within the community and between the community and the larger world. It took up the challenge of managing relations between those who were wealthy and those who were not.

The committee talked frankly about how nonwealthy felt about the wealthy. They recognized that people of modest means sometimes resented the influence of wealth. Yet to take seriously the concerns of the nonwealthy could mean opening up decision making, perhaps even excluding some significant contributors from leadership. That would not be possible.

The committee embarked on a strategy that might be called raising the consciousness of the nonwealthy. The first plan draft acknowledged how those of moderate means felt about the wealthy. In particular, it noted a double consciousness, where those of modest means simultaneously recognize the wealthy and forget about differences in wealth, so as to suppress knowledge of links between wealth and power and avoid resentment over them:

> A fundamental responsibility of the Associated is to raise funds in order to support services. In any such organization, substantial contributors

have a strong claim on the limited number of key positions. The *unspo-ken tradition* of most fund-raising organizations, as of the Associated, is to *ignore that fact*. But *the unacknowledged fact* causes some resent-ment; it seems to some that key positions are monopolized by persons they regard as not representative of the community (Relationships Report 1989:18; emphasis added).

However, it responded to this problem with Recommendation 9, which minimized inequities:

Accept the role of major donors. The influence of large contributors is not a problem to be solved; it is *a natural phenomenon* to be accepted, within bounds. The fact is that, *except at the uppermost level*, many positions of importance in the Associated are held by persons whose monetary contributions are not large (Relationships Report 1989:19; emphasis added).

This text was in bold print. A final sentence, not bold, suggested, "More-over, the desire to open additional positions to persons of modest means can be further satisfied by Recommendation 11," which urged The Asso-ciated to "export" talented leaders to agencies, synagogues, and other organizations where fewer rush to participate (Relationships Report 1989:19).

The final draft included much of this language, but with different emphases. There was no specific recommendation such as draft Recom-mendation 9; that discussion was subsumed in an introduction to a rec-ommendation to export leadership and another to simplify Associated deci-sion making. The differences in language were significant, beginning with

acknowledging a reality. Raising funds in order to support services is, of course, a fundamental responsibility of the Associated. In any such orga-nization, substantial contributors have a strong claim on the limited number of key positions. But that fact is *rarely acknowledged* and may cause resentment. Some will feel that key positions are occupied by per-sons who are not representative of the community as a whole. Our view is that the role of major donors is not a problem to be solved but *a nat-ural and appropriate phenomenon*, to be understood and accepted so long as it remains within bounds. We believe it is well within bounds in the Associated since, *in fact*, many positions of importance are held by persons whose monetary contributions are relatively modest (Plan 1989:15; emphasis added).

This language departed from the earlier draft in two ways. First, it declared a "reality": claims of the wealthy to power positions were not only "natural," but "appropriate."

Second, in contrast with draft references to "unspoken" tradition and "ignored" and "unacknowledged" fact, this text stressed that the reality rarely was and always should be "acknowledged." In this view, there was no place for double consciousness, because there was nothing wrong, nothing anyone should resent. Further, the nonwealthy should take comfort in another "fact," that they held many positions of importance (no longer did the text say "except at the uppermost level").

The plan promulgated a higher, unconflicted, consciousness. The nonwealthy had developed a double consciousness for peace of mind, because they held the federation up to the wrong standards. They focused on its fundraising role and, without understanding fundraising realities, mistakenly expected it to be a grassroots community organization. Instead, they should think of how it provided services they used or could use. In this vein Recommendation 12 argued to *"Better inform the community"* "about the nature and purposes of the Associated and about the services it supports" (Plan 1989:11).

Still more important, the nonwealthy erred even in measuring community members in terms of wealth and power. If they looked at people in terms of ability, they would find wealth was unimportant and anyone with ability could make a difference. Thus the plan included the nonwealthy among the "large number of able and energetic persons" who wanted to be involved in Associated decisions but who could not be included without bogging down the system. Recommendation 19 carried forth the aim of the draft, to *"Insure a sharing of leadership throughout the community"* (Plan 1989:16). The nonwealthy, who were unlikely to gain power in The Associated, could do better, representing both themselves and the federation, in other Jewish institutions or the larger community.

The Federation's Name

Fundraising is a federation reality. Strategic planning decision makers did not shrink from asserting the centrality of the wealthy and the legitimacy of their power. Still, they recognized resentment of their role. The plan's arguments about their authority were subtle, and the plan would not be read by many, particularly the nonwealthy. A more visible intervention would be a change in the federation's name.

A number of Associated leaders were dissatisfied with "Associated Jewish Charities and Welfare Fund." The first plan draft explained:

> The name of the Associated conveys inappropriate meanings and fails to convey appropriate ones. The Associated is far more than a "charity," and it should not wish clients of the service agencies—many of whom are contributors—to regard themselves as recipients of charity. Moreover, the Associated does not duplicate public "welfare" programs; and one of its main missions is community-building, which the name does not suggest (Relationships Report 1989:6).

Significantly, the issue came before the Relationships Subcommittee, in the context of understanding why nondonors shunned The Associated.

Associated agency clients did not want to think of themselves as "charity" cases. This stigma could discourage them from using services. Moreover, in noting many clients were also contributors, the text emphasized a change in the community. Although Jewish philanthropy grew from a concern for the poor, most Baltimore Jews were now middle-class. Federation programs should serve everyone, and the name did not legitimize services for middle-income people.

The name drew too much attention to economic differences. Insofar as clients were also contributors, donors and nondonors alike were only being asked to give to themselves. The Associated was not taking money from one group for another (it was not Robin Hood). It was just helping people take care of themselves. This was an appealing theme in the 1980s, and it corresponded to the Jewish view of *tzedakah*, that everyone will eventually need *tzedakah* and, therefore, should at some time give it.

The text noted The Associated was concerned about "community-building," and the old name did not recognize this. This denotative shortcoming was also a connotative weakness. Federation leaders wanted to emphasize all Baltimore Jews were one community, not divided into contributors of "charity" and recipients of "welfare." When so many were both clients and donors, not only were all similar members of one community, but there was no important difference between wealthy and non-wealthy. If everyone could be the client of some service—whether job placement, recreation, food baskets, or Jewish education—all were alike. If anyone could be a donor, then all, even if not wealthy, were at least well off.

However, neither the Relationships Subcommittee nor the Strategic Planning Committee could agree on a new name to carry all these meanings. Instead, Recommendation 13 said, simply, "*Seek a more appropriate name*" (Plan 1989:11).

In implementation, the Communications, Image-Building, and Community Relations Task Force considered various names, including one that referred to plural "Baltimore Jewish communities," before settling on "THE ASSOCIATED: Jewish Community Federation of Baltimore." The short name was the same as before, and the new words both linked the organization to other local Jewish federations and affirmed The Associated's role as community builder.

Wealth, Banking, and Community

Looking back on the overall impact of strategic planning, a staff member emphasized a development of the kind the namechangers intended: "Now people say we are in the people, community business. Earlier, people thought we were in the banking business." Whether public perceptions changed this way or not, the observation expressed Associated hopes. Relationships in a bank are unequal. It is a place where, literally, those with the gold rule. In contrast, a community of just "people" is a place of equality. No one has or is more than anyone else. No one feels ashamed or resentful for having less; no one feels guilty about having more.

Still, "community business" is a peculiar phrase. Although the first word plays down the role of wealth, the second portrays The Associated as an economic enterprise, where the product is community. Moreover, business and community are uneasy partners. Once people engage one another in business, some profit at others' expense, and inequalities can divide people.

The phrase encapsulates the dilemmas of a community organization that is also a major fundraiser. A community organization needs resources for its activities. However, when fundraising takes a great deal of effort and attention—either because it is urgent but difficult or, as here, because it is so enormously rewarding—fundraising displaces organizing. The organization values persons in relation to their ability to contribute, and it gives priority to those who have the most.

These considerations put the organization in tension with community members who frame their identity in religious, ethnic, or other non-economic terms. In the process, it reduces the organization's authority *qua* community organization—with not only those who have few resources, but, in different degrees, almost everyone who identifies with the community.

The reason is summed up in the staff member's contrast between banking and community. It is expressed, as well, in the fundraiser's observation that people want to be remembered for community contributions, not their wealth. What makes a community special for most people, what moves them to identify with and involve themselves in it in extraordinary ways, is its connections with transcendent ideas and emotions.

Wealth brings the satisfactions and rewards of power, but it is hard to think of wealth as something transcendent. Money is an object of exchange, and one's wealth is always dependent on others. In contrast, religion and ethnicity, for example, are autonomous sources of identity. Ties with ancestors or relations with God have nothing to do with the vicissitudes of the market or other social institutions.

This is the argument—and attraction—of the Orthodox. They have faith that supports a community. The staff member who substituted "community" for "banking" recognized this appeal. So did the Relationships Subcommittee, who recommended in the plan that The Associated "seek a shared vision" with synagogues (Plan 1989:14). When federation leaders created a Joint Commission on Associated-Synagogue Relations to implement that recommendation, they set up a Jewish Continuity Subcommittee. The future of the community, they assumed, depended on faith as well as wealth.

The fate of that search is the story of a later chapter.

CHAPTER 15

Other People's Money:
The Challenges of Implementation
in Southeast

INTERVIEWER: What are some important influences on the future of Southeast?
COMMUNITY ACTIVIST: Money.

In Southeast, wealth isn't so complicated. There isn't enough of it to matter. Incomes vary from the Gold Coast to public housing. However, long-time residents and planning activists identify most strongly with the large group between these extremes. By income, they are working-class. By morality, they are good-hearted homeowners. In contrast with the Jewish community, these people, perhaps of necessity, idealize those with modest incomes. Undoubtedly many envy those with much more, but they do not see them as better.

Most think of wealth as something outsiders have. SECO does little to raise funds from local residents, because returns are small. Southeast has several dozen large firms, including some owned by people who grew up in the area, but few give much to community activities. Implementing the Southeast plan depends on getting other people's money.

MONEY IN SOUTHEAST

Modest Blue-Collar Lives

Blue-collar families in Southeast think of their incomes as modest and their finances as occasionally precarious. Many balance satisfaction about having made it so far with anxiety about whether they can depend on things to last.

Family narratives often begin with stories of privation in the immigrant past. A woman of Slavic descent recalls,

> I remember my mother counting out money for bread and things like that. And I remember she used to ask us what we wanted for Christmas, and we thought that we were poor, and we didn't really ask for hardly anything.

One who grew up nearby in public housing recounts, "My mother made money baking."

Families managed to take care of children; the growth of the factories provided jobs; many bought homes, but most still lived humbly. Years later, retirement and widowhood left many in limited circumstances. The first woman, after talking about eventual economic success, speaks of leaving work: "Of course, I don't have the money to spend that I used to have. I have more time now, but a lot less money, so that makes it hard."

In recent years, industrial decline and recession have eroded even working families' security, as a local leader notes:

> This area is depressed. As it has lost a lot of business, it has lost a lot of jobs. For people in this area, a lot of money, income, spendable income, has gone out of this area in the past ten or fifteen years.

Many government supports that once helped in hard times were cut during the Reagan and Bush years, another remarks:

> With what started happening twelve years ago, the money is drying up, and a lot of people fell through the cracks. The poorer communities weren't served. . . . I think that's really a big difference in the neighborhood. You don't see the people coming in and renovating anymore. You see a lot of houses for sale.

Southeast Baltimore has suffered the hard times of the city. A shopkeeper ties his privation to those broader conditions:

> We don't have any money here. This is a very poor city, and the statistics show that it is getting poorer. . . . I own nothing now. I own what you see inside this shop, and that is what I own in this world. I can't have a home here. I had bought a place a few years ago, and I realized finally that I had the money to either fix up that place and live in it or do my business, and I didn't have the money to do both. And so I had to sell my home. I never had a chance to live in it. I never spent a night in it. It broke my heart.

The Poor

Still worse off are those who work only a little or don't work at all. Public housing residents are among the poorest. Many long-time residents see them as government wards pushed into Southeast; racial differences reinforce feelings these people are outsiders. The elderly whose only asset is their house may earn even less, but they own homes, once worked or were married to wage-earners, and are probably related to several Southeast households. The blue-collar majority, especially their children or other family members, are concerned about their circumstances and sympathetically view them as community members.

The clearest line many long-time working-class residents draw between themselves and those who are poorer is the distinction between owners and renters. Although housing tenure is inexactly correlated with income, the good-hearted homeownership culture divides owners and renters as a way of assigning social and moral status to those with a little more and those with a little less. Blue-collar homeowners are concerned about how the poor push up taxes by making claims on welfare programs, but they are more specifically worried about how renters run down neighborhoods, damage property values, and erode community life.

The Gold Coast

Yet, even amid these privations, the financially successful move into the Gold Coast. Old-time Southeasterners envy and resent the newcomers' comfort. They also paint them in colors that give the working class added virtue. Though few "Gold Coast" residents have the gold that rules at The Associated, the epithet conveys the animosity nonwealthy feel toward the wealthy.

Moreover, nothing balances this feeling, such as the admiration that goes to leading Jewish philanthropists. Not only do Gold Coast residents lack conspicuous wealth, but few are interested in supporting, much less leading, the Southeast community. No sense of peoplehood binds those with more to those with less. Perhaps especially for this reason, Gold Coasters sometimes seem unambiguously irredeemable.

Deliberately or unknowingly, they exploit the vulnerabilities of blue-collar families and victimize them. A social worker links the creation of the Gold Coast to The Road. Twenty-five years ago, the City offered working-class families small sums for their homes, to tear them down and build a highway. After great struggle, the community beat the City:

> Then they started to rebuild on the property, and, instead of the 5 and 6 and 10 thousand dollars they paid the people that were there, they're building 80 and 90 and 125 thousand dollar housing there. It's not housing that people in the neighborhood could afford for the most part. It's bringing in an entirely different class of people in the area. . . . it's very difficult. In some cases, it pushes the property values up on the rowhouses and homes adjacent to the redevelopment areas. It brings speculators into the area, real estate investors instead of homeowners in many cases. That happened a lot when the Anchorage [condominiums were built]. . . . a lot of those homes were bought by investors, were bought by companies who wanted a place in Baltimore where they bring their execs in. And they, if you could afford to buy one at the Anchorage when they opened at $154,000. . . .
>
> That's a lot of money, when you figure the average value of a home in Canton is probably somewhere between 20 and 30 thousand dollars

still, maybe 40. Some of the houses, some of them are 60, and some of the neighbors shriek and laugh and giggle when they see someone trying to list their house for 60 thousand bucks in this area. The houses not in great condition are still available, where there haven't been major modifications, and some of them are smaller still in the 30 to 40 thousand range. And you're talking, this is ten years ago . . . about building 154 thousand dollar townhouses on the edge of the community, and the developers come in and tell them it is not going to affect the community at all, it won't affect their property taxes. Well, it has. Their taxes have gone up.

A man who grew up in Highlandtown details the harm Gold Coasters have inflicted on the poor and elderly:

> When all this stuff came about down on Boston Street where they were building all the condos and things along that little Gold Coast that they had set up with the marinas and stuff like that . . . people had money, moving in to buy those condos there on Boston Street. Well, it raised the property values for a lot of the families that have been there for years and senior citizens that are on fixed incomes, and their property taxes went sky high and forced a lot of them to sell, because they couldn't afford them after the property values were raised.

Middle-Class Activists

The idealization of blue-collar families and resentment of Gold Coast newcomers puts middle-class activists in a delicate position. In the 1970s and 1980s they came to Southeast Baltimore to embrace its urbanity and renovated homes in areas like Butcher's Hill. They have become some of the most effective advocates for Southeast social and economic improvement. Yet they enjoy economic comfort while many working-class families live precariously.

Only a little more than a decade ago, these middle-class householders were dubious "gentrifiers." A craftsman who moved to Southeast twenty years ago describes the transformation of Butcher's Hill:

> When I first moved here, Butcher's Hill was the slum, but it had these big mansions with sixteen, seventeen units in it. . . . People with money came in there and bought the whole thing and renovated it, made it back into the old-style mansion, which it was meant to be. But those people up there, they have a different way of thinking than the regular people who are around here.

The blue-collar ethos makes some feel guilty for their advantage. For example, some old-timers refer indiscriminately to middle-class newcomers as "yuppies," a label connoting individualism and self-indulgence that contrast with good-hearted communitarianism. One young urban professional, active in Southeast organizations, handles the term uneasily when asked to compare Fell's Point with other neighborhoods:

> Well, I think, generally speaking, it's probably a little on the higher end, because these are houses that are in the historic district. And, for lack of a better word, sort of yuppies have moved in, though I don't necessarily classify myself that way, but some people would. So there is a little bit more of an income level in this part of the neighborhood that I live in, because it's the area that the city has put some money into the streets and the sidewalks.

Tiptoeing gingerly around the fact that he has more money than a lot of people, he accepts the view that it is not only unusual in Southeast, but perhaps also unseemly or even illegitimate, to be a financially secure professional.

In the end, working-class leaders recognize they share interests with middle-class activists, who can help get outside resources for improvements both groups want, and they join in a practical alliance.

IMPLEMENTING PLANS: TAKING AND MAKING OPPORTUNITIES

With little community wealth, the Planning Council pursued implementation opportunistically, doing what it could get support for. Their early efforts show ways community organizations can influence outside resources, as well as limits on what communities can control.

Implementing a Community Plan

Anticipating Implementation. Implementing the plan depended on getting authority for the planning process and the relationships that went under the name of the Southeast Planning Council.

As task forces proceeded with developing recommendations, the core group met in June 1993 to talk about adoption and implementation. The first agenda item was "What does it mean to adopt this plan?" And the final item, as someone paraphrased it, was "How should we define the institutional framework to take responsibility for the plan . . . implementation capacity?"

A SECO staff member had collected neighborhood plans from around the country for guidance. They reinforced inclinations to have the plan somehow adopted by the Planning Commission, City Council, and/or Mayor. Mayors did not adopt plans, but the Mayor might endorse this one, though endorsement alone would have little effect. The Planning Commission could adopt the plan in conjunction with its physical plans for the City, but Commission actions lacked the force of law. The City Council enacted laws, but implementation of many recommendations depended on action by City departments, which took direction from the Mayor.

Those talking considered Planning Commission support likely, since its staff had aided Council work and the Commission Chair liked the plan. First and Second District Council members had participated in Southeast planning to various degrees and could be expected to be allies. The City Council had urged Southeast to create a community plan, but it was unclear whether Council members felt committed to Southeast by that directive and, if so, what they considered an acceptable response. The Mayor was a question mark. The group felt he favored downtown and the Inner Harbor over neighborhoods. In addition, First District Council members did not always take his side and thus could not be sure of his support. Further, though no one said so, there was the possibility that Kurt Schmoke, a black mayor, would not strongly aid white Southeast Baltimore.

As discussion went on, political calculations alternated with ambiguities about what plan adoption meant and what the plan was. If it were simply a collection of proposals, the Council should try to influence those with the money, time, or power to make them reality. But the plan was also the community's self-appraisal and vision. Crucially, it represented a new coalition of neighborhood associations, interest groups, and community activists. The alliance was broad, though its depth and endurance were untested. Accordingly, those meeting wanted the plan accepted as a definition of the context for the proposals. And they wanted the plan acted on in a way that would strengthen the coalition as part of Southeast's civic infrastructure.

Someone wondered whether there was a way to get political support for the general principle of community planning, of which this plan could be seen as one legitimate example. Framing adoption in that way might divert heated attention from the merits of Southeast interests vis-à-vis the rest of the City while emphasizing how City government benefited from community initiatives in planning.

A consensus emphasized getting Planning Commission endorsement of the plan and mayoral support for specific projects, with uncertainty about a City Council role.

Over the next few months, the Planning Council and its task forces consulted with a widening circle, including public agencies, private firms, developers, elected officials, independent experts, community notables, and nonprofit organizations. Not only did their advice help craft recommendations, but, as their involvement left them impressed with the Council, they became a growing network of supporters.

Fortuitously, the Council had a powerful ally in a high place whose commitment to them they would test: U.S. Senator Barbara Mikulski. One of the original opponents of The Road and an organizer of SECO, later a city councilwoman, after that a member of the U.S. House of Representatives, now, still a Fell's Point homeowner, she chaired the Senate Appropriations subcommittee that controlled the budget of the Department of Housing and Urban Development. After the Southeast Community Plan was released in November, the Council sent her a copy, and when a small delegation met with her at Christmastime, she talked specifically and enthusiastically about it.

Getting the Plan Adopted. The Coordinating Committee settled on two forms of adoption. One, more literal, was endorsement by the Planning Commission. The Planning Director and his staff member who had worked with the Planning Council both respected the outcome. The Commission Chair also liked and supported the plan.

Coordinating Committee members met with Planning staff to draft a resolution, which the Planning Commission passed on January 27, 1994, stating,

1. The Planning Commission agrees to review all proposed zoning and development projects in Southeast Baltimore in the context of the Southeast Community Plan and to include the affected community groups in that review process at the early and ongoing stages of development, and
2. The Planning Commission will utilize the Plan's goals, recommendations and development principals [sic] as an element in its review of the City's Capital Improvement Program, and
3. The Planning Commission will recommend that appropriate City Departments continue to work with the Southeast Planning Council on reviewing the specific recommendations in the implementation of the Plan, and
4. The Planning Commission will encourage all City agencies to review its development and community notification procedures (Baltimore City Planning Commission 1994).

The resolution's impact would depend on the nature of zoning, development, and capital project proposals, but it declared a receptivity to capital proposals to implement the plan, and it contributed to general City support for the plan.

The Planning Council also aimed for the Mayor's endorsement, to add to the plan's authority and to get him to direct City departments to help implement recommendations. The Planning Commission's action, growing publicity for the plan, and, crucially, Senator Mikulski's advocacy with the Mayor encouraged him to meet with Coordinating Committee members in March 1994. He then put the Planning Council on the agenda for a cabinet meeting, held in Southeast Baltimore. The presentation included a handout linking each agency to specific recommendations. At the end, the Mayor urged department heads to talk with Planning Council representatives.

Those meetings developed relationships, though few led to immediate action. For example, the plan recommended assessing Southeast health needs, and the Health Commissioner acknowledged the value of a study, but it required resources not available. In contrast, however, the Housing Commissioner at different times committed Community Development Block Grant funds to adult literacy programs, housing initiatives, and purchase of a building for a teen center.

Raising Money

Implementing the plan meant influencing outside money. One way was to react to others' plans, supporting them when they coincided with community priorities, trying to shape them to fit community needs, or opposing them when they seemed harmful. The other was to encourage outside actors to put money into specific projects, by appealing either to philanthropy or the possibility of political or financial profit.

Taking Opportunities. Whenever possible, the Council took advantage of opportunities that presented themselves. For example, anticipating President Clinton's Empowerment Zone program, the Council advocated including a Southeast industrial park in Baltimore's proposal. That idea, however, quickly died for technical reasons: because the 1990 Census put a Canton public housing project in its own Census tract, the adjacent territory for the industrial park exceeded Empowerment Zone income limits. Eventually, a small area at the west end of Southeast Baltimore was included in the City's application.

Some opportunities were serendipitous. Grants became available for communities like Southeast, entities like the Planning Council, or activities like those recommended in the plan, and the Council or allies applied for them. For example, in March 1994 the Pew Charitable Trusts announced a Neighborhood Preservation Initiative to form partnerships with community foundations to serve "urban neighborhoods threatened by deterioration and decline yet with clear potential for renewal and growth." It emphasized "the talents and commitments of resident volunteers as an important part of local preservation efforts" (Pew Charitable Trusts n.d.).

The Planning Council took Pew's focus on youth as an opportunity for linking several related recommendations. Coordinating Committee members organized a coalition of organizations serving youth and families and worked with the Baltimore Community Foundation on a proposal that included a teen center, a school-to-work program, and other youth social and economic development projects. The Community Foundation, the Goldseker Foundation, and the City committed matching funds. Although the Council did not get the grant, it has continued working with the coalition and foundations to promote the projects in other ways.

In April 1994 the U.S. Department of Education invited universities to apply for an Urban Community Service Program to "work with private and civic organizations to devise and implement solutions to pressing and severe problems in their urban communities" (U.S. Department of Education 1994:15810). The University of Maryland's Community Planning Program, building on relationships developed in conducting the case study presented here, approached the Coordinating Committee to see if faculty and students could help implement the plan.

Eventually the university prepared a proposal including aid creating an industrial park and expanding port-related industries, promoting well-managed owner- and renter-occupied housing in Patterson Park neighborhoods, increasing the use and safety of Patterson Park, and improving education. A five-year grant was awarded in the fall of 1994, though the Republican Congress would try to cut funding.

The Case of South Shore Bank. Another serendipitous opportunity involved South Shore Bank, a Chicago community development bank that revived the South Shore along Lake Michigan. In 1993 the Goldseker Foundation and the Venable, Baetjer and Howard law firm approached Shorebank Advisory Services (SAS), a subsidiary of Shorebank Corporation, about setting up a community development bank in Baltimore. After initial study, SAS recommended considering a target area around Johns Hopkins Medical Institutions, including parts of the Southeast planning area but characterized as "Northeast Baltimore" (Shorebank Advisory Services 1993:2). SAS hired a consultant to manage further study in Baltimore. Goldseker and Venable, Baetjer and Howard organized an East Baltimore Community Development Advisory Committee to weigh and represent local interests and to raise or commit funds if the bank went ahead.

The possibility that South Shore would start a bank in East Baltimore offered an opportunity to implement the recommendation to establish a community development fund, as well as to further the Patterson Park Neighborhoods Initiative. In addition, a local community development bank could increase homeownership generally, in conjunction, perhaps, with the recommended live-near-your-work program. To turn South Shore's explorations toward implementing these recommendations, the

Council had to get recognition as a legitimate, knowledgeable party, persuade the Advisory Committee and Shorebank to set up a financial institution that would make certain kinds of loans, and include Southeast Baltimore in the target area.

Chance and initiative both played roles. In the fall of 1993 a small club of Baltimore urbanists traveled to Chicago to look at development programs there. One had worked in Chicago, knew South Shore staff, and arranged a tour. The Baltimore entourage included several people from Southeast Baltimore, one a Planning Council member, and a Goldseker staff member.

A year later, Shorebank invited people from East Baltimore to see its Chicago operations, and another Planning Council member, associated with the Patterson Park Initiative, went along. As he and others with the Planning Council and SECO got to know Shorebank people better, they advocated extending the target area to include the Southeast planning area. Tacitly, they urged Shorebank and Johns Hopkins, which would have dominant influence over any program, to think of the problems for which a community bank would be the solution in terms that linked their neighborhoods' interests with Hopkins interests.

Hopkins administrators were increasingly concerned that crime around the medical institutions made it hard to attract staff and patients. They saw a community development bank as a way of enabling middle-income staff and others to buy and fix up homes around the campus. Staff would come to Hopkins and feel secure living cheaply nearby, and their presence would make the neighborhoods safer for patients.

Yet such a neighborhood stabilization emphasis would lead to a narrow geographic focus on the area close to Hopkins. Council members made three arguments for expanding boundaries. Two tied to Hopkins interests. The housing market affecting Hopkins, they said, reached beyond the blocks just around the campus. Stabilizing the Hopkins environs would entail managing the area of racial transition south of the institution and past that.

In addition, Council members encouraged Hopkins to think of a community development bank in conjunction with the plan's recommended live-near-your-work/employer-assisted housing program, arguing the staff Hopkins wanted living nearby would be interested in a much larger area than the adjacent blocks. For both reasons, Southeast advocates urged Hopkins to consider all Southeast its community and housing market.

Finally, the Patterson Park Neighborhoods Initiative and SDI's new Southeast Development Initiative in the southern part of Southeast were good examples with respect to Shorebank interests. These projects had sophisticated analyses of local housing markets. They had ties to community networks. They were strongly committed to promoting home-ownership. And they offered good economic models for neighborhood investment. Shorebank would do better financially if it included the more stable areas farther from the medical campus.

A June 1994 Shorebank proposal for "a community development bank for East Baltimore" applauded three "encouraging processes" in East Baltimore. One was cooperation among Hopkins, City government, and African American neighborhood groups around Hopkins in creating the Historic East Baltimore Corporation, which would represent East Baltimore residents in the City's Empowerment Zone. The inclusion of much of East Baltimore in the Empowerment Zone was the second encouragement.

> The third is the very encouraging work, by a range of groups working to improve South East Baltimore, and the adoption in early 1994 of *South East Community Plan: Towards a Future of Hope and Opportunity* (Shorebank Advisory Services 1994:6).

The accompanying target area map stretched through Southeast to the waterfront.

The Planning Council invited the bank's chairman, other staff, and the local consultant to its January 1995 meeting. One aim was to let Shorebank people present their ideas to residents. The other was to impress Shorebank with the Council's community connections and community members' interest and sophistication. No one was disappointed.

Later, the Council members who had visited South Shore in Chicago arranged a housing tour with small contractors, a group Shorebank liked to support. The tour epitomized the Council's assets. Hopkins was essential to creating a bank, because it would provide a major part of the operating capital. However, Hopkins had little community involvement, and past neighborhood relations had often been rancorous. The Council understood the local housing market because it knew the community intimately.

At the same time, Council members showed Hopkins administrators how they could help employees buy neighborhood homes. The Federal National Mortgage Association offers mortgages for 95 percent of housing value, with 3 percent of the purchase price in cash. Two percent can be a gift or loan, for example, from employers, who could give workers low-interest loans to buy nearby, perhaps with requirements to stay for a certain period and provisions to forgive the loan after that. Council members gave Hopkins staff details of a City government program to help employees buy in Baltimore and similar university programs and took staff to see one at the University of Pennsylvania.

When the bank's Baltimore promoters set up the Advisory Committee, most of the thirty members, including a third from Johns Hopkins, represented institutions that would sponsor the bank financially. However, the committee included two each from the Historic East Baltimore Community Action Coalition and the Southeast Planning Council.

Shorebank and the Advisory Committee still needed to agree on a project. Crucial decisions would involve lending terms, any differentiation of terms within the target area, and board membership. So far, boundaries had been extended to include much of the Southeast; the Planning Council was recognized as a community representative, with two members at the table. Even if their formal decision role was small, they had already exercised power based on community knowledge and connections.

Making Opportunities. Many plan recommendations depended on creating opportunities, interesting others in actions that had never occurred to them. For example, one recommendation advocated revitalizing the Highlandtown business district, and another called for a Canton/Highlandtown housing initiative. They fit together as community development strategies but required significant funding.

To advance the first recommendation, the Planning Council got a grant from the National Trust for Historic Preservation for a Main Street consultation on Eastern Avenue, the center of Highlandtown's business district, and some Council members joined a Highlandtown planning task force.

At the same time, as people began to think about a Canton/Highlandtown housing initiative, during the summer of 1994, a city councilman who had worked on Senator Mikulski's staff called on her. At his prompting, she persuaded the Neighborhood Reinvestment Corporation to put up money for a Southeast housing initiative. With her urging, the Mayor added Community Development Block Grant funds.

Quickly, before people had clear ideas about what a housing initiative should do, $500,000 was available. In intense, sometimes hurried meetings, parties interested in housing and business development discussed and negotiated purposes and responsibilities. The result was the Southeast Development Initiative, administered by Southeast Development, Incorporated, combining business and housing development. Because PPNI already got Block Grant funds for its catchment area, SDI's homeownership activities were tied to the southern part of Southeast. While the two initiatives market different areas, they have members on each other's boards and consult on general strategies for promoting Southeast.

SDI hired consultants to develop and implement a housing marketing plan. Smith, Mead and Associates surveyed recent homebuyers, held focus groups with realtors and lenders, and interviewed community leaders to identify target groups for Southeast housing. The firm prepared promotional materials. SDI set up housing counseling and offered 5 percent closing cost loans to reduce cash requirements for getting a mortgage. Eighteen of the first seventy-five clients bought homes in Southeast.

SDI began working with a group of preferred realtors who were committed to promoting Southeast homeownership. Educating agents about the attractions of the area, SDI encouraged them to sell to families that would settle in Southeast, rather than investors who would treat the properties only as income sources.

SDI's economic development staff offered firms assistance in preparing business plans, marketing their services, and solving other problems.

Still, families will have to find Canton and Highlandtown more attractive than the County, and many will be evaluating schools as well as housing stock. Would-be entrepreneurs will need start-up capital to go with good ideas. Any businesses will have to find Highlandtown more attractive than other parts of the City or suburban malls. Moreover, they will find the odds more favorable if they see other firms simultaneously taking a new chance on the declining business district. SDI incentives can affect the balance in economic calculations, but others, involving social assessments and loyalty, are harder to affect.

The benefits of having an ally like Senator Mikulski are obvious here, where public funds can create implementation incentives. In contrast, implementing a live-near-your-work/employer-assisted housing program requires persuading private firms community interests are business interests.

Managing the Community Economy

Although implementation was opportunistic, each project had a rationale as a strategy for community development. Youth programs would make the next generation emotionally stronger, socially more competent, and better educated. Homeownership programs would give more people economic and social stakes in the community. Economic development programs would bring more money into the area, enable more to buy homes, and provide more stable conditions for young people.

Seen as an approach to managing the Southeast economy, early implementation efforts had two emphases. One, simply, was to increase community wealth in any way possible. Job creation, business promotion, community development banking, homeownership, and housing renovation would all bring money into Southeast and increase the value of living there. They would raise the tide to lift all boats.

Second, consistently, many initiatives focused on recruiting new residents with higher incomes. The South Shore Bank and employer-assisted housing efforts aimed to increase the number of homeowners. Smith, Mead found 75 percent of new Southeast homebuyers had annual household incomes above the Southeast median around $23,000 (Smith, Mead, n.d.). Most new homeowners would probably come from outside the community (see Smith, Mead, n.d.), and they would directly or indirectly displace lower-income renters.

These first implementation initiatives made sense as a strategy for community economic development. Yet they put greater value on some persons over others: those with incomes that could pay for homes. The scarcity of community resources pushed the Planning Council, whatever members' personal preferences, toward serving those with more before, if not necessarily instead of, those with less.

MONEY AND IMPLEMENTATION

Southeast implementation differs from The Associated's in three related ways. First Southeast planning started three years later, and this account leaves implementation there at an earlier stage. Even so, the scarcity of resources, including the loss of staff, held back implementation.

Second, differences in community wealth affected the role of wealth as a topic in and influence on the planning process. At The Associated, people talked openly about wealth, largely because there was a lot to talk about. Southeast planners talked more about the absence of wealth but, nevertheless, drew economic distinctions among community members. In both cases, people in a broadly defined middle class were concerned about others at an end of the economic continuum. In the Jewish community tension turned on the influence of the wealthy, whereas in the economically vulnerable Southeast it focused on that of the poor, as renters.

At The Associated, community wealth directed implementation inward, whereas in Southeast implementation turned outward. Hence the story of Southeast implementation is more about people outside the community. It is tricky to compare the complexity or difficulty of the problems the two communities faced: Is it harder to instill deep Jewish identity in the next generations or to increase homeownership in Southeast Baltimore? Neither is it straightforward to measure how much each community's problems are subject to its control: Is it easier for the Southeast Planning Council to control regional, national, and international economic changes that remove manufacturing from central cities, or for The Associated to modulate the forces of modernity that dissolve religion and ethnicity?

Still, a third difference is that Southeast's limited resources and dependence on the intentions of strangers make implementation much more tenuous. Not only could The Associated easily fund many of the Southeast service recommendations, but the federation and agencies have staffs with time to do the planning and strategizing that must precede implementation. Southeast Planning Council members spearheading implementation have experience and sophistication, but they are few, most of them have full-time employment, even if implementing the plan sometimes fits into their job responsibilities, and they have no overall staff coordination or support.

Nevertheless, the Planning Council has begun to implement recommendations, and the reasons offer lessons for other community organizations with few economic resources. Central to their success has been leadership. A small core group carefully designed the planning process, organized meetings, coordinated cluster groups, design workshops, and task forces, and moved these activities toward production of a plan and, after that, implementation. They had a relatively clear, if occasionally changing, vision of a Southeast community plan that guided decisions about what groups should meet when and what the groups should do. They consistently shared this vision with participants. They persistently pushed the process ahead.

The leaders repeatedly invited people to join planning. As a result, about three hundred persons from dozens of community groups attended meetings, discussed problems, and proposed remedies. They not only provided valuable ideas, but also gave planning authority. Community groups came to feel the process represented them. Equally important, as time went on, outsiders, in government, foundations, and other institutions, accorded the Council growing legitimacy as a voice for Southeast interests.

These leaders organized not only people, but also ideas. With staff help, they analyzed data, studied programs elsewhere, and consulted with experts to define problems and develop proposals. Research presentations at planning meetings often persuaded community members to take common views of their conditions. Carefully reasoned, empirically based proposals gave the Council authority with outside implementors and funders.

The leadership group took initiatives. When planning got stuck, they tried new directions. They went to outsiders for help. They consulted with potential implementors while planning. When time came for implementation, they used their relationships to get to public officials, foundation staff, and anyone else who could help generate support.

They parlayed success into other successes. Each time they got a grant, they built on both the work it paid for and the recognition it gave in soliciting further support.

Finally, Senator Mikulski offered crucial support, especially when implementation started.

Conclusions

Southeast Baltimore and the Jewish community view and value wealth within different economic, social, and cultural frameworks. But in both those who have more have higher status than those who have less, and those who have less often resent those who have more money, status, and power.

For different reasons, planning activists in both communities generally have higher incomes than many others in the community. The link at The Associated is direct: donors make decisions. The Planning Council connection is more subtle: college-educated, middle-class professionals are most likely to have the formal education, cognitive style and skills, confidence, and time to take part in planning. Yet the effects are similar. Planning reflects perspectives and interests of activists with relatively higher incomes (see Cnaan 1991).

In Associated strategic planning, wealthy participants acted with a consciousness of their wealth and interests. They sought to rationalize their influence and reoriented programs to meet the needs of the economically successful. Southeast planning activists held no such thoughts of their own class interests. Yet, confronting a weak community economy, they moved toward building up the middle class. They might have preferred otherwise, but they had fewer choices than The Associated.

PART 5

Continuing the Community

CHAPTER 16

Continuing the Jewish Community: Older Generations and Younger Generations

Southeasterners worried about their community's survival. Planning, they hoped, would bring a good-enough future, where, despite many losses, they could find ways to sustain themselves. Jews have often worried about their survival, but The Associated did not start planning with any sense of crisis. Yet planning entails thinking about the future, and events raised questions about Jewish continuity. The next two chapters look at how these communities thought about and planned for their futures.

As The Associated moved to implementation, data from the 1990 National Jewish Population Survey were released (Kosmin et al. 1991). Every account emphasized that 52 percent of Jews who married between 1985 and 1990 had non-Jewish spouses. The percentage had risen for decades. Of those who married before 1965, only 9 percent married non-Jews (Kosmin et al. 1991:14).[1] Further, only 28 percent of children of mixed marriages were being raised as Jews (Kosmin et al. 1991:16).

Around the country, "52 percent" became shorthand for trends portending a sharp decline in the Jewish population.[2] The Council of Jewish Federations urged local federations to plan for "Jewish continuity." The *Journal of Jewish Communal Service* devoted its summer 1992 issue to the survey. The title of one section put the issue graphically: "Jewish Continuity—Will Our Grandchildren be Jewish?"

References to "our grandchildren" not only concretized concerns about continuity, but also established an emotional premise that both enabled discussion and seemed to assure success. The language of family was unifying because everyone belongs to a family. Not only did it identify adults as parents, but it invoked and evoked the deepest human feelings: love, it implied, could bridge or avoid a generational break.

The phrase "Jewish continuity" itself encouraged assumptions and feelings of harmony. "Continuity" implied older generations were all right, and their task was simply to pass on their beliefs and practices to the young. Just as having children is in the natural order of things, parental love could directly produce not only Jewish children, but Jewish grandchildren.

DYNAMICS OF GENERATIONAL RELATIONS

The older generations concerned about continuity identify strongly with the community, though they hold widely ranging views of Jewish identity and community. They are probably affiliated with The Associated, a synagogue, or, most likely, both. They see a threat to their community, not in the wrath of an enemy, but in the tolerance of the larger society. They worry that Jewish community membership has become voluntary and fear the young will not identify with the community. Associated activists are concerned that philanthropists' children will stop giving to the federation.

These older members want the young to affiliate with the community. As we have seen, many regard the unaffiliated ambivalently, wishing them to join but also fearing and disdaining them as possible traitors. Putting affiliation in generational terms changes its emotional valence. Younger-generation family members are seen as affiliated or affiliable. Whereas the affiliated are ambivalent about the unaffiliated, older generations care about and invest in younger generations.

Anxiety about Assimilation

Intermarriage is the most consequential act of assimilation into the larger society. It is also a departure from Baltimore patterns. It raises disturbing questions of continuity in an old Jewish community, where some families go back six or seven generations and where federation leadership has rested comfortably in the hands of a small number of families.

Some Orthodox, emphasizing their lower (albeit rising) intermarriage rate, argue the problem belongs to the non-Orthodox, as one rabbi says: "There is hardly a family in the Reform or Conservative movement where there isn't a mixed marriage." He exaggerates, but many, particularly non-Orthodox, see enough in their own families to worry. "Maybe," a federation leader says, accepting responsibility,

> we are failing the younger generation in infusing Jewish commitment. I am very troubled by intermarriage, the lack of any affiliation. It is a matter of survival, the perpetuation of the species. In my day you didn't marry a non-Jew.

Another measures the odds of Jewish continuity in his own family:

> I can't predict the future. I don't want to predict it. I wouldn't like what I saw. My son married a non-Jewish woman. She didn't convert, but she

agreed to bring up the children Jewish. As of now, I haven't gained anything, but I haven't lost anything either.

Older leaders worry about not only intermarriage, but also growing involvement in the larger society. Many recall hostility and discrimination in Baltimore and doubt the Gentile society will truly accept their children. In addition, leaders who have given years of their lives to Jewish communal service both worry who will carry on their work and feel rejected by children who show little interest.

Many leaders are proud when their children continue to be committed to community service but chagrined when the community is not Jewish. These philanthropists' children are like others in Jewish communities elsewhere (Mayer 1988; Tobin 1992). Their choices affect the continuity of the overall Jewish community and the federation community.

A woman reflects on how her children encounter a different world than the one she grew up in. She notes many generations in her family have been active in the Jewish community, but, as for her children,

> I am very concerned about that. We are concerned. Nationally there is great concern. . . . My oldest daughter said, "Mom, you will have to recognize that your children will express their Jewishness differently." We are trying to use different strategies to involve our next generation. . . .
>
> Are we appealing to enough young? No. One reason is, they are more interested in social causes. When I and my generation were younger, the general community was not open to us. And these young people go to the general community and shoot to the top. And they are not willing to wait in line at The Associated. This is true [that you need to work your way up at the federation]. And we are not going to change that.

An Associated staff member adds to the picture:

> The younger generation will not buy in the way their parents did. We are competing with other communities. At one time we were the only game in town. Now they choose between being active in the Jewish community and the Baltimore Symphony and the Walters.

Still, the Symphony and the Walters, though outside the Jewish community, are traditional objects of Jewish philanthropy. Beyond them, many of the young have more interest in "social causes," as another leader comments:

> Younger people are growing up in this world where the issues of homelessness are far more prevalent today. . . . They focus on it more than I do. I've got a kid who works in a soup kitchen. He will do that instead of working with The Associated.

A federation activist speaks of his children's generation:

Their interests . . . are different. They are more concerned about AIDS
than a sixty-year-old, because for them it is a reality, while for a sixty-
year-old it concerns someone else.

Jewish tradition includes the obligation of *tikkun olam*, "repair of the
world," an admonition to do social justice to make the world whole.
Some Jews consider social activism a basic expression of Judaism (Fein
1988). Yet, a woman active in both the Jewish and larger communities
laments, many of the young see no Jewish basis for their civic involvement:

I worry a lot. They are very far from the Holocaust. They don't associate any kind of social activism with being Jewish. If they are marching
for Planned Parenthood, there is nothing Jewish about it. Or child abuse.
Sarah Glickman [a young activist at The Associated] feels it is important
to have social issues on the women's agenda. She says women want it. I
have mixed feelings about it.

Federation leaders get their children appointed to boards or involved
in other Associated activities, to stimulate their interest. Some children
take up their parents' cause. Others are inactive. Some do not want to
work their way up a hierarchy when they can have quick influence and
prominence elsewhere.

Wealthy children may be glad to write checks, but, as the head of a
prominent family observes, they often dislike leaving their families to
attend meetings or make speeches. This comment points to another generational change affecting communal activism. Young women are much
more likely than their mothers to have professional careers, usually in the
larger community. Women of earlier generations managed the household, enabling their husbands to participate in civic activities. In wealthy
families, women were also expected to be professional volunteers, usually
in a women's division. Younger career women have little time either to
manage the household to let their husbands participate in communal
activities or to take part themselves.

The woman who remarks on the distance of the Holocaust from the
young alludes to the emotional meanings of these changes. She believes
Jews must stay together to defend against a future Holocaust. But, more
than that, many who witnessed the Holocaust feel all Jews owe it to the
dead to redeem them by participating in and strengthening the Jewish
community.

The federation leader who says "we are failing the younger generation in infusing Jewish commitment" acknowledges the responsibility
many feel for their children's choices. Because they did not do enough to
make Jewish life meaningful and attractive, their children moved into
the larger community.

But there is another way to see the children's actions. Their parents and grandparents wanted to be Americans (Fein 1971). They only worried, on the basis of old European experiences or new Maryland ones, whether they would be accepted. The distance from the Holocaust has different meanings for the generations. The old fear the young will forget its warning about the illusions of assimilation, whereas the young see a world that is, at last, safe.

All the same, those hovering on the community's boundaries, who superficially affiliate or do not affiliate, threaten community members politically, financially, and psychologically. Parents who wanted their children to make it in the larger society may feel guilt for this unintended result.

Concern about Jewish Continuity

Hence older generations, anxious about their children's and grandchildren's choices, commit themselves to "Jewish continuity." While this effort affirms something positive about Jewish life, it leads to the question of what to continue.

The traditional answer is religion. Its proponents want the younger generations to observe rituals, acquire religious knowledge, and take on the beliefs—and even faith—that arise from and motivate observance. An Associated leader asserts, "Jewish continuity is part of Jewish values and beliefs." Another says he would like to hear someone say, "I like this rabbi, and I will go to synagogue next week." Or, a third adds, "I will light Shabbat [Sabbath] candles."

Yet, if Baltimore Jews are like others nationally, the declining Jewishness of the younger generations is a continuation of the older generations' patterns, not a break with them. Cohen finds both diminishing ritual observance and communal affiliation from older to younger Jews (1988:60). Comparing first, second, third, and fourth generations, he finds steadily declining ritual observance, synagogue membership, affiliation with Jewish organizations, and contribution to Jewish charities, as well as movement from Orthodox and Conservative to Reform and "other" denominations (1988:44).

However, within this trend, parents' observance matters. Highly observant, more likely Orthodox, parents generally succeed in transmitting their level of observance to their children. Moderately observant parents' children, as a whole, observe less than their parents. At the same time, many children of minimally observant and nonobservant parents seem to "bottom out," holding on to some rituals or adding a few (1988:75–81).

In other words, if Baltimore is like other American Jewish communities, "Jewish continuity" as an ideal defined religiously would require discontinuity with these trends. In fact, mainly the Orthodox define continuity in strictly religious terms. Many non-Orthodox offer views of continuity that emphasize ethnicity, culture, customs, and social relations.

Those who think of Jewish continuity in these terms want the younger generations to identify with other Jews and to involve themselves in Jewish institutions and society. An Associated leader puts this position succinctly: "The basic bottom line is Jewish continuity: 'I am so glad I am Jewish.'" She does not specify what this feeling should be based on, nor does she require that it be accompanied by particular practices.

Those who take the ethnic view are pluralists. They recognize diverse ways of being Jewish and acting Jewishly. Often they value religion, though they may not be observant themselves. They consider synagogues one of many community institutions, alongside restaurants, bookstores, social agencies, schools, and cultural centers.

In private, many non-Orthodox speak ethnically in describing their Jewish identity and what they transmit to their children. They observe fewer and fewer rituals, and faith is elusive. But they live and socialize with other Jews, think of themselves as Jews, and identify with the Jewish community.

Still, on the record, many of them talk of Jewish continuity religiously. Few have confidence a diluted ethnicity can carry the community for a long time. Many are not sure how they differ from non-Jews other than in their choice of neighbors and friends. Moreover, many feel those who emphasize religion represent the essence of Judaism.

In addition, religion is an apt American answer. Given a choice between being an ethnic group or a religion, most find it safer to be a religion (Elazar 1976). America was created as a religious nation. Though there would be no established church, everyone was expected to belong to some church. The churches would inculcate common moral teachings that would foster social harmony.

Periods of ethnic acceptance or pride notwithstanding, America has been wary of ethnic groups. They arouse suspicion for insisting on separate attachments. They participate in politics uncompromisingly: there is no middle ground between electing or giving patronage to a German or a Pole—or, to use a clear contemporary example, a black or a white. The metaphor of the melting pot declared war on ethnicity, taking it as an alien loyalty. Common schools and settlement houses were designed to Americanize immigrants by scraping away foreign origins.

Jews are sensitive to charges of dual loyalty. When they are seen as an ethnic group tied to Jews in Israel or elsewhere, some question their attachment to the United States. Jews are considered safer Americans when they are only a religious group. Religion, unlike ethnicity, is usually private. Churches and synagogues neither compete with the larger society for individuals' fidelity nor intrude into public affairs.[3]

Denominations differ, but they are assumed to teach a common ethic, often characterized with homogenizing hyphenation as "the Judeo-Christian tradition." In fact, many in the older generations found a melting pot with three compartments, what Herberg (1955) called the "triple melting pot." Every American became Jewish, Protestant, or Catholic. This is what the federation leader quoted earlier meant when he said,

> I don't think it is important whether a person is Jewish, Catholic, or Protestant. I happened to be born Jewish, and so I participate in the Jewish community.

Thus many Baltimore Jews consider religion essential to "Jewish continuity," even though they disagree about its importance. An Orthodox rabbi recognizes "Jewish continuity" means different things to different groups, including The Associated and synagogues, but he asserts the Orthodox view: "For us it means halachically committed. . . . We carry a heavy load to guarantee continuity of the Orthodox community." A federation staff member replies, "We need to learn from the Orthodox success in Jewish continuity with your children."

Yet a non-Orthodox leader offers the response of those who emphasize ethnicity:

> There are some who think Jewish continuity will be helped by becoming an observant Jew. My greatest complaint, concern about Jewish education is, we don't tell young people about what is the big deal about being Jewish. . . . Rabbis think of being Jewish in terms of religion. For me, being Jewish is a way of life. Fasting [on Yom Kippur, which I do,] doesn't make me more Jewish. The Ten Commandments as a way of life. I can be the most zealous practitioner of halacha and still be a crook. I am very concerned about religion generally. If you look around the world today, there are very few conflicts that are not religiously motivated.

The lowest common denominator for those who take an ethnic view is identification with the community, as with the lay leader who wants to hear more people say, "I am so glad I am Jewish."

Yet the religious find this position inadequate. It does not derive from specific knowledge or commitment. A rabbi answers someone who has talked about how good she felt observing a traditional Jewish ceremony:

> You emphasize that a group of Jews gathered for a minyan [a gathering of ten or more men for prayer]. You have feelings about what they were doing. Our definitions of Jewish continuity shouldn't be based on *feelings*. We should [emphasize] what Jews should be *doing* if we win at the continuity game.

Planning for Jewish continuity would test these positions and the possibility of finding common ground.

PLANNING FOR JEWISH CONTINUITY

When the Commission on Jewish Education talked about Jewish continuity, members quickly locked into opposing sides, divided roughly between Orthodox and non-Orthodox. Anxiously avoiding conflict, people shied away from volatile issues, even at the cost of not planning. When the Joint Commission on Associated-Synagogue Relations[4] was asked to plan for Jewish continuity, there was no reason to expect it could escape these splits, and yet it apparently did.

To be sure, the Joint Commission's first meetings, in early 1992, were acrimonious. Rabbis and synagogue leaders complained The Associated lured wealthy and talented people with more glamorous rewards than synagogues could offer. At the same time, they argued, synagogues made the community Jewish, and the federation did not recognize this debt. Associated leaders, in turn, impatiently attacked synagogue representatives for creating division: those present were involved in synagogues and the federation and should be loyal to both.

Part of this conflict grew from Orthodox–non-Orthodox differences, but most, as the rationale for the commission suggested, reflected differences between a civil institution and religious institutions. Some from the synagogues considered the openness of the disagreements a refreshingly honest moment, but Associated staff worried dispute would alienate federation participants.

In response, the commission chair opened the next meeting by announcing three focused subcommittees. The Jewish Continuity Subcommittee would develop joint synagogue-federation projects to promote continuity. A second would look at how community organizations could implement those projects, and a third would consider how to get needed resources. We follow the Jewish Continuity Subcommittee.

The Jewish Continuity Subcommittee

The Jewish Continuity Subcommittee was set up with seventeen members, six of whom, including two rabbis, were affiliated with Orthodox congregations. Most of these were modern Orthodox, though modern Orthodox rabbis are politically responsive to traditional colleagues. Most members were younger than those on the Commission on Jewish Education. In addition, whereas two-thirds of Commission members were men, nine of seventeen Subcommittee members were women. Although the federation and synagogues each designated members, and even though the committee had federation and synagogue co-chairs, nearly everyone had taken part in both worlds. While getting synagogue and federation people to talk with one another was the rationale for the Joint Commission, and even though early meetings were sometimes bitter, in this Subcommittee these roles quickly lost importance, and people focused on promoting "Jewish continuity."

Members represented an intermediate generation. They saw themselves as a rising generation of Associated leadership. Some were children of senior leaders. At the same time, they had their own children and thought of themselves as both immediately and generally responsible for the community's next generation.

They shared some of the older leaders' worries. One was that many children in wealthy families did not participate in Jewish institutions. More broadly, they were concerned that many in their generation did not identify strongly with the Jewish community and did not pass on either religious practice or ethnic identity. They saw their task ambitiously: they would define what members of a properly continued Jewish community should do and be, and they would find ways of promoting this continuity.

Defining Jewish Continuity and the Community

Talk at the first Subcommittee meeting moved fluidly, though without clear aim, around definitions of "Jewish continuity," until a rabbi suggested listing "behaviors" that would signify continuity. At once, an Orthodox woman invoked the generational link with "children's Jewish education." Others rapidly called out the following items, recorded on an easel:

- majority of children have visited Israel [suggested by an Orthodox woman]
- synagogue membership [non-Orthodox staff male]
- attend synagogue [non-Orthodox rabbi]
- lower intermarriage rate [Orthodox rabbi]
- lifetime Jewish education [non-Orthodox staff male]
- contributing to the federation [non-Orthodox woman]
- and other Jewish philanthropy [same woman]
- families celebrating Jewish holidays [non-Orthodox woman]
- and life cycle events [same woman]
- Jewish home observance [non-Orthodox staff male]
- Jewish leaders and Jewish organizations providing exemplary role models for society, the world [Orthodox woman]

- actively contributing to tikkun olam beyond financial giving [Orthodox woman]
- synagogue attendance, active participation in Jewish life [non-Orthodox woman]
- ethics [non-Orthodox man].

The man mentioning "ethics" told a story about friends who adopted a boy and did not circumcise him, as required by Jewish law; this, he said, was an ethical problem. Not coincidentally, it was also a breach of the generational chain. Following this theme, a woman observed, "The birth or adoption of a child is a wonderful opportunity" to affirm continuity, through, "for example, the choice of a name" that remembers a deceased family member. Another woman emphasized people should "participate in meaningful formal and informal Jewish education at all life cycle stages."

A rabbi invoked "Torah" as a guide to Jewish education, but the woman speaking next built on previous comments: "We want something about the family." A liberal rabbi called attention to the diversity of family forms. For example, "Where do single people and couples without children fit in?" A woman abruptly retorted, "They don't. There is no continuity with these people." Consistently, a male staff member suggested "increasing the Jewish birthrate." However, one woman, thinking of converts, mentioned "more Jews by choice." The woman who had just insisted on transmission through children summarized the discussion with "community support for Jewish families."

The next meeting began with a staff definition of "Jewish continuity." An Orthodox rabbi praised it but asked why five paragraphs were necessary. It would be enough to say "making sure our children and grandchildren are Jewish." Others endorsed the text until another rabbi complained it was in secular federation language, ignoring spirituality. Everyone agreed on this point, a group was designated to revise the definition, and discussion turned to groups "at risk" of not meeting the terms of continuity suggested at the first meeting.

After much talk, a rabbi argued for focusing on "families with children":

> They meet the criterion of rich with opportunity. They are not the group at greatest risk, perhaps. But they are at the point in life when their faith community becomes important or doesn't become important. It is the do-or-die time about what kind of Jew you will become. . . . Jewish continuity [means] children and grandchildren will be Jewish.

Another rabbi advocated for single persons:

Survivability risk and continuity opportunity. Many singles are not interested in marrying and are not having children. I want to emphasize that these single people are children of very committed Jewish families.

The committee agreed to look at both groups.

Nevertheless, at the third meeting, when the Subcommittee turned to programs to promote continuity among target groups, members focused on families with young children, unambiguously taking the position the community continued itself by bearing and rearing children. With this population in mind, members discussed family camps, seminars on college issues for parents and young adults, a program to educate families about *tzedakah* and contributing to the federation, and scholarships for family trips to Israel.

Afterwards, the co-chairs concluded members were most interested in developing family camps and asked staff to research these camps for the next meeting. The fourth meeting opened with presentations on family camps, leading into principles for a model camp to be jointly sponsored by The Associated and synagogues. The discussion was characterized by much good-willed, easy-flowing talk toward what members saw as the successful completion of their mission.

A Family Camp

A staff member set out the premises relating family camps and Jewish continuity:

> Jewish family education is based on a very simple idea: identity is shaped in the home. All lifetime behavior is patterned after parental roles. . . . Jewish education views the parent and child as the target to educate. Education directed only at the child that is not reinforced in the home is not very effective. We as parents have to be involved. It is our Jewish heritage. . . . We as parents need Jewish education as well. That is why a Jewish family camp setting really lends itself to it. . . . Spending a lot of time together as a family. . . . There is a balance between study, recreation, inspirational moments, prayer. It creates a sense of community. . . . There is one caveat: it is not an end in itself. It is a jump-start experience.

Ensuing discussion had two themes, one about generational continuity within families, the other about community.

Regarding families, the staff member identified herself and committee members as parents, an older generation taking responsibility for a younger generation. And yet, she acknowledged, parents often did not know enough to continue the community alone; they, too, needed attention. As committee members endorsed these premises, they took the view that the camp's aim would be to repair families, both generations together. The federation, its agencies, and synagogues would temporarily take over and model parental roles while teaching parents how to fulfill obligations of the older generation. The institutions would aid families by offering the first installment in lifetime learning.

Discussion of camp location elaborated assumptions about an ideal, albeit temporary, community that would help families continue themselves and, in turn, the larger community. Committee members quickly agreed the camp should be in the country. It was important that families remove themselves from everyday work, school, and home surroundings to have the freedom to think extraordinary, transcendent thoughts and glimpse possibilities for deeper relationships.

In considering target groups for the program, committee members articulated an inclusive model of community. Denominational differences did not divide them, and they believed the camp should, and could, include Orthodox and non-Orthodox. Differences in eating and ritual practices could be accommodated, and the camp would thus let Orthodox and non-Orthodox learn about each others' beliefs. A rabbi named Orthodox, Conservative, and Reform congregations whose members would get along and could be invited to the first camp to demonstrate possibilities for interdenominational community.

The meeting adjourned with general satisfaction.

Continuity through Fantastic Families

At the end of the first meeting, committee members remarked on the easy flow of discussion. Perhaps, some suggested, it resulted from the group composition—except for one young man and an older man, all young women and rabbis. The implication was that women are better than men at seeing common interests and reaching agreements. There is also another way to consider the meeting's sexual makeup: looking at the young women in relation to the rabbis.

The discussion between the young women and rabbis resembled the ease and deference of daughter–father talks. At least symbolically, and perhaps unconsciously, the deliberation on Jewish continuity was a dialogue between an older generation and a younger generation. The absence of "mothers" avoided potential sources of generational conflict. Whatever the conversation's overt content, its flow enacted generational continuity.

This relationship can be seen in the dual themes of the list of "behaviors" for Jewish continuity. One was religious: ritual observance, study, and synagogue participation. One might wonder why these people, few of whom studied or observed as much as the list called for, might, nevertheless, define continuity in these terms. Such "continuity" would require change. One explanation is the authority of religious definitions of the

Jewish people. Another, undoubtedly, was the rabbis' presence, even though, as the mention of "Torah" showed, lay members did not necessarily take the rabbis' counsel.

The inattention to the rabbi's remark sheds some light on the ease of conversation: it seems moved in part by fantasy. Perhaps at some level it was a fantasy of daughters saying what they imagined fathers wanted to hear, even if they had no intention of doing what fathers might want. Closer to the surface, there was a fantasy of gaining the rabbis' approval for being good Jews by giving the "correct" (religious) answers to questions about Jewish continuity, even if the responses did not reflect participants' lives.

The other theme in the discussion was family—beginning with children's Jewish education, moving through intergenerational religious observance, encouraging having more children, and ending with support for all Jewish families. Much of this had little specific link to the religious standards for continuity. It is compatible with an ethnic view of Jewish life, where religion is part of identity. In addition, it introduced values important to committee members in their lives.

It would be reductionistic to characterize the "family" talk as merely women speaking about having and raising children. Still, the exciting discussion began and ended with children. On the one hand, the women, Orthodox and non-Orthodox alike, listed religious "behaviors" they might assume the rabbis would approve, and which, in various degrees, they enacted, but they talked most easily of family matters, including, finally, a family camp. These women, who had high-powered careers and were community activists, were also literally reproducing the community in their families. The ease of discussion probably reflected pride in this fact. Perhaps the talk also represented an unconscious fantasy that the symbolic pairing of the young women and rabbis would produce good religious offspring.[5]

In any case, the family camp was largely the creation of young women and rabbis, with staff help. The absence of symbolic "sons" may have eased conversation. However, in realistic planning terms, it was hard to know whether young men, who were fathers, were interested in family camps. At the fourth meeting, several women joked about how much trouble they had dragging their husbands away from work to anything like these camps. The committee made a proposal without a need assessment.

They did not know, for example, who would be interested in such a camp. Nor did they know who would want to increase their religious knowledge or ritual observance. They did not discuss their own knowledge or observance, to see how they compared with the standards they articulated, and to understand why, where they diverged, someone might choose differently. In short, as planners, they knew little about what shaped the religious behavior of those they wanted to influence. They could be confident of getting an enrollment for the camp, but they could not be sure who would come or how they would be affected.

In part, the situation reflected lay leaders' federation role. They provide general ideas, and staff flesh them out. Because committee members can be big contributors, staff are interested less in testing suggestions against data, standards, and alternatives than in finding ways to make them workable.

The camp might change some families in ways its proponents wished, and it would thus be an incremental success in a larger effort. Yet the federation and synagogues' first joint proposal to continue the community grew on fantasies of harmony. Conceptualizing community continuity in terms of family continuity emphasized what is the same among Orthodox and non-Orthodox: they have families. But there are real differences.

Overcoming Differences

Committee members expected the camp to overcome religious differences. When they considered whom to recruit, a staff member asked, "Could we develop programs of religious observance that would appeal to all?" and a rabbi confidently answered,

> If it were an open-ended invitation, that would be discouraging. . . . If we targeted congregations that we thought would be compatible, that would be a model.

When he named the three congregations whose members might get along, someone asked uncertainly, "How do you see three congregations with three rabbis for a weekend?" Quickly he answered, "It is the ideal community model."

The camp would overcome other differences. When discussing finances, members recognized a camp would be expensive and felt it should pay for itself. They wanted people to pay enough to make a commitment to the experience but also wanted the camp within reach for a wide range of families. Addressing these dilemmas, a member suggested variable fees, a staff person endorsed "a scholarship component," and another member called for "a sliding scale." Still, someone voiced "a concern":

> we will get the end that can pay, and we will get the end that can't pay, through subsidy. What we will miss is the middle—synagogue members who would never ask for money.

Sympathetically, further discussion suggested "patrons," "sponsors," and other arrangements to ensure not only that any family could afford to come, but also that the camp would model *tzedakah* between wealthy and nonwealthy. The reference to "patrons" was perhaps not accidental: in casting the wealthy as "fathers" to the nonwealthy, it was still another family metaphor that dissolved differences and unified groups.

In the end, one group remained outside the "ideal community model": the unaffiliated. The committee briefly discussed whether to recruit them, and someone active in both the federation and a synagogue settled the question in this way:

> I want to say something in terms of participants. We are the Joint Commission on Associated-*Synagogue* Relations. So obviously we are targeting people affiliated with synagogues. But further down the line we should invite unaffiliated people, and have a group of rabbis there.

Later, they might be brought together with a group of rabbis, who, as symbolic fathers, could move them to join the community. Still once more, Subcommittee members imagined family relations to overcome social divisions.

The family camp's significance must be emphasized: this was the first joint proposal of The Associated and synagogue representatives aimed at "Jewish continuity." Centrally, it was a creative compromise between Orthodox and non-Orthodox positions. Traditional Orthodox would not go along with its pluralistic worship, and the Orthodox congregation proposed for the first session was modern. But Orthodox would approve an emphasis on Jewish education that included religious observance, even if brief. And, not at all incidentally, the camp would remove families from the city: it affirmed the Orthodox view that a community could thrive only by isolating itself from modern life. Committee members designed a program that gave participants in modernity a moment aside to find faith.

In most talk about the community, the Orthodox–non-Orthodox split represented the greatest danger. By imagining the camp to overcome this difference, committee members could envision—and promulgate the vision of—a unitary community. Other differences also seemed to melt away. The camp represented more than an "ideal community model" within a larger, divided community: it seemed to transform the community into the ideal.

The Jewish Continuity Subcommittee mirrored Associated and synagogue activists' images of their community. They expressed shared hopes, and they joined in common defenses against shared anxieties about the dangers of recognizing and exploring differences. Fantasies of easy generational continuity let them avoid facing the reasons for splits between Orthodox and non-Orthodox. They also avoided examining why continuation of the contemporary community would not lead to the "Jewish continuity" they framed in religious terms. They affirmed an emotional unity between generations, but they sidestepped the challenges of creating realistic ways for Orthodox and non-Orthodox, wealthy and nonwealthy, and affiliated and unaffiliated to identify and live with one another in a Jewish community.

Family language played an important role in this planning effort. References to children and grandchildren forced attention to the future. They enabled people to move past present conflicts to an open time period. And yet this mental act, which allowed people to imagine the potential rather than get stuck in the seemingly intractable, also encouraged them to believe anything might be possible by thinking it so. It let people simultaneously imagine their grandchildren would be acceptably Jewish and displace responsibility for resolving denominational and other conflicts onto them.

TAKING STOCK

The story of Associated strategic planning is many stories. One is an account of a community federation that raises and spends an annual budget of $30 million to provide community services. The federation involved several hundred people in setting service priorities, finding revenues, and improving community relationships. The scale and scope of the effort are impressive, and outcomes can be seen in new directions and renewed donor commitments.

An organization's actions reveal its character, or culture, and another story centers on The Associated's relations with contributors and concern with consensus. The federation culture, as well as fundraising practicalities, make The Associated mainly accountable to a relatively small constituency of big donors. When decision makers are also funders, staff and lay leaders seek agreements that include all or most and offend none. To avoid conflict, participants try to negotiate differences behind the scenes, avoid decisions, or decide ambiguously.

These considerations are not purely economic or political. They are also psychological. They reflect a community character or culture that anxiously wishes for unity. In particular, it reflects the fears of Jews who have seen recurrent persecution, including the Holocaust. In general, these are the concerns of most minority groups living in societies that do not fully embrace them. Thus the story of Associated planning can be read in terms of the community.

We have attended most here to a community story, of how group relations influence planning by an organization that in various ways represents and claims to represent community members. The central theme in this story is the tension between Orthodox and non-Orthodox. This is much more than a conflict over worship. In their disputes, the parties inexplicitly debate the role of religion and the possibility of faith in modern life. Along the way, they challenge anyone to reconcile fundamentalism and liberal pluralism. Centrally, though their debate is not new in Jewish history, they argue passionately about what the community should be.

Community anxieties about differences make it virtually impossible to look at conditions realistically and plan for a future that is more than a mirror of the present. The Associated has had exemplary success in raising funds and planning programs, and it continues to follow tried patterns. Yet combined political, economic, and psychological concerns make it hard for federation activists to analyze community changes, imagine new directions, and realistically plan programs to fit. The story of "Jewish continuity" shows how complicated the challenges of community planning are and how much anxieties about differences constrain initiatives.

We examine lessons from the two community planning efforts together after looking once more at Southeast Baltimore.

CHAPTER 17

Continuing the Southeast Community: Old-Timers, Newcomers, and Schools

While Associated leaders look out on religious, economic, social, and generational differences and speak of the Jewish community's "unity," Southeast activists talk often of their community's "diversity." The Associated saw unity as the basis of "Jewish continuity." Was there a common Southeast future in diversity? One Planning Council member worried so many differences among Southeasterners would pull everyone apart: "There might be too diverse groups within the [planning] cluster to reach common goals."

In fact, many who extol Southeast's diversity moved there from elsewhere. They wanted the heterogeneous contacts they associate with urban life. But they are "consumers" of Southeast diversity, not its "producers" (except, perhaps, as a new group).

Significantly, some born in Southeast talk differently of diversity. A Highlandtown resident remarks,

> I am kind of surprised at how outsiders assess it. The people who live there and grew up there, we can cut it like a pie. It is not diverse. High-landtown was almost all white—predominantly Italian, German, Polish, a few Jews. It had a handful of blacks. The people in the neighborhood are very sacred about where the line is drawn.

Indeed, as diversity grows, old-timers resist it. A Canton resident catalogues his neighbors:

> We've got pretty much everything except Asians that I know of. We've got a large contingent of Lumbee Indians that live in Southeast Baltimore. The Hispanics are the fastest-growing section of Southeast Baltimore. We have blacks and, of course, the big pocket of whites.

Yet in the neighborhood association dominated by long-time white residents, "there is just one point of view that is being heard. . . . And they don't want any diversity."

The traditional American metaphor for the variety of immigrants was a "melting pot": differences would be merged into one American alloy. In the ethnic revival of the 1970s, the "ethnic mosaic" replaced the "melting pot." This metaphor accented groups' irreducible separateness and affirmed the beauty of an overall picture formed from distinct shapes and hues. Many Southeast natives believe the area remains a mosaic, where most want to keep with others like themselves. The "diversity" that many enjoy is produced by discrete communities, each trying to perpetuate a stable, homogeneous population and culture.

Thus one might frame a comparison between Southeast Baltimore and the Jewish community in either of two ways. One would take each community at its public word: the Jewish community is homogeneous, and the Southeast is diverse. In these terms, planning for the Jewish community's continuity entails identifying its core identity and nurturing the conditions where it can flourish. Planning for Southeastern continuity more complexly involves creating the conditions for many different communities to grow together.

A second view would look at the meanings of each community's public presentation in terms of community dynamics. In the Jewish community, assertions of unity often aim to deny religious or class differences. One might ask whether Southeastern emphasis on diversity might be meant to obscure certain similarities. In the 1970s, in reaction to black pride, descendants of European immigrants resurrected ethnic identities. One aim was to assert their own specialness and pride. Another was to avoid dichotomizing society into white and black by introducing myriad group identities (Stein and Hill 1977). Both purposes can be seen in the SECO history describing Southeast as

> a patch-work quilt containing identifiable neighborhoods of Polish, Greek, Italian, Ukrainian, German, Finnish, Irish, Czech, Black, Appalachian, and Lumbee Indian immigrants (Truelove 1977b:6).

Blacks are like Czechs, and differences between them are no different than those between Polish and Greeks. This "patch-work quilt" has dozens of colors; it is not simply black and white.

Thus emphasis on "diversity" has two meanings. It responds to concerns about what special qualities join Southeast residents and what planners should nurture to keep the community alive. Here "diversity" refers to parallel efforts to honor ethnic antecedents. But it also defends against racial division. By legitimating certain differences, the language vitiates others.

RELATIONS BETWEEN OLD-TIMERS AND NEWCOMERS

Changes

Though race is Southeast's most anxiety-laden difference, one might argue it is not the difference most threatening old-time white residents.

Racial change is a sign of a larger transition. African-Americans are moving into the area to live near other blacks and to take advantage of housing prices. Whites are doing similarly. Blacks are more likely than whites to rent, but many of both treat Southeast first as a housing market, rather than a community. This new diversity separates old-time whites from newcomers, mostly white, who think of Southeast Baltimore as a cheap, convenient place to live and have little or no attachment to the old-timers or their traditions.

The analogy in the Jewish community juxtaposes older and younger generations. They differ in religious and ethnic orientation, including commitment to Jewish communal life, but they find common ground in family dining rooms. Whatever their disagreements, they take their kinship for granted. When people worry whether their grandchildren will be Jewish, they know who the grandchildren are.

There is no such familial certainty in the Southeast. More and more, families of school-age children move to the suburbs, leaving aging parents alone in the old neighborhood. If they sell their home—as more and more do—they are likely to list with a realtor, who will sell to the highest bidder, who will not be a family member.

Smith, Mead and Associates (n.d.)[1] found that children selling family homes, because they lived in the suburbs, often listed with suburban realtors. Only 20 percent of listings were with Southeast Baltimore offices. Agents unfamiliar with Southeast did not aim at buyers who lived or might fit in the area, and buyers were often outsiders. Just over half (54%) of buyers came from Southeast. In transitional Patterson Park neighborhoods, the proportions of outside listings and buyers were higher.

The buyers include three main groups. One is adults with grown children, who have decided to move back from the suburbs to the City. A second comprises individuals and couples who have not had children. Many are young professionals who come to enjoy urban life and proximity to work until they are married or have children. Together, these groups make up two-thirds (64%) of new Southeast homebuyers. The last third are adults with children, who, when their children reach school-age, are as likely as old-timers' children to leave for the suburbs. Only 16 percent of buyers considered schools important when purchasing.

The continuity of old-timers' families is not the same as the continuity of the Southeast community. And the converse must also be true. But if family relations do not sustain the community, what about family feelings? It would only stretch the imagination slightly to think of newcomers with small children as themselves potential adoptive children for the old-timers.

Planning participants who reviewed a draft report for the Services Task Force had such a sense. A Southeast native commented on the order of recommendations: "I see seniors first. Maybe youth ought to be first."

A newcomer agreed: "They are our future." Shortly afterward, a service worker, also a newcomer, asked, "Is there nothing for the family?" He pushed: "How about something on parenting?" The first newcomer agreed. Strikingly, the parenting recommendation echoed arguments for a family camp across town at The Associated. Literally and figuratively, this coalition of old-timers and newcomers wanted to continue the community through family relations.

Old-Timers' Wariness toward Newcomers

Yet many old-timers think the newcomers neither look nor act like their children. Far from inspiring feelings of kinship, the newcomers arouse anxiety and hostility. Those with money who buy expensive houses or fix up cheaper ones push taxes up and force old-timers from their homes. Because of the cultural centrality of homeownership, this move means much more than a physical relocation, even if the owner who can no longer afford taxes moves in with family. The loss of a home takes community status.

Some old-timers associate newcomers with all the changes that upset their lives. They single out blacks, Hispanics, drug users, children with behavior problems, and criminals. A pastor describes how his congregants feel about their new neighbors:

> There remain a number of long-time residents, and they are basically living in transitory situations. It is just amazing that I talked to someone who has lived in the same house for eighty years. . . . So you have stability and also the level of interest that is represented by the older people.
>
> You have the younger people that are moving in and buying. . . . I think they are people from outside, essentially. The children of the people who live here have actually moved out or are in the county. They are not particularly interested in repurchasing or moving back in, which means that there are more houses for sale. . . . The other thing that is happening here, too, is that, because the houses are cheap, there are investors who can purchase and rent them.
>
> You have the old community lamenting what has been lost, finding a few around that are still neighbors that they can still count on, but pretty well ignoring the new people except to complain. And the new people may be kind of rootless and rudderless, and so they don't share the old values. {*Interviewer*: What are the complaints of the old against the new?} They leave a mess. They don't care. There's more fear than there used to be. The old don't go out at night because they don't know them. It's kind of funny because I think it's one of the safest neighborhoods in the City around. . . .
>
> What is happening is that the old-timers could control the people who might have moved in and that they are no longer able to do that, and that sense of closeness . . . it has gone from a closed community to a divided community or area.

Although many whites worry about blacks, concerns about new-comers are not essentially racial. A long-time black resident voices identical worries about her community:

> Southeast Baltimore . . . has changed because the people who lived here have moved away and sold their homes to people. . . . So the new people came in the neighborhood who didn't have that sense of belonging. . . . This was a little small community here. . . . So that kind of changed this neighborhood a lot.

Old-timers of all races experience neighborhood change as taking something. A service provider observes they "identify with the fact this is their turf. They were here as kids." Yet, the minister explains, old-timers make things worse by keeping newcomers at arms' length, not offering contact that might restore community closeness, if not necessarily closedness:

> The issue is of disconnectedness. . . . There is some connection with the old. They are not connected with the new, and the new themselves are not particularly connected.

Many newcomers not only have no connection to old-timers, but also are hardly connected to one another. Residents who come to Southeast Baltimore from the same part of Latin America, for example, do feel linked, but they are exceptional. Many who have moved to Southeast recently are tied to a dwelling unit through the housing market, but not to the surroundings or neighbors. A Butcher's Hill activist observes of those who have moved into that renovated area, "The reason we all live here . . . is probably because of the housing stock."

A newcomer who tried to get involved in his community association, however, tells of resistance. He has lived in his neighborhood

> seventeen years, since 1976; that's about sixteen years, I guess. And I am really a newcomer compared to, like my neighbor was born in his house, and he is about seventy-something, and the neighbor I had just before this was born in her house, and she died when she was about eighty-two, last year. I mean, sixteen, seventeen years is a relative newcomer in some cases.

He reports that he

> and a couple of other new board members have been trying to get more, some of the younger people on the board of directors, and it's been a real fight. . . . The president of the association, she just wants the people like that, that she can pretty much manipulate, and some of these people . . . they have just sort of like lost it, like a lucidity factor of maybe 50 percent, it being elusive to finish a thought, and so forth, and not fall asleep at the meeting. And I think that's why she wants all these people. . . .

At the last board meeting I nominated two people. One was fifty-two, and the other one was fifty-five. . . . They are not young, but at least they are vital, still, and everything. And she nominated three people that are just, you know . . . I think the youngest one is probably around eighty. . . . I am forty-nine. I am probably the youngest person on the board of directors. . . . I just don't know what the problem is, because the president of the organization is probably fifty-five, too.

He feels old-timers want newcomers to buy houses at prices that do not raise taxes, and then keep quiet. He realizes old-timers don't want to lose control over organizations or the community. Still, he wants to join them, but the only relationship they seem to offer is silent subordinance. He says he will set up a new organization. These old-timers do not evidently wish to adopt newcomers.

Choosing to Live with Newcomers

Yet families and geographic communities are similar in that one has little power to get rid of members one does not like. For those old-timers who will stay in Southeast, newcomers are part of their future. Perhaps the most apt familial metaphor is that many old-timers feel forced to be foster parents for children they are not sure they want.

At the same time, newcomers' focus on housing leads old-timers to recognize they depend on them, however they feel about them. When 11 percent of housing units are vacant, when many older residents cannot keep their homes or are dying, homebuyers offer assets: not just their money, but also physical stability and at least potential community concern. They patronize local merchants and may work in local businesses. Some send children to neighborhood schools. A few attend the churches.

Hence the community association president just described as obsessed with control views newcomers pragmatically:

We figure that the young people that have the children may be the ones to target for homebuying. . . . To resolve housing problems [we should] encourage new people to move into the community, encourage the people that are here to stay.

And perhaps, as the man who talks of good-heartedness hopes, the place will civilize them: "If all this [finding good people to buy homes] goes well, then the ethic that is East Baltimore will stay here, after us."

It would be better, some conclude, to aid this civilizing process than to leave newcomers on their own. Indeed, more than anything else, it is concern about their children that keeps them from putting down roots in Southeast. A community activist who came to Southeast in the 1970s summarizes many accounts of families that came and went according to their children's ages:

When those people had come in, they were mostly young professionals, and when they started having children . . . because the schools never changed in the area, we have those people leaving. They never developed a stake, a whole community stake. While they were there, that was fine. You have to have people stay in those neighborhoods in order to keep that. . . . Until the schools become good, you are never going to keep them here—the young families—which means the children won't grow up in the neighborhood. Or the only thing you are going to keep here are the people who can afford to send their children to private school, or are too poor to leave the neighborhood. That's not good for a community like Southeast.

These forces make Southeast a place of transit, as a social worker summarizes:

I would see the newcomers as people who have as much need, who have families, and they can be part of the community. There are people who are looking for community. . . . Instead of a place where you are going to come and live for the rest of your life . . . it is seen as a stopping place. I have had people tell me, while the kids are in the elementary school, they will stay here, but once they head for the middle school, they'll move out.

Nevertheless, some newcomers put down roots. They find it not so easy to move, as they may have planned, after only a few years, when they have children or their children reach school-age. They develop stakes in Southeast Baltimore, including stakes in good schools. No old-timer can quarrel with that.

When Associated activists think of affiliation as a response to social conditions, they view the unaffiliated sympathetically and try to supply the resources that would make affiliation possible. Southeast old-timers who see newcomers' "rootlessness" as a reaction to poor schools see them with similar compassion and think of ways of improving the schools. Many old-timers and newcomers take a modest view of community continuity. It may be anachronistic to expect successions of generations to occupy the same territory, but it should be possible for families to raise children in Southeast.

Hence, as in the Jewish community, they focus on education as the key to the future. Few can afford private school; they want good public schools from kindergarten to twelfth grade. Here religion is a private matter, but the public schools teach about ethnic heritages. Many have no qualms about putting prayer back in schools. Many more feel it would not be too much to expect the schools to teach the good-hearted culture once again.

PLANNING FOR SCHOOLS AND COMMUNITY

The group that launched Southeast planning defined Southeast as a physical space. Transportation, housing, and economic development were on the agenda. Sanitation and crime would be left to neighborhood associations. Education was too complex. Yet planning participants, particularly old-timers, could not help thinking about social ties. Talk of "ethnicity," references to "community," and appreciations of good-hearted culture affirmed and bespoke wishes for connection. Even though participants wanted to avoid divisive issues, the importance of these attachments pushed planning toward social concerns.

Social Talk in Planning

From the start, planning participants brought up social issues. At the first cluster workshop, in April 1992, a Coordinating Committee member showed demographic data. Southeast had dropped from 97,000 residents to 77,000 residents between 1970 and 1990. What, she asked, were the reasons? Someone answered at once, "People move out to County schools." When the group later listed issues and problems, a businessman named "Better schools." Discussing opportunities, a young man urged, "Improve the schools."

The last exercise was to advise hypothetical developers. Donna Miller, a Coordinating Committee member who advocated for social services planning, wanted to get "industry that works with schools" finding jobs for graduates. Moments later, someone admonished developers to "encourage schools to have partnerships with business and industry."

As if simply picking up this discussion after a three-week pause, Miller opened the next workshop talking about issues planning could address: "for example, how to create partnerships between schools and businesses, leading to training and job opportunities." People talked often of schools and social concerns.

Identifying neighborhood issues, problems, and obstacles, a minister mentioned "Schools." A Southeast native agreed at once, "They are an obstacle." The minister insisted the school system needs reform: "*We* need this kind of input into schools." The other man took a broad perspective:

> The Big Two: Schools, and drugs and crime. Because of them nobody wants to live here. The value of the properties is such that nobody wants to fix them up. They are this incredible obstacle. If you could fix these, you wouldn't have to worry about anything else.

Soon after, another old-time Southeasterner named his issues: "schools and senior centers." And shortly after that, still another said, "drugs and crime, and schools."

People were asked to think about community building blocks and resources. Someone who had moved into the area in the 1970s said, "Improve race relations . . . community involvement in schools, job training for local residents." Discussing what to advise a developer, a young mother suggested, "Adopt a school."

When the meeting moved to future steps, a woman summarized the morning's talk: "We can build up our housing; we can have wonderful housing. But if we don't have good schools, people will not move in—or stay." The moderator for that part of the meeting immediately repeated the original ground rules:

> There are certain issues this group will not address, because local neighborhood groups can do them better. Code enforcement, sanitation, crime—these are for local community groups. We have thought of this process as concerned with guidelines for development and housing.

The cluster workshops were a continuing conversation among Southeast residents. Thus Miller, starting up the next workshop, ignored those last words at the previous meeting. Once more, for a new group, she talked about the issues they could raise: "for example, education and job training for kids—this might become a task force on business partnerships with schools." Leading a visualization exercise before a bus tour, she asked the roomful of people with closed eyes to think about future residents' lives: "What kind of schools will they see?"

After the tour, education came up in connection with neighborhood issues, problems, and obstacles:

JACK TAFT: Schools.

ARNOLD GUNTHER: Absolutely! Is there any group trying to organize . . . I know SECO is trying to get . . . school-based management in Southeast schools.

DONNA MILLER: We would need to worry about schools.

MARY RILEY: Sixty-five percent of the community according to the Census don't have high school diplomas. What can we do? There is a need for massive outreach in this area. . . .

MILLER: There is a need for literacy.

GUNTHER: The schools fight giving up control to community people.

A community activist later named "schools" and "social services" as obstacles to Southeast development.

In advising future developers, Miller listed what was acceptable: "child day care center . . . senior facilities . . . strong input into local schools, facilities for children."

In December, after the four cluster workshops, the Planning Council met. Staff had been asking civic and business leaders and experts for advice, and interview summaries were passed out. A woman with strong educational interests picked up on one suggestion: "What does it mean, 'SECO should run a community-based school'?"

Her question could be heard as a summary of a nine-month conversation. People were leaving Southeast because schools were bad. It would be hard to attract newcomers without good schools. Many public schools resisted community ideas and participation. Therefore, why not run an independent school?

That meeting set up task forces to address overall Southeast issues. Miller convened a task force on services and infrastructure. She recruited people interested in schools and other services, and the group began social planning.

Social Planning

While the task forces worked, the March 1993 Planning Council meeting surveyed progress and assessed priorities. The task force chairs reported. People got a "Summary of Findings from Southeast Plan Process: March 1992–March 1993." Members divided into groups to consider what was missing from task force reports or the summary and to identify priority issues.

Miller led a group. Early on, a SECO staff member sitting in observed, "Nobody is marketing the City or Southeast." The solution, he said, was, "We have to figure out how to market *education* in the area. For example, a community school that you can promote." Miller took up the theme: "I get so discouraged with all the problems in the schools. If people could just run their own school." "We could start a school," he replied. "The Mayor has said to us, start a school." A businessman liked the idea, "the neighborhoods taking their own initiative." "Schools," he went on, "could do a lot better without North Avenue [the central school administration]." The staff member continued, "We could start one. [A local foundation] would give us money for a feasibility study. We could do it at [a neighborhood church]." When Miller reported back to the whole Council, she mentioned a recommendation for a "community school."

A second discussion leader reporting on her group's "missing issues" mentioned "a magnet school." Another group leader said, "There is an education project at CPHA [Citizens Planning and Housing Association, a civic organization] to promote community schools. One outcome could be a school within a school."

The Services and Infrastructure Task Force continued to work. Its April meeting was concerned with framing recommendations for the plan. Miller summarized two: "Create trade schools with work-study programs," and "Create business-linked schools." After further discussion, she concluded, "And recommend, as everyone wants: create a community school." A woman affirmed, "That's how it was in the past, and it kept the community together."

In May the Planning Council convened a group to review an outline for the plan. Miller circulated her task force report and opened discussion by saying,

> We looked at geographic gaps in services in the Southeast community and mapped that. We looked at it from two perspectives: from the perspective of generations—seniors, child care—and targeted particular types of services—general education, libraries. Then we looked at gaps, and made recommendations about the gaps.

When the meeting moved on to articulate the main themes of the emerging plan, someone mentioned "schools" and no one protested.

In June the Council reviewed task force recommendations to set priorities before presenting a draft plan to a Community Assembly. The group discussing services went over proposals on recreation, a teen center, and jobs for adolescents before settling on schools:

TOM MALKOVIC: This would be a chance for us to say something. For example, "The Southeast recommends schools for Tesseract [a program where the city school administration had contracted with a private firm to run nine schools] or enterprise schools." Should we say that? I don't think anybody here knows whether we should say anything about this.

SARA TAYLOR [A TEACHER]: Teachers don't want Tesseract schools.

MALKOVIC: That is probably a clue that it's a good idea. . . . On Number Five, work-study programs through trade schools and business linkages, we see a new emphasis on vocational schools. They should train kids sixteen, seventeen, eighteen on how to put back together a vacant house. We will see a lot of willingness to look at proposals for vocational education.

DONNA MILLER [who is leading the group and reviewing recommendations in order]: Child day care: The number of day care providers, there are . . . almost none in Butcher's Hill, Fell's Point, Highlandtown, Greektown, right on over. . . . Seniors: . . . Seniors need someone to animate them. It could be volunteers. Adult and family education. . . .

THERESA BORGE: This makes perfect sense.

MILLER: Health: Southeast has a density more than any other sector of Baltimore. . . . The O'Donnell Heights Clinic . . . Spanish population. . . . Require a study of Southeast community groups' needs.

MALKOVIC: We need to identify "underserved communities." . . .

MILLER: "Other": Schools and education, libraries and parks. We thought about doing studies of them. . . .

BORGE: What group is aware of everything going on in the schools in Southeast?

While interested in including schools in the plan, the group acknowledged how little they knew. Hence they talked of studies.

The Council invited Southeast residents to a Community Assembly in July. About sixty came. They were asked to comment on the draft plan and vote on priorities. A Coordinating Committee member read the plan's statement of principles. One said, "Promote continued development of Southeast Baltimore as a complete community that provides affordable housing, employment, and recreational opportunities." "Did we get it right?" she asked when finished. "Got it right!" someone chorused. Yet at once someone else urged including education in "a complete community."

After task force presentations, the chair asked whether anything should be added to suggested priorities. A father of two said, "The school system." Again the chair reviewed the boundaries: "Rats, crime, schools are all issues, but we are not tackling them at this time." Still, he went on, "One suggestion was, start a community-based school."

When the Council met in September, members congratulated themselves on good work. A staff member was finishing the plan, and now they needed people to work on implementation. The chair read the list of recommendations and asked for volunteers and suggestions for each. At one point, someone interrupted to object, "There is no recommendation to do research on a charter school," and several people quickly volunteered to look into such programs. Finally, the chair referred to a Recommendation 25:

> It isn't on your list—to establish study-action groups for schools, libraries, and parks. . . . It would include a study of the notion of charter schools. Should the Southeast Planning Council do this study?

At once, a woman volunteered to work on the school project. The man who mentioned charter schools earlier now insisted,

> You've gotta do something about the schools. A community is based on the schools. You are not going to get any families moving here without the schools. Regardless of the job base.

The chair once more recited the statement about planning boundaries, but now with a different ending: "We purposely left out rats, trash, and the school system from the plan. I would argue for keeping it in there." The man who had just spoken jumped in: "I agree. There is already a group looking at [setting up a community school in Memorial] Stadium. We should talk with them."

The Southeast Community Plan, published in December 1993, reflected a successful push to treat the community socially. It contained eleven recommendations on services, plus one to

> SUPPORT RICH (REJOICING IN COMMUNITY HARMONY): Advocate for RICH in its efforts to form a strong coalition, which will address racism, and create ways to appreciate and value the multi-cultural diversity in southeast Baltimore (Plan 1993:52).

Although race was an unspoken topic during planning, the plan supported those who would discuss it.

Priority recommendations sketched a community that cared for its young because it considered their growth essential to the community's future. For the early years of life, Recommendation 18 would

> EXPAND LICENSED DAY CARE SERVICES FOR INFANTS AND CHILDREN . . .
> Provide employment and entrepreneurial opportunities for parents who
> want to care for children in their own homes . . . particularly for low and
> moderate income families (Plan 1993:38).

Recommendation 14 encompassed education from early childhood through adulthood: "EXPAND COMMUNITY-BASED LITERACY, HEAD START AND GED PROGRAMS" (Plan 1993:34), and Recommendation 20 would "ESTABLISH A STUDY-ACTION GROUP FOR SCHOOLS." The text explained,

> Throughout the southeast planning process, citizens all over southeast
> Baltimore expressed a desire to improve and diversify the uses of existing
> community service resources. Schools were a topic of grave concern.
> Time did not permit an in-depth study, nor would it have been wise to
> deal with Southeast schools outside the context of the City of Balti-
> more. The Services Task Force recommended, therefore, a Southeast
> Study-Action Group on schools (Plan 1993:40).

To help support these programs, Recommendation 19 aimed to establish an annual Southeast grassroots fundraising campaign.

The plan was especially concerned about adolescents. Recommendation 15 would "REDESIGN NEIGHBORHOOD RECREATION CENTERS [by changing hours to be] more accessible to working families and children, especially teenagers" (Plan 1993:35). Recommendation 16 aimed to "FUND A YOUTH COMMUNITY SERVICE CORPS . . . an opportunity for providing early, positive work experiences" (Plan 1993:36). Clearly linking youth to the community's future, Recommendation 17 proposed to

> CREATE A SOUTHEAST TEEN CENTER . . . with a program aimed at: scholas-
> tic improvement, substance abuse prevention, life skills building, and
> recreation. . . . Surrounded by crime, violence, and substance abuse,
> many teens are without adequate support systems to enable them to
> make healthy choices. . . . Overall benefits of the Teen Center include
> promoting a healthy atmosphere for positive growth in teens, which
> will result in attitudes and actions benefiting the wider community (Plan
> 1993:37).

Schools, Social Services, and Southeast

Recommendations treating Southeast as a social and cultural, as well as geographic, community can be credited to Miller's stubborn campaign for schools and social services. Overruled in the decision to restrict planning to physical and economic development, she advocated for services and organized a task force. In a loosely structured process where intellectual and other human resources were scarce, she succeeded by putting in time and effort to articulate broadly shared concerns.

Many service recommendations involved motherhood issues. Anyone could support day care, youth jobs, adult literacy, recreation centers, and parks without insisting on details, and implementation was unlikely to spark controversy. Schools were different. Few might disagree about "community input" and "community control," perhaps many would support "community-based schools," but no path led directly to the "quality education" everyone wanted (Plan 1993:40). Ten thousand Southeast students attended 16 public schools under 2 assistant superintendents in a system with 113,000 students in 182 schools.[2]

On the west end of Southeast, poor single African American mothers in public housing worried the elementary school was not teaching their children to read. On the east side, working-class white parents were upset the high school could not guarantee their children's learning or safety. In between, parents of various incomes, races, and ethnicities found both things they liked and things that concerned them. Although many families shared potential common ground, school study and action would entail a dialogue that crossed lines rarely transcended. And change would require unprecedented cooperation with the school system.

In the face of such challenges, "Establish a study-action group for schools" was as much as could be said. The recommendation resembled Associated education recommendations, describing minimum grounds of agreement. Leaving the schools alone would certainly change the community for the worse. That was the undeniable argument for going on.

Yet, after all this, it was unclear whether such a diverse community would have more than a geographic identity. Good schools were a precondition for the stability from which something deeper might be formed. Old-timers hoped to continue the good-hearted homeownership culture. New residents, many with more income, formal education, and outside attachments than the old-timers, might become good neighbors and share interests. Whether all could or would see themselves as having something fundamental in common was a more complicated question than Southeast planning had addressed, and any answers lay ahead.

TAKING STOCK

Southeast planning is the story of a group of activists who organized and managed a planning process involving three hundred people from several dozen organizations. With creativity, commitment, and strategic outside resources, the group directed attention to a shared Southeast community and its future.

The process involved simultaneously planning with and for a community and organizing the community. For all the talk of "the Southeast community," Southeast Baltimore is a collection of communities. Some are socially and culturally coherent, perhaps organized about race, ethnicity, or a way of life. Some are defined by shared problems. Others are geographic concentrations. One of the successes of the planning process was to focus attention on common conditions and aspirations. One hindrance to holding that attention was the difficulty of making a Southeast identity rewarding.

Confronting growing losses, many Southeasterners hope to regenerate community life. They are buoyed by a tradition of activism with a history of successes. Yet they struggle against long odds: conversion from industry to services, public and private abandonment of the City, the City's consequent impoverishment, and declining schools. In a contest between hope and despair, these conditions alone would defeat many communities.

Southeasterners have lost the confidence that went with economic security. Racial differences conveniently divert attention from these problems, and racial conflicts easily channel frustrations, anger, and desires for simple villains. Economic decline and race are at the center of both the community and planning stories. Race collects and arouses anxieties that get in the way of realistically analyzing groups' needs and planning to address them. And declining community resources provide few incentives for trying.

It is premature to judge the outcomes of Southeast planning, since the plan is new and implementation is just starting. The challenges to this community's continuity show the economic, political, and psychological difficulties of community planning in American cities. Cacophonously, several voices compete to tell the story's end.

PART 6

Community, Organizations, Planning, and the City

CHAPTER 18

Community Identities

What communities do people identify with today? We have looked at two organizations whose members think of themselves as belonging to, planning for, and shaping communities. Although their particulars do not exhaust the possibilities (for example, they include few African-Americans, middle-class white Protestants, or poor people), they test the role of general factors: geography, culture, wealth, ethnicity, and religion.

We have asked how perceptions of their fellows encourage people to interact richly and identify deeply with them. In part, this is a question of whom people find around them who are similar enough to constitute a community. In part, too, this question concerns how people collectively choose to see those among and around them in order to create a community.

The two communities we have studied differ in some obvious ways, with many of the consequences one might expect. Yet their traits combine complexly, sometimes producing subtle differences but also leading to striking similarities. Both communities struggle to define themselves. Both ponder the contemporary meanings of ethnicity and religion. Both test whether community is possible in modern society.

Those of us who identify with communities assume and emphasize their uniqueness. Southeast Baltimoreans talk of the exceptional co-existence of their diverse ethnicities. The Jews are proud of their community's size, institutional richness, and cohesiveness, as well as Jewish religion and culture generally. To take the latter example, it would be tempting to argue the Baltimore Jewish community is representative of only Jewish communities and any lessons from that case apply, at best, only to those communities.

Certain aspects of the Baltimore Jewish community most easily fit other Jewish communities. Tensions between Orthodox and non-Orthodox over Jewish education are an example. Yet if one thinks of that dynamic in terms of the predicament of making decisions when groups disagree on fundamental principles, the specifics look less important than the general challenge. Moreover, part of this dynamic, as well as other relations in the Jewish community, reflect a history of being a periodically victimized minority, a condition shared by blacks and certain other groups. This experience sensitizes members to boundaries, leads some to polarize the world into good insiders and bad outsiders, and pushes some anxiously to emphasize unity and loyalty over differences. In these respects Orthodox–non-Orthodox conflicts parallel opposition between good-hearted white homeowners and black renters in the Southeast.

In other words, we can best learn from the cases by recognizing what is general in their particulars.

COMMUNITIES OF MEMORY, COMMUNITIES OF HOPE

Robert Bellah and his colleagues describe "a real community" as a

> "community of memory," one that does not forget its past. In order not to forget that past, a community is involved in retelling its story, its constitutive narrative, and in so doing, it offers examples of the men and women who have embodied and exemplified the meaning of the community (1985:153).

In addition,

> The communities of memory that tie us to the past also turn us toward the future as communities of hope. They carry a context of meaning that can allow us to connect our aspirations for ourselves and those closest to us with the aspirations of a larger whole and see our own efforts as being, in part, contributions to a common good (1985:153).

We have the testimony of two community organizations that community is problematic, that continuity from a community of memory to a community of hope cannot be taken for granted. The reasons are complex—some societal, some idiosyncratic to the two types of communities here, and some peculiar to cities like Baltimore.

Belonging to a community is a matter of faith. People must identify collectively with something sufficiently uplifting to move them to give priority to community affairs over everyday business. Community is also a matter of spirituality, the sense that everything, no matter how apparently trivial, is connected, ultimately to something exalted. The sense of community is the feeling that everyone is tied to everyone else, every action participates in the community, and every person shares the power and love of all.[1]

The loss of the spiritual or transcendent is a modern problem. The juxtaposition of a panoply of practices, religion among them, not only calls any one into question, but questions the possibility of an overarching connection or encompassing meaning (Berger, Berger, and Kellner 1973; Douglas and Tipton 1983). Any activity becomes as potentially meaningful as any other, and sure proximate rewards displace gambles on possible distant ones. Self-fulfillment looks like a better bet than community membership (Yankelovich 1982).[2]

Creating a community of hope depends on building a bridge of transcendence from a community of memory. That struggle has been at the center of planning in both communities here.

TWO COMMUNITIES AND TWO MODELS

Two Communities

The Baltimore Jewish community and Southeast Baltimore differ in three consequential ways. First, the Southeast is a territory, whereas the Jewish community is a culturally defined group. Second, the Jewish community is wealthier than Southeast. Third, the Jewish community has a history and language that enable it to speak of being "one," whereas the Southeast is an aggregation of similar but discrete communities.

The different community definitions—geography and culture—produce distinct community processes and form different lenses for viewing them. In both corners of Baltimore, members of the great middle class are leaving the City for the suburbs in search of proximity to work, good schools, adequate housing, lower taxes, safety, separation from frightening populations or conditions, or, most likely, a combination of these things. Members of the Jewish community see one another as they move more or less together. Members of the Southeast community view the trends and their consequences within geographic boundaries.

The Jews, as a cultural community, have considerable freedom to define themselves. They can decide how to live Jewishly without external constraint. Although they will always live in a world with Gentiles, many can choose to leave social, political, or economic conditions that limit them. Wherever the community goes, it develops strategic relations with local organizations, but Jewish institutions define and center the community.

In contrast, Southeast, as a territory, cannot escape environmental problems or constraints. Annexation to a suburban jurisdiction would make a difference but is unlikely (Rusk 1996). Thus the City's government, economy, and social infrastructure become centers of attention and the focus of remedial efforts. This is one reason why Southeast's boundaries have corresponded to political districts and why the First District Democratic machine was a source of cohesion.

Economic differences reinforce these tendencies. Money brings the Jewish community autonomy. Wealthy city neighborhoods enjoy similar advantages. Residents' resources, including professional skills and involvement in the City's elite, enable them to influence government, escape some of the City's fiscal constraints, and, generally, do much on their own. Southeast's relative poverty reinforces its dependence on the City and surroundings.

Unity and division are matters of reality and perception, as debates over Jewish "one-ness" and Southeast "diversity" show. Stalemate over Jewish education testifies that significant differences divide that community. Yet this conflict occurs because the contending parties consider themselves members of the same community. Jews disagree about whether they are an ethnic group or also a religious group and, if the latter, what worship is appropriate. This is an old, well-practiced argument. It is never resolved, but millennia of Jewish history and religious and cultural languages of Jewishness give Jews ready terms for considering themselves one community.

The appeal to common Jewishness overcame national and class conflicts between Germans and Russians. Similar tensions were continually re-created in the Southeast without benefit of a unifying ideology. Immigrants brought national and religious differences from Europe to Baltimore, they lived as separately as they could, and they joined different churches.

When manufacturing flourished, a common class identity cut across ethnic lines. Yet much of this identity was negative, defined in terms of victims who fought industrial bosses for decent pay. In recent decades, manufacturing and ethnicity have both declined. National differences divide European descendants less, but working-class status has less power to unify them.

The 1970s ethnic revival was an effort to establish a common white identity. However, part was just oppositional, asserting white specialness against black pride, and much of the content was symbolic. Goodhearted homeownership, as a secular expression of ethnicity, may be taken for granted as a community value, but it is a weak basis for a Southeast identity. It does not invoke a deeply shared history, and no language of ethnicity has the force to hold even whites close.

Now identifications with geographic neighborhoods take the place of ethnically defined neighborhood identities. For many, they are derivatives of ethnic pasts; for some, they are simply territorial matters. In either case, whatever the positive nature of this identity, sharing geography has often led people to identify with one another as victims of common troubles. Thus the Democratic machine, in dealing with these problems, offered pragmatic unity that substituted for an overarching identity.

Southeast's diversity is partly an artifact of its geographic definition. Almost any large urban area will be heterogeneous. Limited incomes prolong the diversity. If more residents had means to move to homes near others more like themselves, they might leave Southeast more homogeneous.

Historically, the area was more diverse than the Jewish community, but most contemporary differences are less salient and arouse less passion than those in the Jewish community. Race is the great divide in the Southeast. Religion is similar in the Jewish community, with the crucial difference that it is balanced by a powerful unifying identity.

Two Models

These are the reasons why Baltimore Jews and Southeast Baltimoreans think of community in the different ways identified with Bellah's ideals and Gans' "middle Americans," respectively. These correspond to Fowler's (1991) communities of tradition and participatory communities.

In the former, the present is rooted in the remembered past, and authoritative traditions order contemporary affairs. Thus personal identity is tied to communal activity. Family life takes meaning from connections to a shared culture, and community affairs matter deeply because they build on and reinforce childrearing practices, worship, and the like. Thus the public domain and what many think of as private activities are linked. Hence people trust public activities. This community is measured by the preservation of traditions, the enabling of intimacy, and authenticity.[3]

The participatory community is concerned less with intimacy than with democracy. Its proponents design and measure it politically (see Barber 1984). Although they would like public harmony, they take differences of interest and culture as a premise. Although they would like greater congruence between public and private activities, they do not unhesitatingly trust public institutions to raise children or shape personal identity. Such responsibilities may be best left to small groupings. A participatory community would enable these groups to articulate their interests and find common ground, but it would also provide resources for groups to meet their needs autonomously.

Talk of "community" at The Associated describes a community of tradition. Liberal, especially secular non-Orthodox draw lines between public and private domains, and Orthodox, particularly the traditional, have little social contact with non-Orthodox. Nevertheless, in each group most assume similarities in interests and outlook that warrant close ties among religious congregations, communal organizations, helping agencies, families, schools, and so forth. Communal activists assume community membership is central to personal identity. For fundraising and community reasons, The Associated recruits individual members. Consistently, the strategic plan asserted members' common interests as the basis of community unity.

Early Southeast ethnic communities had these characteristics. They remain as communities of memory, and neighborhood and family are now the foci of deep loyalty. In recent years political organizations have pragmatically shaped community, often with a focus on "foreign relations" (Crenson 1983). In contrast with The Associated, SECO is an umbrella organization, whose constituents are neighborhood associations. The Southeast Planning Council was created on a similar principle, that individual members represent groups. Although the plan referred to a "Southeast community," planning participants spoke often of "interests" and "representation." The plan recognized neighborhoods' importance by including recommendations for each major participating group.

COMMUNITIES OF HOPE

With these differences, Jewish and Southeastern planners aimed to formulate community identities that could give meaning to and guide future action. Their efforts tested the power of geography, class, ethnicity, and religion to draw people together, constitute the core of a collective identity, and move people to act with others.

Southeast Baltimore is defined by specific geography, whereas the Baltimore Jewish community is generally located in "the Northwest." The imprecision of the latter description testifies at once to the value of propinquity for interaction but also the inferiority of geography to other definers of community identity for at least the Jews.

Although Southeast Baltimore is bounded by lines on a map, its history shows the limited force of geography as a basis for community identity. It may demarcate common interests, which can draw people together for collective action. Physical features, such as Patterson Park or the waterfront, can symbolize a common identity, but it is more likely shared problems, such as crime in the park or waterfront development, which mobilize people.

Still, problems, though they can cement a coalition, offer only the negative identity of victim. Righteous indignation can motivate a campaign but does not define an enduring identity. People need something to live together for, not just against. And in Southeast it is not geography alone, but social relations and culture, which move people to act collectively. Opposition to The Road was couched as a defense of working-class ethnic families. Truck traffic is seen as a threat to families and small businesses.

Both communities have distinct economic images. The Jews see themselves as solidly middle-class, with a large proportion upper-middle-class and some quite wealthy. Southeasterners cherish a blue-collar identity.

Many Jews point with pride to community wealth. In American society, influenced by the Protestant tradition, it is possible to equate wealth with virtue. At the least, wealth makes it possible to act virtuously. Nevertheless, even though fundraising leads those around The Associated to attend to money, no one asserts wealth has anything to do with Jewish identity.

Some in Southeast Baltimore make other claims—that humble blue-collar conditions are virtuous and constitute a core element in community identity. They can be good-hearted, they say, because they are not burdened or tempted by too much money. Moreover, the good-hearted ethos is emotionally and culturally tied to the immigrant experience. This generic expression of ethnicity, framed in class terms, can define what disparate Southeast groups have in common.

However, the ambiguities of "blue-collar" spoil it as a foundation for community identity. On the one hand, because the phrase is not tied to the class continuum, some who call themselves "blue-collar" can, without contradiction, claim middle-class manners, aspirations, and status. Still, it is hard to avoid equating "blue-collar" with "working-class" and recognizing economic differences that put many Southeasterners below the middle and American norms for success.

Problems with "blue-collar" illustrate the general weaknesses of class as a basis of community identity. Wealth, whether a little or a lot, cannot give activities extraordinary meaning because it is an object of exchange. Those who have little must compare themselves unfavorably with others. Those who have much can take satisfaction in their superiority but must recognize the contingency of their position on social arrangements. Moreover, crucially, no matter how successful they are, because everyone has and can be measured in dollars, they may always be better off than others but can never be absolutely different—the quality of transcendence that justifies community.

In the end, both communities try to articulate their specialness in terms of ethnicity and religion. The effort can be seen as a reflection of their histories, imagining a community of hope like the community of memory. The Jews disagree about the role of religion and its relation to ethnicity. Their opposing positions grow, in part, from their specific European origins and the eras their families came to America. They measure their arguments by what American culture values about ethnicity and religion and by the demands and opportunities of modern life. Yet they contend with one another in languages of traditions that go back centuries.

Many Southeasterners, while emphasizing ethnicity, also associate ethnicity and religion. Catholics, Eastern Orthodox, and Protestants draw on old faiths. When they came to America, they took on identities asso-

ciated with the regions they left. They consider religion part of their ethnicity, and the two reinforce one another. In public life, speaking of what
Southeasterners have in common, they focus on a general European ethnicity, leaving religion to a private domain. In part, that is a compromise with a reality of ethnic differences. In part, as ethnicity loses force, it
is simply the American way. Liberal Jews argue similarly for the private
importance of religion.

There are historic reasons for believing in religion and ethnicity.
Yet it is important to note why they have offered enduring identities.
Religion speaks directly of transcendence. It links the everyday to the
godly, ennobling the community of the faithful. It sets off worshipers
from others.

Roman and Greek myths tell of ethnic groups' divine origins. These
groups command loyalty and identification not simply because they are
familiar and safe, but because they, too, connect to the transcendent.
Sometimes, when ethnic groups have their own religion, as with Italian
Catholics, Jews, and Greek Orthodox, the link is explicit. Other times,
when people experience ethnicity as civil religion, it is tacit.

The Jews' and Southeasterners' approaches to community identity
have similarities and differences. They agree ethnicity should matter. In
Southeast, it is increasingly a generic European ethnicity that acknowledges largely symbolic national differences. Jewish ethnicity is more elaborated, but it, too, is becoming more symbolic, less part of everyday
affairs.

Many Jews couple religion with ethnicity, because the two have
always gone together in Jewish life. In debate about community identity, the most specific statements refer to religion. This is one reason why
advocates of religion often get the upper hand over advocates of ethnicity.
More powerfully, religious proponents seem to have faith in something
transcendent that can give the community special meaning.

Southeasterners similarly split between believers and nonbelievers
but do not talk overtly of a religious basis for community identity. The
diversity of ethnic and religious origins would make such a dialogue
problematic. The assertion of good-heartedness substitutes as a generic
secular moral position. Theological discussions are confined to separate
churches.

After all has been said, both groups, each with their own formula,
would like to create a community future based on ethnicity somehow
joined to religion. The Jews have the advantage in public discussion,
because they can more easily talk of ethnicity and religion together. Yet
both communities reveal more challenges than solutions. The central
problem, simply, is faith—finding a credible object for human impulses to
feel attached to and supported by something greater.

Each community faces the challenge of defining its character in ennobling terms and prescribing specific ways of participating in the sublime. At the same time, for communities such as these, which have histories, these efforts must be tied to traditions. Moreover, community obligations should fit with mundane affairs, both permitting and explaining them.

Yet community building is not simply an intellectual project. Belief in community arises from the experience of community, just as faith emerges from the experience of something compellingly trustworthy. Communities that see their identity in ethnic and, especially, religious terms at least tacitly recognize these facts. Yet simply using these languages, as many in the two Baltimore communities do, does not create the experience of community.

A community identity is shaped in the experience of a community based on that identity. In these two cases, planning recommendations rest on assumptions about shared identity and, if implemented, could encourage community members to see themselves attached in those ways. The Baltimore Jewish community aims at a community of tradition, Southeast Baltimore at least a participatory community.

LESSONS

We see here two models for community: a deep, intimate community of tradition and a participatory community of political interests. As aspirations, they reflect differences in taste and opportunities. Culturally defined communities are especially likely to follow the first model in defining a community of hope. They will draw as they can on ethnicity and religion, because they offer transcendent meaning for everyday affairs and because, for that reason, they constitute communities of memory.

Geographic areas of any size probably have heterogeneous populations. If residents consider themselves a community, they are likely to define their community of hope in terms of equitable norms for interest group politics. Insofar as people aspire to a deeper, more encompassing, positive identity, they will try to define themselves in terms of shared culture.

In defining a community of hope, the Baltimore Jewish community resembles other culturally defined communities, such as African-Americans, certain religious groups, and vital ethnic groups (most likely nonwhite and/or recent immigrants). These communities have traditions, languages, social relations, and norms that define and shape common experiences. The Baltimore Jewish community illustrates the aspirations and challenges to contemporary American groups in forming deep communities.

Southeast Baltimore is typical of many old "ethnic" neighborhoods in American cities. They are defined mainly geographically because they have lost earlier social and cultural cohesion. Ethnic political machines, with all their virtues and vices, governed many of these areas. Most have gone down with citywide reforms, racial shifts in local politics, suburban migration, or grassroots community organizing. Typically, the result is less concentrated or salient ethnic identity and less political power. Southeast Baltimore shows the disadvantages of these neighborhoods in forming political communities, much less something deeper.

We look next at the two planning processes as efforts to solve the problem of community while solving the problems of their communities.

CHAPTER 19

Community Organizations Planning for Community

TENSIONS BETWEEN COMMUNITY AND PLANNING

People live in communities of memory. Planning calls them to create and join communities of hope. The language of the lived community is the language of origins and the past. The language of planning is the language of the future.

It is not easy to move from the language of community to the language of planning. When we note it is hard to imagine a future different from what we are used to, we speak of emotional obstacles much more than intellectual ones. We hesitate to give up what is familiar, no matter how troubled. If we have succeeded in the community, imagining an alternative seems foolhardy. Being part of a community, we may think of creating another as betrayal. Planning inevitably arouses anxiety.

If the present is troubling enough, if the future is enough in jeopardy, and if the past provides pleasurable enough memories to motivate preserving what issued from it, deliberate planning is likely. If, however, the future seems overwhelmed, or if past memories provide a gratifying refuge from the present, inaction or active immobility is more likely. Under some conditions, community memories motivate planning, whereas under others they lead away from it.

When the possibilities of planning arouse too much anxiety, communities defend themselves by assuming the future will easily mirror and continue the past. Planning participants may agree problems require new policies, programs, or relationships but find themselves unable to think of any that differ much from the present. They may assert present practices are good enough, at most requiring more effort or funding.

Alternatively, people may retreat to nostalgic images of community glory. Reminiscing on fantasy-enhanced memories, they find it so satisfying to recall the "golden era" that planning has no appeal. If they speak of planning, they do so to restore the lost past (see Gabriel 1993). They may conjure up an idealized community image and project it onto the future, as if just imagining it could make it so. It gives pleasure, but its sketchiness precludes action, and people stay where they started.

Planning must allow people safely to say what they think. They must be able to talk about the community and their discontents with it, their desires for it, and their anxieties about it. Crucially, the planning process must be a transitional space where people can speak without having to act on what they say.[1] It is a moment when the community of memory exists but need not be lived in and when a community of hope, not yet existent, can be entered into. Planning must permit the illusionary experience of being secured to the community while stepping away from it and experimentally situating elsewhere. Planning must allow those holding responsibility for the community momentarily to give it up so they can reflect, analyze, criticize, and consider alternatives.

People must be able to hold their hopes and imagine a community that realizes them, without anxiety they are abandoning the community of memory. Then they can return to the present, where they are members of a community and responsible for it, and consider, newly inspired, how to transform the community in which they live into the hopeful one they envision.

To say loyalty to the community of memory affects planning for a community of hope is another way of noting that community dynamics shape community planning. Tacitly, unconsciously, community members use planning processes to manage community relations. Thus community planners proceed against powerful conservative impulses. We analyze these challenges in three respects: whether participants represent the whole community, whether they recognize community diversity, and whether they plan for a community that diverges from tradition.

REPRESENTATION: PLANNING BY A COMMUNITY AND PLANNING FOR THE COMMUNITY

Associated and Southeast organizers talked of choosing participants to represent the community. But in similar, though not identical, ways, each organization planned in the name of the whole community with participation from only certain sectors.

The Associated

The Associated directly asserted the "reality" the wealthy were entitled to influence. The federation, after all, was created by philanthropists to manage giving. Consistently, most planning participants were representatives of wealthy families, usually men. Most were from older generations, though some were younger family members. A majority were Reform or Conservative, rather than Orthodox, reflecting the choices of major donors and roughly matching general community affiliations. This membership gave little or no formal representation to the unaffiliated, lower-income families, agency staff and clients, and synagogues.[2]

Participants were chosen to include major contributors who could "buy into" recommendations. Committee composition fairly represented the Associated community. More broadly, participants represented those who remembered a community where successive generations of wealthy families stayed and worked in the Jewish community, giving their time and money.

Yet committee members acknowledged and worried that younger generations of all incomes were moving away from Jewish life. Moreover, The Associated aimed to be the "central address" of the overall community. The group that represented the federation community of memory did not include Jews whose habits and choices linked them to different remembered pasts.

This pattern limited the group's representativeness as planning *by* the community of 92,000 Jews. It also limited participants' ability to plan *for* either that larger community or the smaller Associated world. Planning for a community requires representing a community of hope, a community of the future. This is an old problem in planning: how to include the voices of the not yet arrived. It is a pointed problem in any community that declares its future in jeopardy.

The future of the larger Jewish community depended on the desires and actions of many besides federation activists. Even The Associated's future depended on not just donors' wishes, but also others' inclinations. Planning without them would limit the interests, perspectives, and information going into decisions.

The absence of the unaffiliated made it unlikely planners would consider a future in which the federation was differently involved with the larger community—for example, organizing new groups or offering services not traditionally considered Jewish. Because synagogues had no formal representation, participants would be unlikely to weigh more explicitly religious norms for The Associated or the community. Because moderate-income persons were not involved, no one would advocate to give them a place in the federation, nor would anyone likely consider their economic needs if they fell outside conventional programs. Thus planners would have difficulty examining particular trends and imagining a community that responded to certain groups' desires.

The Southeast Planning Council

Southeast organizers tried to create a planning council broadly representative of the community at-large. They invited known community organizations and tried to contact public housing tenant associations and racial and ethnic minority groups.

Yet in the end active Council members were predominantly white. Most were associated with well-organized, particularly gentrified, neighborhoods. Many were middle-class, a number of them professionals, most in their fifties or younger, many people who had moved to Southeast in the past decade or two. The older generations, Southeast natives, nonwhite minorities, and poorer people were weakly represented.

Some explanations were similar to those at The Associated. The core group invited those they knew or knew about, and strongest responses came from people familiar with them or SECO. In articulating an image of Southeast, the core group most clearly appealed to the good-hearted homeowner community of memory. These attachments most effectively engaged middle-class activists and some working-class neighborhood leaders. Single parents, low-income persons, and those whose native language was not English, even if they wanted to take part, faced various obstacles. Some nonwhites felt unwelcome.

Council members sought to speak for groups that did not take part, but lack of familiarity limited what they could say. Many found it hard even to represent the remembered community of white ethnicity and good-hearted homeownership, not only because they had come from other communities, but also because that community's weaknesses had motivated planning to begin with. Many activists, in fact, had educations and professions linking them to a postindustrial future inaccessible to many Southeasterners.

Still, the absent groups would be part of the geographic community's future. Working-class families, if more involved in planning, would have raised urgent questions about education and jobs. Greater African-American participation would have pushed race relations and race-related issues, such as low-income housing, onto the agenda. Excluding these voices, planners could not consider a community embodying a broad range of hopes.

Community Dynamics in Planning

Although both organizations, particularly the Southeast Planning Council, tried to include a wide range of participants, both ended up without members from significant groups. One explanation concerns the difference between organizations and communities. Organizations have structures that, no matter how flexible, cannot match a community's fluidity. However well an organization may once have fit its community, the two will diverge over time without deliberate effort to re-create the organization (see Mansbridge 1983). Thus planning participants picked by a community organization are more likely to represent the organization than the community.

One might say more simply that organizational elites try to maintain control (see Cnaan 1991). Associated leaders acknowledged such an interest, though Southeast activists did not. Yet more is involved than crude self-perpetuation. Activists come to share an image of the community. It is their community of memory, linked but not necessarily identical to the community remembered by other community members. Activists are likely to select participants who represent their community of memory, which they often assume is everyone's. Thus The Associated picked people who fit in with the philanthropic tradition, and the Southeast core group most easily reached those who identified with the good-hearted homeowner culture.

Another explanation for participants' relative homogeneity was anxiety about recognizing differences within the community. The organizations deliberately or unconsciously defended against that anxiety by avoiding groups who could divide the community. We turn now to that issue.

THE PROBLEM OF DIVERSITY:
SEEING DIFFERENCES REALISTICALLY

Both the Jewish community and Southeast are diverse, the Southeast proudly so, but planners in each avoided examining a central difference: religion in the Jewish community, race in Southeast.

The Associated

Associated planners referred often to religion in deliberations but did not speak deeply or reflectively about it. One explanation is that the federation is a civil institution. But Associated practices involve religion in many ways. Leaders choose committee members to represent all denominations. The federation closes for all religious holidays, food at meetings conforms to religious laws of kashrut, and the Jewish Community Center is closed on Friday night and Saturday for the Sabbath.

In these ways, the federation not only incorporates religion, but defers to specific, particularly Orthodox practices, even though most of the community does not observe them. The Associated gains Orthodox support and benefits from seeming more Jewish. Nevertheless, talk of religion in strategic planning was notable for one unexamined conflict and one unexamined consensus.

In education, divergent religious beliefs led to different policy preferences, and these disagreements, reinforced by competition for scarce funds, introduced years-long conflict. No one tried to analyze and resolve underlying issues. Their inherent intellectual complexity was manifest.

Moreover, religious differences were accompanied by guilt, shame, doubt, envy, and resentment. Committee leaders avoided public conflict because of political interests in unity. In addition, planning participants, as members of a small minority with memories and fears of anti-Semitism, steered clear of discussion that could divide them before the outside world.

These tactics limited conflict but could not resolve it. Indeed, paradoxically, as people suppressed complex feelings, they went underground and seemed still more dangerous. The Jewish Continuity Subcommittee took a lesson from this experience.

Most discussions of Jewish continuity were characterized by easy agreement that community members should study Torah and incorporate worship into their lives. Although committee members practiced Judaism in many ways, including some at variance with this consensual standard, no one moved to look at the differences for what they could tell about the range of motives, abilities, attachments, and interests that influenced community members' current practices and desires for the future. The Jewish education stalemate discouraged them from disagreeing about religion, and the rabbis' presence encouraged them to espouse more or less traditional norms.

Personal feelings and group pressures deterred those who observed differently or less from raising questions about differences, much less trying to resolve them. Consensus on Jewish continuity concealed differences packed with strong feelings and tacitly affirmed the more traditional in a way that secured them and the less traditional from exploring uncharted ground between them.

The Southeast Planning Council

With similar determination, the Southeast Planning Council avoided talking about race. Whereas federation planners held diverse religious positions but spoke of religion without examining its meanings, Southeast planners were largely white and barely mentioned race.

A rare exception involved Angelo Buono, who gave vehement voice to white anxieties about blacks. Some planning leaders considered his position morally unacceptable. Most worried racial conflict would scuttle planning. Council leaders sent out word he was not welcome, and he did not return.

Whites like Buono were willing to speak of race, but what they said would anger blacks and make some whites anxious. The safer course, which organizers chose, was to exclude those likely to introduce race in a dangerous way. Participants generally accepted a norm of saying little about race. Blacks were more likely than whites to mention it. Sometimes people used class or tenure to refer to race, equating blacks with renters or the poor, but those frameworks, tied to housing and income, led quickly away from race. Middle-class whites especially preferred to characterize people in class terms, a perspective that might disparage renters or the poor but denied differences between blacks and whites.

Racial anxiety is so American as not to require special explanation in Southeast Baltimore. Fear of explosive emotions hindered looking more specifically at racial differences or at racially implicated issues, such as low-income rental housing or education. On top of this, as at The Associated, a sense of being a minority in a hostile world discouraged opening issues that jeopardized unity. The result was not only to suppress discussion of race, but, in excluding those who would introduce it, to avoid issues they would raise.

Community Dynamics in Planning

Both planning groups worked hard to avoid looking at differences out of fear they could produce conflict. While each group planned creatively in some areas, difficulties reflecting on differences hindered them in others. Some important issues were neglected, related issues were ignored, and some groups were not included in the community imaged by the plan. Sometimes planners preferred stalemate to struggle with touchy problems. Occasionally fantasy displaced planning.

One explanation for the avoidance of differences is that religion and race are, indeed, volatile. Yet both groups faced other differences, including class, affiliation, and generation in the Jewish community and class, tenure, and generation in Southeast, and none of these was much more examined than religion or race. Some of these, too, were tied to religion or race. But the broader explanation is that planners avoided them because they were, simply, differences, matters of conflict or anxiety.

Perhaps these communities each focused on not discussing one especially dangerous difference as a way of expressing anxiety about many differences. The choice was not arbitrary, because race and religion matter, but its tacit purpose was to give good reason not to see the community divided in any way.

The wishes that lead people to idealize a community discourage analysis that makes it seem divided, smaller, or imperfect. Excluded or persecuted minorities are especially loath to see differences that would split and weaken them before outside danger. Paradoxically, it then becomes nearly impossible to see realistically not only how groups differ, but also what they have in common. Abstract assertions of unity displace specific realistic recognition of shared, if not identical, views and interests. People lose opportunities to build superficial, fragile attachments into deeper, stronger ones.

PRESERVING THE COMMUNITY OF MEMORY, PLANNING A COMMUNITY OF HOPE

Both planning groups honored their community of memory, sometimes by realistically linking it to a community of hope, but other times by ignoring challenges to it, trying to re-create it unchanged, or simply asserting its continuity. We look first at how the groups preserved the community of memory and then at how they made progress in planning a community of hope.

Preserving the Community of Memory

The Associated. Those who initiated Associated planning felt confident of the community's strength and success. They wanted to raise more money, and they were concerned fewer families gave to the federation, but they saw no serious problems, much less crisis.

Participants crafted a conservative plan. Many recommendations might have been reached without strategic planning. Some endorsed decisions already made. Some involved administrative matters more than general policy. Service priorities would change a little, and The Associated would do more in suburban Owings Mills. The federation took new approaches to recruiting and directing volunteers, and it embarked on new fundraising initiatives. Jewish education was a focus of controversy, and specific decisions were put off until later, but even there no one felt forced to take new ground.

The 1990 Jewish National Population Survey, prominently discussed at the 1991 Council of Jewish Federations General Assembly in Baltimore, recast things. Federations across the land spoke of intermarriage as the symbol of a crisis in Jewish continuity, and they endorsed Jewish education as the prime response. Thus Associated activists, beginning to implement their plan, came to regard the future anxiously.

They faced hard questions: What should their community of hope do and be? And why was the community of memory not leading toward it? Why were people making choices that apparently jeopardized the community's biological, social, and cultural continuity?

Normative conflicts hindered agreement on what the community should be, and, as a result, there was no single framework for analyzing conditions. The Orthodox, religious liberals, and secularists were each free to delineate the "continued" community they desired and to analyze conditions in their own terms. Yet such an analysis, particularly for those not traditionally Orthodox, would be thorny, because, until the concern about Jewish continuity, everything seemed all right. Turning sociological and psychological lenses toward the community could cast unwanted light on practices that gave great satisfaction.

Hence planning for Jewish continuity took two courses, both intended to reaffirm the community of memory against these challenges. One, exemplified by the Commission on Jewish Education, was to avoid conflict over the future and anxiety about analyzing the past and present by taking almost no action. While arguing for a newly patterned community, members proposed incremental changes in past practices. The Joint Commission on Associated-Synagogue Relations' Jewish Continuity Subcommittee illustrated the other approach. In proposing a weekend camp that would bring together all denominations to create a unified community, it imagined away past traditions and present practices that would restrain the desired future.

The Southeast Planning Council. Southeast planning, in contrast, began with long recitals of community problems—loss of jobs, increasing renting, decline of schools, aging, and suburban migration, to name a few. Facing an uncharitable future, people began planning with faith in their past. Yet they faced the question whether good-hearted homeownership could still sustain communal life.

On the one hand, the Planning Council acknowledged societal changes that would, at the least, redirect Southeast Baltimore. On the other, they found it easiest to build incrementally on institutions and practices that might support blue-collar white ethnic life. Though no ingenuity could re-create industrial boom times, the plan recommended expanding port-related industries and creating an industrial park. Some Southeasterners had moved to the suburbs to be near good schools, and the car made it less important to live near employment. The small, self-sufficient urban community was becoming a memory. Yet simply closing down neighborhood shopping strips would be difficult, and someone had to live in the thousands of Southeast housing units. Hence the plan urged revitalizing commercial districts and developing an employer-assisted housing/live-near-work initiative.

These proposals were worthy experiments. There are middle-tech jobs in a higher-tech economy. Mom-and-pop stores give way to regional and national firms, but neighborhood strips might retain some traditional social and economic functions. Few workers at Johns Hopkins, the biggest potential prize in the employer-assisted housing campaign, were from Southeast, but if they bought homes there, they might become good enough neighbors.

Nevertheless, Southeast planners, as those at The Associated, hesitated to start with a hard, broad question: What was the best realistically possible future for the community? What were the alternatives? For example, how did the growing movement of low-income blacks into

Southeast affect the area's future? Was that only a danger to be defended against? If so, what was to be defended, and how? If not, did it suggest the value or necessity of creating a multiracial community?

How did the decline of public schools affect future possibilities? Did it make improvement of public education a priority? If so, could the schools be improved enough, and quickly enough, to serve today's children? Or should Southeast write off the public schools, at least in the short term? Should the area become a residence for those without children—a way station for young professionals and a haven for empty nesters?

Addressing such questions was essential for identifying realistic futures for the geographic Southeast that had some connection to the past. Planning participants avoided doing so, as did their Associated counterparts, because they liked what they remembered and idealized about the past, and their own situations offered hopeful evidence the community could continue. Taking on the big questions could disable them. Instead, they harnessed general wishes for a better future to opportunism and focused on a variety of projects that, in fact, were feasible.

Planning a Community of Hope

While the plans conservatively represented community traditions, the planning processes nurtured originality that went beyond the written text.

The Associated. During strategic planning, when participants met socially, they often talked excitedly about what they were doing. In this extraordinary way, they testified to leaders' success in encouraging them to think of the community as an entity they could, and should, actively shape. It was not simply something they received from the past, but something they could design for the future. In part, this urging simply reinforced contributors' views that they molded the community with their philanthropy. But, more than that, strategic planning was framed as an effort to think comprehensively about the community.

Those who gave money were urged to think about the needs and services toward which their contributions should be directed. Those with interests in one service or agency were exhorted to consider the range of programs the community should have. Associated activists were encouraged to think about their relations with synagogues and the larger Baltimore community. People were asked to look at their interests in the context of what a good Baltimore Jewish community required, to see how pieces of a community fit together.

The choice of strategic planning chairperson was meant to balance convention with realism and creativity. The first woman chair of The

Associated Board, moderately wealthy, she was internationally respected as intelligent, hard-working, selfless, and independent. Her designation signaled the project would be serious, not ritualistic. She convened planning with an admonition of "no sacred cows."

To reinforce calls for independent thinking, as well as to provide it, the leadership hired an outside consultant. Jewish but unfamiliar with the federation world, he was a national consultant from Washington who had worked in Baltimore. He raised questions about federation relationships. He organized focus groups of the unaffiliated. He interviewed non-Jewish Baltimore leaders about the Jewish community. He spoke and wrote candidly about conflicts between Orthodox and non-Orthodox. Thus he opened difficult topics to discussion. In presenting an example of someone who could talk about them without untoward consequences, he tacitly offered to contain others' anxiety if they would join the conversation. Planning, he implied, could be a place to talk safely without obligation to act.

The Associated president, by assigning the community planning and budgeting director full-time to strategic planning, showed lay leaders how much management valued their efforts. In addition, the planning director's prominence conveyed a more subtle, perhaps even contradictory, message. Strategic planning would differ from normal committee work. Because the issues were much more complex, consensus decisions would have to be shaped by expert knowledge. The planning director would provide information to help lay leaders decide rationally.

He talked with committees and individuals to explicate questions and develop frameworks. Some efforts aimed at specific outcomes, such as adoption of constituency-based budgeting. Other times he simply sought agreement among conflicting parties. He tried to conceptualize issues so as to get decision by identifying common ground. Although more committed than the consultant to conventional federation positions, he, too, tried to make opportunities for disagreeing parties to agree even while moving in separate directions.

Most participants were members of an elite with strong ties to the past, and, as major donors, they wanted to see their ideas and interests in the agenda they supported. At the same time, these aspects of the planning process encouraged them to think of themselves as active designers of a community that must change to continue and offered them expertise to balance tradition in guiding the community to a realistic future.

No community, even if apparently facing crisis, changes quickly. Hence one must speculate about longer-term outgrowths of strategic planning and planning for Jewish education that followed. Religion is a focal concern. The Associated treats it ambiguously: it is valued, present, and acknowledgeable, but not discussable. Yet differences over religion's importance, role, and substance stymied planning for Jewish continuity and Jewish education. Many argued that, as attachment to the Jewish community declined, only religion could provide a compelling basis for a transcendent identity.

As long as philanthropists give to The Associated, it will continue as a fundraising organization. However, if it is to play a role in broader struggles over community identity, it will have to create a more enduring space where people can safely examine the role and practice of Judaism.

The Southeast Planning Council. The Southeast core group believed community planning entailed enabling a community dialogue as much as analyzing issues rationally. They assumed planning depended on creating a Southeast community identity. One reason was that neighborhood associations were too small to affect social, economic, and political conditions threatening the area. The other was that many neighborhood associations were bound by traditions that made it hard to imagine new directions. An organization representing all Southeast might have the power and autonomy to shape the future. The core group aimed to create such an organization, authorize it to act on behalf of Southeast, and establish organizational leadership for it (Giloth 1994).

Bus rides, slide shows, statistical presentations, and workshops encouraged planning participants to think about their neighborhoods in the context of all Southeast, or, to put it differently, to think about all of Southeast as a context. Residents knew about visual relations between neighborhoods and the waterfront. They were urged to see connections between residential and industrial areas. They were invited to think about commercial strips in relation to housing and jobs. They readily linked housing and schools.

The core group set up planning to encourage creative thinking about the future. They created clusters as political and psychological middle ground between neighborhoods and all of Southeast. These reinforced feelings of locality while pulling residents to think in larger units. Cluster workshops urged people to look at a bigger picture but brought them together with neighbors with whom they were comfortable.

Bus trips not only acquainted residents with a much larger area than they knew, but impressed riders with Southeast's diversity. In revealing differences in views and interests, the tours supported the position that planning should produce a variety of programs. Diversity might make agreement difficult, but it also argued for alternatives.

The planning process balanced local knowledge with expert knowledge. Cluster workshops, set up to elicit residents' views, were introduced with statistics, maps, and surveys. Design and planning workshops brought architects, planners, environmentalists, and scientists to consult on problems raised in clusters. Task forces invited housing, economic development, transportation, and social service experts. They introduced independent views in ways similar to The Associated's consultant. Southeasterners listened because they felt threatened, the experts had obvious experience, and most of their advice involved noncontroversial matters.

One effect of these efforts could be seen in recommendations that reached for a future unprecedented in Southeast. Economic development proposals, while aiming to keep and create manufacturing jobs, also endorsed biotechnology and the life sciences. They encouraged mathematics and science education and wanted employers to form partnerships with schools. Social service recommendations, while supporting traditional values, urged educational and service innovations to enable young people and their parents to adjust to societal changes.

The planning process offered Southeasterners a space in which to reflect on their community. Nearly two years of planning, when people looked at their community and talked about how they would take charge of it, encouraged many to think of themselves as knowledgeable actors in and for a community, rather than victims of outsiders' aims. The plan, even if often conservative in its recommendations, articulately represented and promulgated a growing belief that something called Southeast Baltimore was a context for people's lives and change efforts. That political community was a means for residents to promote their interests, and the Planning Council became an instrument and model.

One must speculate about longer-term effects of Southeast planning. Much depends on success in securing educational opportunities and jobs for residents and stabilizing neighborhoods. Much also depends on whether Southeasterners can come to terms with racial changes and imagine a community with both blacks and whites. This is an American problem, and the consequences of failure are visible throughout Baltimore and many other cities. Thus a key challenge is to create a secure space where whites, blacks, and others can begin to discuss and make sense of racial and ethnic differences.

COMMUNITY DYNAMICS IN PLANNING

In everyday details and as examples of community types, the Baltimore Jewish community and Southeast Baltimore differ. Their resources and cultures affect the problems they encounter, the organizations they create to address them, and the organizations' approaches. But the organizations face similar challenges in planning in, with, and for their communities. They must act within traditions that simultaneously guide and constrain them. They must touch the future without losing hold of the past. To do otherwise would be meaningless.

Communities plan to prepare their future. They do so also to honor their past. We should never be surprised to see a community planning as if its future could recapitulate the past. Planning is the organization of hope, but to say that does not gainsay the pull of the past, where many of the deepest hopes lie once satisfied. What calls for understanding is those hopeful efforts that extend toward the unknown future, imagining settling there as if it were a distant, but reachable, planet.

The stories here tell us such successes depend on leadership. More than any specific knowledge or skills, leaders build on faith in their community and the possibility of sustaining it. They offer a vision that holds others, creating a space where they can rest, looking forward and back without moving. Time is important in planning. Even when community members say they want to plan, it may take years to work through obligations to the past before they are free to create something they have not seen.

Vision and time offer an opportunity to appreciate differences. Differences unsettle us by suggesting criticism, competition, or, worse, annihilation. They suggest we are only part of the world, not all-powerful, all-knowing, or all-loved. At the same time, as we may say, differences can be interesting, even stimulating. Yet it takes time for communities, as for individuals, to be comfortable with differences, and it takes a vision to sustain them as they struggle.

Community members are always trying to make their communities meaningful and rewarding. Formal planning activities are a way of assisting and guiding these ubiquitous efforts at community governance. We should be impressed in these two cases at how planners helped community members look at themselves, consider possibilities of improving their situation, and take actions they would not otherwise have thought of.

CHAPTER 20

Communities and the City

Communities have attached individuals to the city by offering proximate objects with which they could identify, a domain where they could care about others who cared about them, and means whereby they could exercise control over the larger world. Today there are few communities that serve these functions. We have looked at two groups with city roots that think of themselves as communities. What do they suggest about the future of urban communities?

Community membership is a matter of calculation, albeit not always conscious or rational. Whether people belong to communities depends on what they desire and what the world allows. In general, people identify with or take part in a community when it offers them something of psychological, social, economic, or political value. Some wish to identify with a cultural community whose traditions offer transcendent meanings. Others want to be part of a political community that provides means for promoting local interests.[1] Often people seek both.

The question for the city is whether it can provide values communities need, ideally attaching members to the city, but at least allowing people to find communities in, if not necessarily of, the city. The city can offer comfortable conditions in which people shape communities of tradition, but the meaning that sustains such communities is not subject to public policy. Political communities, on the other hand, need the services government can provide, and these communities' vitality depends on whether government pays off.

We have seen people of different classes, ethnicities, religions, races, generations, life stages, and lifestyles who desire attachment to a community that gives their lives special meaning. Often they define themselves in terms of ethnicity or religion, because these affiliations matter greatly, because people want them to matter more, or at least because they offer a credible language for expressing communitarian wishes.

At the same time, we have seen the difficulties of maintaining old communities or refashioning them to fit new circumstances. Geographic and social mobility have stretched or torn old ties, more people work farther from home, fewer families have a parent who stays home and socializes with neighbors, and the basic interactions that constitute a community are harder to sustain. On top of that, fewer find the faith that could give any social group extraordinary meaning. Thus community declines in the city, as elsewhere.

Still, we have seen culturally defined communities of tradition that satisfy their members' yearnings well enough: the Jewish community and good-hearted homeowners. We could have found other such communities in Southeast, for example, among the Greeks, Lumbees, or Salvadorans. Yet, though such communities may form in the city, they do not depend on it. As the suburban movement of both Jews and Southeasterners suggests, a growing population regard city residence as voluntary.

Pointedly, many who want community feel the city gets in the way. Schools are bad, the streets seem unsafe, and the poor or other races frighten them. Moreover, although cultural community rests on similarity and requires contact, members need not be closely concentrated. Jews and Southeasterners leaving the city represent those of at least moderate means who can and choose to live elsewhere and who, if they join cultural communities, will do so in the suburbs.

In the groups we have studied, those who want to stay include cosmopolites who cherish urban life and have any necessary means to pay for private school. Traditional Orthodox Jews like the city because its housing density allows them to live close enough to support a synagogue they can walk to on the Sabbath, but they want little contact with others.

The largest number interested in city living are Southeast's working-class residents. Partly from familiarity with people and places, partly from inertia, they are looking for reasons to stay—not just as individuals but as members of a community. Insofar as they have choices, whether they stay depends on how they calculate the costs and benefits of city and suburban life.

Besides comprising cultural communities, these Southeast groups share overlapping, if not exactly congruent territory. To varying degrees, they are part of a political community defined by city geography. Their desires for such a community are similar to those of many city residents: they want to promote interests resting in the place they share. Once party machines offered identity, representation, and power. Now organizations like SECO and the Southeast Planning Council may do so.

Civic leaders interviewed in the 1970s for SECO's official history noted that organization performed functions city government should but did not (Truelove 1977b). Not only did Southeasterners gain from better conditions, but the city and government benefited from residents' satisfaction. When the Planning Council organized people to articulate community goals, the City Planning Commission endorsed their plan with the position that active community planning makes it easier to govern the city. Clear expressions of community interests help government make fairer, more reasonable decisions, and residents represented in public decisions are more likely loyal citizens. The case of Southeast, which is dependent on outsiders, shows how participation in a political community attaches members to city government. People attend to it because it can help them.

Local governments have choices. Conceptualizing the city as constituted by communities, policy makers can allocate resources to strengthen communities and tie their members to the city. Alternatively, they can regard the city as a collection of individuals of varying economic value. Then they would aim at attracting residents who like what the city can passively provide (cheap housing), demand few programs such as schools, public health care, and social welfare, and do not run up charges for police or fire services. The young and the childless fit these criteria well, young professionals especially well.

The latter view has short-term attractions but longer-term drawbacks. Even when young individuals or couples purchase homes, they are often like the renters good-hearted homeowners disdain. They are there only temporarily; neither they nor the landlord (city government) has an incentive to invest effort or money in lasting improvements or relationships.

Moreover, such an approach founders on another reality. Large numbers of city residents of little immediate economic value will stay. The very poor, especially those who depend on subsidized housing, have scant freedom to leave. Racial minorities may have limited choice simply if they are poor, but they are often also more comfortable living near others like them in the city, rather than in largely white suburbs, whose residents may not want them. These people have normal yearnings for community, and some belong to communities, traditional, participatory, or both.

City government need do nothing to retain these people, and, given the choice, many administrations would be glad to see them gone. Yet few will leave. With limited resources and leverage, local governments cannot greatly improve the lives of the poor, but they can support and reward efforts at community organizing. Especially among the poor, organizing is not easy, but where it succeeds, community members and city gain from both improved conditions and stronger ties (Berry, Portney, and Thomson 1993).[2]

Both cases here point to the centrality of education in building community. Schools teach knowledge and skills for work and citizenship, and they pass on cultural traditions that guide individual decisions and social interaction. When schools fail to serve these purposes, parents with choices use them, removing their children to private schools or moving to the suburbs. Interests in community add to all the obvious reasons for improving city schools.

The stories in this book do not lead to a neat summary or conclusion. What they show, above all, is that community is a question that matters. For individuals, it is a question whether there is more to life than making a living. For the collectivity, it is a question whether civil life is possible. We should be grateful to Baltimore's Southeasterners and Jews, and all groups like them, who are wrestling robustly with these questions.

NOTES

CHAPTER 1. INTRODUCTION

1. Fowler (1991) summarizes communitarian concerns and positions.

2. For example, Medoff and Sklar (1994) offer an account of planning by a Boston community in many ways like Southeast Baltimore. Stoecker (1994) presents a Minneapolis case.

CHAPTER 2. THE BALTIMORE JEWISH COMMUNITY, THE ASSOCIATED, AND STRATEGIC PLANNING

1. All statistics on the Baltimore Jewish community come from this source, which is the most recent survey of Baltimore Jews.

2. Unless otherwise noted, all statistics about Southeast Baltimore or Baltimore City come from these sources.

3. The following account of Baltimore Jewish history relies on Fein (1971).

4. This account of the development of community institutions relies on Cahn (1970); Fein (1971); and Kellman (1970).

5. In 1986 the Park Heights–Reisterstown Road area had 17 percent of the metropolitan Jewish population; 44 percent were Orthodox. In contrast, suburban Owings Mills had 8 percent of the Jewish population; 17 percent were Orthodox, virtually all modern Orthodox, in contrast with the largely traditional Orthodox population of Park Heights.

6. "Lay leaders" is the federation term for community members actively involved in the organization.

7. Elazar (1976) links federations' concern with public unity to the corporate background of board members.

CHAPTER 3. SOUTHEAST BALTIMORE, THE SOUTH EAST COMMUNITY ORGANIZATION, AND SOUTHEAST COMMUNITY PLANNING

1. The numbers add up to 29 percent because of rounding off.

2. This is the source of other data on Baltimore in this chapter.

3. The significance of this gift was not lost on the recipients. A copy of a 1969 "Report and Proposal of the Southeast Community Organization" has handwritten marginal notes next to the budget. Someone divided the $19,000 committed or requested as follows: "Jews = 5,000.00, Prot. = 9,500.00, R.C. =

4,500." The Jewish contribution stood out against earlier marginal comments counting 24,300 Roman Catholics and 13,500 Protestants (and no Jews) ("Report and Proposal" n.d.:8, 20).

CHAPTER 4. COMMUNITY, IDENTITY, AND PLANNING

1. Similarly, McMillan and Chavis describe "sense of community" as "a feeling that members have of belonging, a feeling that members matter to one another and to the group, and a shared faith that members' needs will be met through their commitment to be together" (1986:9).

2. Tönnies (1963 [1887]), a psychologically astute sociologist, associated the desire to identify with a community with the wish to restore a symbiotic relationship with a loving, powerful, perfect mother. For psychoanalytic interpretation of these desires, see Chasseguet-Smirgel (1985) and Freud (1959 [1921]). Schwartz (1990) shows how they influence organizational behavior.

3. For examples of how group and organization members retreat from realistic problem solving when anxious, see Baum (1987), Bion (1961), Diamond (1993), Hirschhorn (1988), Schwartz (1990), and Stein (1994).

CHAPTER 5. SETTING JEWISH COMMUNITY BOUNDARIES: THE AFFILIATED AND THE UNAFFILIATED

1. In 1985, 58 percent reported giving to The Associated (39% said they did not give, and 3% did not say; Tobin 1992:62). These individuals represented about a third of the estimated 36,000 Jewish households. For example, the 1994 federation annual campaign received 20,000 contributions, including 7,000 through the Women's Department, most in addition to spouses' or other family contributions (Stone 1995:55). Slightly more than half (55%) of Baltimore Jews are members of a synagogue or temple, though others belonged in the past or say they will join in the future (Tobin 1986:10).

2. Jewish community quotations come from shorthand interview notes. Some Southeast quotations come from such notes, and some were transcribed from taped interviews. The notes are imperfect but close to the speakers' words. Ellipses denote gaps in the notes or edited quotations.

3. Although local agencies agree to depend on federation fundraising, synagogues, local Jewish social and political organizations, and national and international Jewish organizations solicit funds independently.

4. Halacha is the body of Jewish law consisting of the Torah (the Five Books of Moses) and sixty-three books of rabbinic commentary known as the Talmud, compiled between approximately 450 B.C. and A.D. 500. The Talmud applies the Torah to everyday situations.

5. This definition is not as precise as it appears, since Orthodox and non-Orthodox disagree about whether certain mothers are Jewish and what conversion requirements are. In addition, Reform rabbis now recognize children of Jewish fathers as Jews.

6. Kosmin et al. (1991) found 52 percent of Jews marrying in the previous five years to have wed non-Jews. This finding became the national symbol of problems of assimilation and Jewish continuity.

7. Stein (1978) argues these dual impulses are deeply embedded in Jews' thinking about the assimilated.

CHAPTER 6. PERMEABLE SOUTHEAST BOUNDARIES: DUMPING, LOSS, AND THE DECLINE OF ETHNICITY

1. This is a typical problem of lower-income communities. Medoff and Sklar (1994) tell a similar story of the Dudley Street neighborhood in Boston.

2. The identities of individuals and some businesses have been changed, but the names of streets, geographic locations, prominent firms, and elected officials are real.

3. These figures count all households where neither English nor Spanish is the primary language. They include non-English speakers from Asia, but their number is small.

CHAPTER 7. ESTABLISHING THE BOUNDARIES: INVESTING AND REGENERATING

1. The Johns Hopkins Medical Institutions, including the Johns Hopkins Hospital and the Bayview Medical Center, as well as Hopkins' medical and other health professions schools, all in Southeast Baltimore, represent the economy's change from manufacturing to services. Johns Hopkins, including the university campus in North Baltimore, is the City's largest employer, with more than 16,000 on the payroll. Hopkins eclipsed Bethlehem Steel several years ago.

2. For example, Planning Council members considered urging Johns Hopkins Medical Institutions to purchase supplies from Southeast firms and to help set up local suppliers where none existed.

CHAPTER 8. DEFINING THE JEWISH COMMUNITY AND GOOD MEMBERSHIP: THE ORTHODOX AND NON-ORTHODOX

1. The reported numbers do not add up to 100 percent.

2. The Baltimore survey was conducted in 1985 and the national survey in 1990. More recent surveys would show a higher proportion of Orthodox in Baltimore and greater divergence from the rest of the nation.

3. Fein (1988) enunciates the view that political liberalism is the modern meaning of prophetic Judaism.

4. Baltimore Hebrew Congregation ended up Reform, and Chizuk Amuno eventually became Conservative.

5. This mental process, similar to that whereby wealthy non-Orthodox attack the Orthodox over money, is projection. One who dislikes certain aspects of himself (herself) unconsciously denies he has them, splits them from the rest of himself, attributes them to someone else, and attacks the other for them. See Freud (1946), Klein (1946), and Schafer (1968).

6. Modern Orthodox are less likely than traditionalists to believe that God definitely exists, the Torah was revealed by God to Moses at Sinai, or there is a Messiah who will definitely come. They are less likely to see the hand of God in everyday life, less observant, and more likely to interpret the world scientifically (Heilman and Cohen 1989). They participate more extensively in secular institutions and are more likely to support secular education.

CHAPTER 9. THE ORTHODOX, THE NON-ORTHODOX, AND STRATEGIC PLANNING: THE CASE OF JEWISH EDUCATION

1. Liebman (1973) calls this a "communal" perspective on Judaism, in contrast with the other, which he calls "religious."

2. Jewish preschool is considered supplementary education, though it is often more child care than schooling.

3. "Silver" is a composite of the person who formally chaired the meetings and another person who occasionally carried out the chair's responsibilities. This device obscures the actions of the designated chair, but it accurately represents the role of lay leaders managing the Commission.

4. "Aaronson" is a composite of the primary staff member serving the Commission and other staff members who assisted. This device obscures the actions of the main staff person, but it fairly represents the staff role with the Commission.

5. Requests and allocations were divided into two parts. One would give each agency a sum to restore its FY93 budget to the FY92 level. The other would go for specific initiatives. The first part came to $146,875, with $41,641 (28%) to the Day School Council. The Council asked $147,731 for teacher salary supplementation from the second part.

6. All revised requests included the sum to bring the base budget to 100 percent. Changes scaled back other initiatives.

CHAPTER 11. DEFINING GOOD MEMBERSHIP IN SOUTHEAST BALTIMORE: GOOD-HEARTEDNESS, HOMEOWNERSHIP, AND THE PROBLEM OF RACE

1. They exemplify what Gans (1988) calls "middle American individualism."

2. A member of an old-time family, he calls the area "East Baltimore." "Southeast Baltimore" is a more recent label, reflecting a growing differentiation of neighborhoods. Today, the names are racial as well as geographic, and "East

Baltimore" generally describes African-American areas, while "Southeast Baltimore" denotes largely white areas.

3. Shesgreen and Smith (1995) describe blockbusting practices in Southeast Baltimore.

CHAPTER 12. HOMEOWNERSHIP AND COMMUNITY PRESERVATION

1. Housing meanings, possibilities, and patterns differ in other countries. They show alternatives to homeownership as a means for exercising long-term control over housing. See Bratt, Hartman, and Meyerson (1986) and Hays (1993).

2. Nineteen percent had incomes above $35,000. These calculations come from a Census analysis by the Baltimore City Department of Planning.

3. The proposal called the project the Patterson Park Neighborhoods Intervention Initiative; the name was later shortened to Patterson Park Neighborhoods Initiative.

4. See Gabriel (1993) on nostalgia for "the Golden Age."

5. Schwartz (1990) analyzes a similar psychological process of idealizing organizations.

CHAPTER 13. RESOURCES IN THE JEWISH COMMUNITY: THE WEALTHY AND THE NONWEALTHY

1. Smith (1994) estimates there are 7.5 million grassroots associations in the United States, with 124 million members. Taking one local census as an example, he found only 16.6 percent to be incorporated. In his community near Boston, the average annual budget for 51 grassroots organizations was $7,805, with the median $2,000.

Because of this informality, those who study the independent sector, even if they recognize voluntary action (e.g., Lohmann 1992; Van Til 1988), give little attention to community organizations (e.g., Salamon 1992). Hodgkinson and Weitzman (1989) report on incorporated nonprofits, but the category "civic, social, and fraternal organizations" includes the Fraternal Order of Police and the Elks as well as community organizations. Still, the data show limited finances. In 1987, 59 percent of these organizations' staffs were volunteers (compared to 76% in religious organizations and 41% in the whole independent sector). Paid staff got salaries 56 percent of the sector average. The organizations spent 92 percent of budgets on current operating expenditures and only one percent on construction and capital improvements (compared with 80% and 5% for the sector).

2. Because the wealthy are a small group and because their assets protect them from at least financial problems, lower-income groups constitute the largest proportion of clients at most agencies. Tobin found these patterns for Jewish Family and Children's Service (now Jewish Family Services), Concord House (senior housing), the Jewish Big Brother/Big Sister League, the Jewish Community Center, and Sinai Hospital (1986:61, 74, 88, 91, 97).

3. The lowest household income category in a 1985 survey of agency clients was less than $30,000. Though a poor measure of poverty, it allows comparisons. Forty-four percent of Jewish Family and Children's Service clients came from households earning less than $30,000, in comparison with 31 percent for the Jewish Community Center and 30 percent for Sinai Hospital (Jewish patients only) (Tobin 1986:74, 91, 97).

4. No specific dollar figure distinguishes the "wealthy" and "nonwealthy." These are subjective categories differentiating a relatively small group who have considerable assets from others who have less and see themselves as having less. This latter group includes not only the poor, but also many in a broad "middle class."

5. Different people number the very rich differently, but the general impression is accurate: in the 1985 survey, 76 percent of Associated contributors reported giving $1 to $500; 3 percent reported $501 to $1,000; and 8 percent reported giving $1,000 or more (13% did not state an amount; Tobin 1992:62).

6. Actually, at the annual meeting dues-paying members can vote on a slate put forth by the Board's nominating committee. What he emphasizes is that only Associated members, not the community at large, vote and that Associated leaders restrict nominations to a queue of big givers.

7. In the interests of linking with religious leaders, The Associated has put two or three rabbis on the Board, including a leader of the traditional Orthodox.

CHAPTER 14. SETTING COMMUNITY PRIORITIES

1. Budget data come from The Associated (1991, 1995).

2. These calculations compare an agency's percentage of FY96 local service spending with its share of FY91 spending, expressed as a percentage change in the 1991 percentage.

3. This includes the Day School Council, the Board of Jewish Education (later the Council on Jewish Education Services, which provides services to education programs), the Joint Commission (which helps teachers meet Jewish education certification and licensing requirements), and the Synagogue Council (which supports professional development programs).

4. The 1991 formation of the Harry and Jeannette Weinberg Foundation, with assets of nearly $900 million, the largest Maryland foundation and the 24th largest in the country, made it easier to forego public money. Between 25 percent and 75 percent of the foundation's grants would go to Jewish causes. In 1992 Weinberg gave $2 million to The Associated (Magida 1993:21). In 1995 less than one percent of Associated funds came from the federal government, in contrast with other federations, such as New York, where the federal government provided up to 40 percent (Conn 1995:51).

CHAPTER 16. CONTINUING THE JEWISH COMMUNITY: OLDER GENERATIONS AND YOUNGER GENERATIONS

1. The Jewish intermarriage rate was still lower than other rising religious and ethnic intermarriage rates. A decade earlier, about half of recent Catholic

marriages involved non-Catholics (Alba 1981). In the largest European ancestry groups, high proportions of those born after 1950 married outside the group: 44 percent of English, 50 percent of Germans, 60 percent of Irish, 75 percent of Italians, 77 percent of French, 82 percent of Polish, and 85 percent of Scots (Alba 1990:13).

2. The roughly corresponding figure in Baltimore was 40 percent: the proportion of marriages for everyone under forty, whenever married, which included a Jew and a non-Jew by birth (Tobin 1986:11). However, discussion did not refer to this number.

3. The civil rights movement and conservative Christian activism are examples of religious movements aiming to influence the public domain. Douglas and Tipton (1983) and Reynolds and Norman (1988) analyze tensions between religion and public policy.

4. As synagogue representatives noted, it was not really a joint commission. The Associated set it up and invited synagogues to participate.

5. Groups that struggle with difficult tasks sometimes unconsciously switch from frustrating instrumental activity to "magical" ways of solving problems. One pattern is tacitly to pair two members, as if they were "parents" whose mere presence could give birth to a solution for the group's efforts (Bion 1961). Perhaps in the Subcommittee the women and the rabbis tacitly paired to become symbolic parents of good Jewish children. The constant talk about families and children would encourage this fantasy.

CHAPTER 17. CONTINUING THE SOUTHEAST COMMUNITY: OLD-TIMERS, NEWCOMERS, AND SCHOOLS

1. Data on new Southeast homebuyers come from this source.
2. About 1,500 more attended seven Southeast Catholic schools under the Archdiocese.

CHAPTER 18. COMMUNITY IDENTITIES

1. This is what community psychologists mean by "sense of community," though they shy away from speaking of feelings and spirituality (e.g., McMillan and Chavis 1986).

2. An alternative is fundamentalism, of which certain traditional Orthodox offer an example. As an act of faith, a defense against anxiety about unlimited possibilities, or something else, it asserts that everything is linked to the divine, and tightly so. Fundamentalism is not simple self-fulfillment, but it is self-concerned, giving primacy to personal relations with an object of faith over spontaneous, reciprocal social relations.

3. This description best fits Bellah and his colleagues (1985). Fowler (1991) describes variations, especially among conservatives who distinguish freedom in the public sphere from devotion to tradition in the private domain.

CHAPTER 19. COMMUNITY ORGANIZATIONS PLANNING FOR COMMUNITY

1. This discussion draws on the psychoanalytic concept of the transitional object, identified by Winnicott (1953) as the means by which a child enables himself (herself) to grow from his original symbiosis with the mother to autonomy in choosing his actions. For example, a child may clutch a blanket or teddy bear that represents ties with the mother while he moves out on his own. In this experimental period, the blanket lets him "have it both ways." The planning process is a similar transitional object. Diamond (1993), Hirschhorn (1988), and Stein (1994) show how consultants create transitional spaces to help organizations change.

2. The Associated tried to include members of all denominations, but synagogue representation is complex. Synagogues range from small, informal Orthodox shtiebels to large congregations. Moreover, rabbis, administrators, and members have different interests and perspectives. Hence no one person may represent a synagogue.

CHAPTER 20. COMMUNITIES AND THE CITY

1. Fischer (1991) observes that, even as people become involved in longer-distance social and work relationships, many are becoming more rooted residentially and, as a result, organize more to promote shared local political interests.

2. Putnam (1993), studying Italian civic associations, finds participation in community affairs fosters a competence for cooperation that pays off in economic ventures. Thus community development contributes to economic development.

REFERENCES

Alba, Richard D. 1981. "The Twilight of Ethnicity Among American Catholics of European Ancestry." *Annals* 454:86–97.

——. 1990. *Ethnic Identity*. New Haven: Yale University Press.

Amin, Ruhul, and Mariam, A. G. 1987. "Racial Differences in Housing: An Analysis of Trends and Differentials, 1960–1978." *Urban Affairs Quarterly* 22:363–76.

The Associated: Jewish Community Federation of Baltimore. 1991. *1992 Community Planning & Budgeting Manual*. Baltimore: The Associated: Jewish Community Federation of Baltimore.

——. 1995. *Allocations Report, Fiscal Year 1996*. Baltimore: The Associated: Jewish Community Federation of Baltimore.

Baltimore City Department of Planning. 1992a. "Basic Social and Economic Data." *CensusNews 1990*. Baltimore: Baltimore City Department of Planning.

——. 1992b. *1990 Community Profiles Baltimore City*. Baltimore: Baltimore City Department of Planning.

Baltimore City Planning Commission. 1994. Resolution. Approved January 27.

Barber, Benjamin. 1984. *Strong Democracy*. Berkeley: University of California Press.

Baum, Howell S. 1987. *The Invisible Bureaucracy*. New York: Oxford University Press.

——. 1990. *Organizational Membership*. Albany, N.Y.: State University of New York Press.

——. 1996. "Money, Work, and Legitimacy in Voluntary Community Organizations: How Dilemmas About Participation Affect Planning." Unpublished manuscript.

Bellah, Robert N. 1967. "Civil Religion in America." *Daedalus* 96:1–21.

——. 1975. *The Broken Covenant*. New York: Seabury Press.

Bellah, Robert N., and Hammond, Phillip E. 1980. *Varieties of Civil Religion*. San Francisco: Harper & Row.

Bellah, Robert N.; Madsen, Richard; William M. Sullivan; Swidler, Ann; and Tipton, Steven M. 1985. *Habits of the Heart*. New York: Harper & Row.

——. 1991. *The Good Society*. New York: Alfred A. Knopf.

Berger, Peter L. 1977. *Facing up to Modernity*. New York: Basic Books.

Berger, Peter L.; Berger, Brigitte; and Kellner, Hansfried. 1973. *The Homeless Mind*. New York: Random House.

Berger, Peter L., and Neuhaus, Richard John. 1977. *To Empower People*. Washington, D.C.: American Enterprise Institute for Public Policy Research.

Berry, Jeffrey M.; Portney, Kent E.; and Thomson, Ken. 1993. *The Rebirth of Urban Democracy.* Washington, D.C.: Brookings.

Bion, W. R. 1961. *Experiences in Groups.* New York: Basic Books.

Bloom, Allan. 1987. *The Closing of the American Mind.* New York: Simon & Schuster.

Bratt, Rachel G.; Hartman, Chester; and Meyerson, Ann, eds. 1986. *Critical Perspectives on Housing.* Philadelphia: Temple University Press.

Bryce, Herrington J. 1992. *Financial and Strategic Management for Nonprofit Organizations.* 2nd ed. Englewood Cliffs, N.J.: Prentice Hall.

Bryson, John M. 1988. *Strategic Planning for Public and Nonprofit Organizations.* San Francisco: Jossey-Bass.

Buber, Martin. 1958. *Paths in Utopia.* Boston: Beacon Press.

―――. 1992. *On Intersubjectivity and Cultural Creativity.* Chicago: University of Chicago Press.

Burke, Daniel. 1978. *The Catholic Church in the City.* Unpublished master's thesis, Georgetown University.

Cahn, Louis F. 1970. *Man's Concern for Man.* Baltimore: Associated Jewish Charities and Welfare Fund.

Cardin, Shoshana. 1989. "The Future of the Profession: A Lay Leader's Candid View." *Journal of Jewish Communal Service* 66:131–35.

Cassidy, Robert. 1979. *Livable Cities.* New York: Holt, Rinehart & Winston.

Chasseguet-Smirgel, Janine. 1985. *The Ego Ideal.* Translated by Paul Barrows. New York: W. W. Norton.

Clay, Philip L., and Hollister, Robert M., eds. 1983. *Neighborhood Policy and Planning.* Lexington, Mass.: Lexington Books.

Cnaan, Ram A. 1991. "Neighborhood-representing Organizations: How Democratic Are They?" *Social Service Review* 65:614–34.

Cohen, Maxine A. 1993. "Wake Up And Find Us Unaffiliated Jews." *Baltimore Jewish Times,* April 2, 8, 14.

Cohen, Michael D., and March, James G. 1986. *Leadership and Ambiguity.* 2nd ed. Boston: Harvard Business School Press.

Cohen, Michael D., March, James G., and Olsen, Johan P. 1972. "A Garbage Can Model of Organizational Choice." *Administrative Science Quarterly* 17:1–25.

Cohen, Steven M. 1983. *American Modernity and Jewish Identity.* New York: Tavistock Publications.

―――. 1988. *American Assimilation or Jewish Revival?* Bloomington: Indiana University Press.

Commission on Jewish Education, The Associated: Jewish Community Federation of Baltimore. 1993. *A Strategic Plan for Jewish Education.* Baltimore: The Associated: Jewish Community Federation of Baltimore.

"Conceptual Outline." N.d. Draft working document. Baltimore: The Associated: Jewish Community Federation of Baltimore.

Conn, David. 1995. "Budget Cuts & Bruises." *Baltimore Jewish Times,* July 14, 48–53.

Crenson, Matthew A. 1983. *Neighborhood Politics.* Cambridge, Mass.: Harvard University Press.

Cunningham, James V., and Kotler, Milton. 1983. *Building Neighborhood Organizations*. Notre Dame, Ind.: Notre Dame Press.

Dial, Adolph L., and Eliades, David K. 1975. *The Only Land I Know*. San Francisco: Indian Historian Press.

Diamond, Michael A. 1993. *The Unconscious Life of Organizations*. Westport, Conn.: Quorum Books.

Douglas, Mary, and Tipton, Steven, eds. 1983. *Religion and America*. Boston: Beacon Press.

"Draft introduction." N.d. Draft working document. Baltimore: The Associated: Jewish Community Federation of Baltimore.

Eagle, Jeffrey, and Newton, Peter M. 1981. "Scapegoating in Small Groups: An Organizational Approach." *Human Relations* 34:283–301.

Elazar, Daniel J. 1971. "Community." In *Encyclopaedia Judaica*. Vol. 5. New York: Macmillan.

———. 1976. *Community and Polity*. Philadelphia: Jewish Publication Society of America.

Espy, Siri N. 1986. *Handbook of Strategic Planning for Nonprofit Organizations*. New York: Praeger.

Etzioni, Amitai. 1993. *The Spirit of Community*. New York: Crown.

Fackenheim, Emil L. 1967. "The 614th Commandment." *Judaism* 16:269–73.

Fee, Elizabeth; Shopes, Linda; and Zeidman, Linda. 1991. *The Baltimore Book*. Philadelphia: Temple University Press.

Fein, Isaac M. 1971. *The Making of An American Jewish Community*. Philadelphia: Jewish Publication Society of America.

Fein, Leonard. 1988. *Where Are We?* New York: Harper & Row.

Fischer, Claude S. 1991. "Ambivalent Communities: How Americans Understand Their Localities." In *America at Century's End*, edited by Alan Wolfe. Berkeley: University of California Press.

FitzGerald, Frances. 1987. *Cities on a Hill*. New York: Simon & Schuster.

Fowler, Robert Booth. 1991. *The Dance with Community*. Lawrence, Kans.: University Press of Kansas.

Frazer, James George. 1940. *The Golden Bough*. Abr. ed. New York: Macmillan.

Freud, Anna. 1946. *The Ego and the Mechanisms of Defense*. Translated by Cecil Baines. New York: International Universities Press.

Freud, Sigmund. 1959 [1921]. *Group Psychology and the Analysis of the Ego*. Translated and edited by James Strachey. New York: W. W. Norton.

Gabriel, Yiannis. 1993. "Organizational Nostalgia—Reflections on 'The Golden Age.'" In *Emotion in Organizations*, edited by Stephen Fineman. London: Sage.

Gans, Herbert J. 1979. "Symbolic ethnicity: the future of ethnic groups and cultures in America." *Ethnic and Racial Studies* 2:1–19.

———. 1988. *Middle American Individualism*. New York: Free Press.

Gilman, Sander L. 1986. *Jewish Self-Hatred*. Baltimore: Johns Hopkins University Press.

Giloth, Robert P. 1993. "From Cannery Row to Gold Coast in Baltimore: Is This 'Development'?" In *Comparative Studies in Local Economic Development*, edited by Peter B. Meyer. Westport, Conn.: Greenwood Press.

————. 1994. "In Search of Collaboration: Community Planning in Baltimore 1988–1994." Unpublished manuscript.

Girard, René. 1977. *Violence and the Sacred*. Translated by Patrick Gregory. Baltimore: Johns Hopkins University Press.

Goering, John M. 1971. "The Emergence of Ethnic Interests: A Case of Serendipity." *Social Forces* 49:379–84.

Goetz, Edward G., and Sidney, Mara. 1994. "Revenge of the Property Owners: Community Development and the Politics of Property." *Journal of Urban Affairs* 16:319–34.

Hansen, Marcus L. 1964 [1940]. *The Immigrant in American History*. New York: Harper & Row.

Harris, Lis. 1985. *Holy Days*. New York: Summit Books.

Hays, R. Allen, ed. 1993. *Ownership, Control, and the Future of Housing Policy*. Westport, Conn.: Greenwood Press.

Heilman, Samuel. 1992. *Defenders of the Faith*. New York: Schocken Books.

Heilman, Samuel, and Cohen, Steven M. 1989. *Cosmopolitans & Parochials*. Chicago: University of Chicago Press.

Herberg, Will. 1955. *Protestant, Catholic, Jew*. Garden City, N.Y.: Doubleday.

Hirschhorn, Larry. 1988. *The Workplace Within*. Cambridge, Mass.: MIT Press.

Hodgkinson, Virginia Ann, and Weitzman, Murray S. 1989. *Dimensions of the Independent Sector*. 3rd ed. Washington, D.C.: Independent Sector.

Housing Task Force, Southeast Planning Council. 1993. "The Southeast Plan Housing Mission Statement." Baltimore, September 10.

Jordan, Winthrop D. 1968. *White over Black*. Baltimore: Penguin.

Kaplan, Mordecai M. 1981 [1934]. *Judaism as a Civilization*. Philadelphia and New York: Jewish Publication Society of America and Reconstructionist Press.

Kellman, Naomi. 1970. *The Beginnings of Jewish Charities in Baltimore*. Baltimore: The Jewish Historical Society of Maryland.

Klein, George S. 1976. *Psychoanalytic Theory*. New York: International Universities Press.

Klein, Melanie. 1946. "Notes on Some Schizoid Mechanisms." *International Journal of Psycho-Analysis* 27:99–110.

————. 1955. "On Identification." In *New Directions in Psycho-Analysis*, edited by Melanie Klein, Paula Heimann, and Robert Money-Kyrle. New York: Basic Books.

Kosmin, Barry A.; Goldstein, Sidney; Waksberg, Joseph; Lerer, Nava; Keysar, Ariella; and Scheckner, Jeffrey. 1991. *Highlights of the CJF 1990 National Jewish Population Survey*. New York: Council of Jewish Federations.

Kuttner, Bob. 1976. "Ethnic Renewal: How ordinary people in East Baltimore have created a model answer to inner-city blight." *The New York Times Magazine*, May 9, 18–19.

Lasch, Christopher. 1978. *The Culture of Narcissism*. New York: W. W. Norton.

————. 1984. *The Minimal Self*. New York: W. W. Norton.

————. 1995. *The Revolt of the Elites*. New York: W. W. Norton.

Levin, Marshall S., and Bernstein, William S. 1991. "Community in Concert: Baltimore's Vision Toward the Year 2000." *Journal of Jewish Communal Service* 67:194–204.

Liebman, Charles S. 1973. *The Ambivalent American Jew*. Philadelphia: Jewish Publication Society of America.

———. 1988. *Deceptive Images*. New Brunswick, N.J.: Transaction Books.

Lohmann, Roger A. 1992. *The Commons*. San Francisco: Jossey-Bass.

Magida, Arthur J. 1993. "The Weinberg File." *Baltimore Jewish Times*, July 30, 21–22.

Makofsky, Abraham. 1971. *Tradition and Change in the Lumbee Indian Community of Baltimore*. Unpublished doctoral dissertation, Catholic University of America, Washington, D.C.

Mansbridge, Jane. 1983. *Beyond Adversary Democracy*. Chicago: University of Chicago Press.

Marris, Peter. 1975. *Loss and Change*. Garden City, N.Y.: Anchor Doubleday.

Mayer, Egon. 1988. "Discomforts with Jewish Philanthropy: Some Perspectives from the Children of Philanthropists." *Journal of Jewish Communal Studies* 64:223–33.

McMillan, David W., and Chavis, David M. 1986. "Sense of Community: A Definition and Theory." *Journal of Community Psychology* 14:6–23.

Medoff, Peter, and Sklar, Holly. 1994. *Streets of Hope*. Boston: South End Press.

Miller, Lynn E., ed. 1989. *Managing Human Service Organizations*. New York: Quorum Books.

Morrow-Jones, Hazel A. 1993. "Black-White Differences in the Demographic Structure of the Move to Homeownership in the United States." In *Ownership, Control, and the Future of Housing Policy*, edited by R. Allen Hays. Westport, Conn.: Greenwood Press.

Nisbet, Robert A. 1962. *Community & Power*. New York: Oxford University Press.

Nutt, Paul C., and Backoff, Robert W. 1992. *Strategic Management of Public and Third Sector Organizations*. San Francisco: Jossey-Bass.

Ogden, Thomas H. 1979. "On Projective Identification." *International Journal of Psycho-Analysis* 60:357–73.

Olson, Sherry H. 1980. *Baltimore: The Building of an American City*. Baltimore: Johns Hopkins University Press.

Patterson Park Neighborhoods Intervention Initiative. 1993. "Project Proposal: Patterson Park Neighborhoods Intervention Initiative." Baltimore, February 4.

Perin, Constance. 1977. *Everything in Its Place*. Princeton: Princeton University Press.

———. 1988. *Belonging in America*. Madison, Wis.: University of Wisconsin Press.

Pew Charitable Trusts. N.d. "The Neighborhood Preservation Initiative." Philadelphia.

Putnam, Robert D. 1993. *Making Democracy Work*. Princeton: Princeton University Press.

Relationships Subcommittee of the Strategic Planning Committee, Associated Jewish Charities and Welfare Fund. 1989. "Report of the Relationships Subcommittee of the Strategic Planning Committee, AJC&WF." In "Building A Stronger Community: Toward the Year 2000; Report of the Strategic Planning Committee, Associated Jewish Charities and Welfare Fund." Vol. II. Baltimore.

"Report and Proposal of the Southeast Community Organization." N.d. Baltimore.

Reutter, Marc. 1988. *Sparrows Point*. New York: Summit Books.

Reynolds, Charles H., and Norman, Ralph V., eds. 1988. *Community in America*. Berkeley: University of California Press.

Richey, Russell E., and Jones, Donald G., eds. 1974. *American Civil Religion*. New York: Harper & Row.

Rosenberg, Babette H. 1976. *Remembering When*. Baltimore: Associated Jewish Charities and Welfare Fund.

Rusk, David. 1996. *Baltimore Unbound*. Baltimore: Abell Foundation.

Salamon, Lester M. 1992. *America's Nonprofit Sector*. New York: The Foundation Center.

Schafer, Roy. 1968. *Aspects of Internalization*. New York: International Universities Press.

Schwartz, Howard S. 1990. *Narcissistic Process and Corporate Decay*. New York: New York University Press.

Selznick, Philip. 1992. *The Moral Commonwealth*. Berkeley: University of California Press.

Shesgreen, Deirdre, and Smith, Van. 1995. "Blockbuster." *City Paper*, April 5, 19–24.

Shorebank Advisory Services. 1993. "A Community Development Bank for Baltimore: A Concept for Discussion." Draft paper. Chicago: Shorebank Advisory Services.

——— . 1994. "A Community Development Bank for East Baltimore: A Proposed New Institution." Chicago: Shorebank Advisory Services.

Smith, David Horton. 1994. "The Rest of the Nonprofit Sector: The Nature, Magnitude, and Impact of Grassroots Associations in America." Paper prepared for the 1994 annual convention of the Association for Research on Nonprofit Organizations and Voluntary Action, Berkeley, Calif.

Smith, Mead and Associates. N.d. "East Side Story." Baltimore: Smith, Mead and Associates.

Southeast Planning Council. 1992. "Southeast Community Plan: An Overview." Memorandum, February 14.

——— . 1993. *Southeast Community Plan . . . Towards a Future of Hope and Opportunity*. Baltimore: Southeast Planning Council.

Stein, Howard F. 1978. "Judaism and the Group-Fantasy of Martyrdom: The Psychodynamic Paradox of Survival Through Persecution." *Journal of Psychohistory* 6:151–210.

——— . 1994. *Listening Deeply*. Boulder, Colo.: Westview Press.

Stein, Howard F., and Hill, Robert F. 1977. *The Ethnic Imperative*. University Park, Pa.: Pennsylvania State University Press.

Steinberg, Stephen. 1989. *The Ethnic Myth*. 2nd ed. Boston: Beacon Press.

Stoecker, Randy. 1994. *Defending Community*. Philadelphia: Temple University Press.

Stone, Amy. 1995. "Posed For Power." *Baltimore Jewish Times*, May 26, 50–55.

Strategic Planning Committee, Associated Jewish Charities and Welfare Fund. 1989. *Building a Stronger Community: Toward the Year 2000*. Vol. I. Baltimore: Associated Jewish Charities and Welfare Fund.

Subcommittee on Congregational and Communal Religious School Education, Commission on Jewish Education, The Associated: Jewish Community Federation of Baltimore. 1991. "Report of the Subcommittee on Congregational and Communal Religious School Education to the Commission on Jewish Education of The Associated." Baltimore.

Subcommittee on Informal Jewish Education, Commission on Informal Jewish Education, The Associated: Jewish Community Federation of Baltimore. 1991. "Report of the Subcommittee on Informal Jewish Education of the Commission on Jewish Education of The Associated." Baltimore.

Sullivan, William M. 1982. *Reconstructing Public Philosophy*. Berkeley: University of California Press.

Taylor, F. Kraupl, and Rey, J. H. 1953. "The Scapegoat Motif in Society and Its Manifestations in a Therapeutic Group." *International Journal of Psychoanalysis* 34:253–64.

Thompson, Ginger. 1991. "City Council OKs plan for 5 majority black districts." *The Baltimore Sun*, March 19, 1, 10.

Tobin, Gary A. 1986. *Jewish Population Study of Greater Baltimore*. Baltimore: Associated Jewish Charities and Welfare Fund.

——— . 1992. "Trends in American Jewish Philanthropy: Market Research Analysis." Policy and Planning Paper 8, Maurice and Marilyn Cohen Center for Modern Jewish Studies, Brandeis University, Waltham, Mass.

Tocqueville, Alexis de. 1945 [1862]. *Democracy in America*. Translated by Henry Reeve, revised by Francis Bowen, edited by Phillips Bradley. New York: Vintage Books.

Toker, Eugene. 1972. "The Scapegoat as an Essential Group Phenomenon." *International Journal of Group Psychotherapy* 22:320–32.

Tönnies, Ferdinand. 1963 [1887]. *Community and Society*. Translated and edited by Charles P. Loomis. New York: Harper & Row.

Truelove, Lee. 1977a. "The Director Wears Blue Jeans: The Story of SECO." Draft manuscript. Baltimore: South East Community Organization.

——— . 1977b. *SECO History*. Baltimore: South East Community Organization.

Ukeles Associates, Inc. 1993. "Community Needs for Higher Jewish Education in Baltimore." New York: Ukeles Associates.

U.S. Department of Education. "Urban Community Service Program; Notice Inviting Applications for New Awards for Fiscal Year (FY) 1994." 1994. *Federal Register*, April 4, 59, 94:15810.

Urban Planning Workshop. 1980. *The Baltimore American Indian Community*. Baltimore: University of Maryland, School of Social Work and Community Planning.

Van Til, Jon. 1988. *Mapping The Third Sector*. New York: The Foundation Center.

Volkan, Vamik D. 1988. *The Need to Have Enemies and Allies*. Northvale, N.J.: Jason Aaronson.

Waters, Mary C. 1990. *Ethnic Options*. Berkeley: University of California Press.

Wilson, William Julius. 1980. *The Declining Significance of Race*. Chicago: University of Chicago Press.

————. 1987. *The Truly Disadvantaged*. Chicago: University of Chicago Press.
Winnicott, D. W. 1953. "Transitional Objects and Transitional Phenomena." *International Journal of Psycho-Analysis* 34:89–97.
Woocher, Jonathan S. 1986. *Sacred Survival*. Bloomington: Indiana University Press.
Yankelovich, Daniel. 1982. *New Rules*. Toronto: Bantam Books.

INDEX